DOING GRAMMAR

Second Edition

Max Morenberg

New York   Oxford
OXFORD UNIVERSITY PRESS
1997

Oxford University Press

Oxford   New York
Athens   Auckland   Bangkok   Bogota   Bombay
Buenos Aires   Calcutta   Cape Town   Dar es Salaam   Delhi
Florence   Hong Kong   Istanbul   Karachi
Kuala Lumpur   Madras   Madrid   Melbourne
Mexico City   Nairobi   Paris   Singapore
Taipei   Tokyo   Toronto

and associated companies in
Berlin   Ibadan

Copyright © 1997 by Oxford University Press, Inc.

Published by Oxford University Press, Inc.,
198 Madison Avenue, New York, New York 10016

Oxford is a registered trademark of Oxford University Press

Library of Congress Cataloging-in-Publication Data

Morenberg, Max, 1940–
    Doing grammar / Max Morenberg. — 2nd ed.
      p.   cm.
    Includes index,
    ISBN 0-19-509783-1
      1. English language—Grammar.   2. English language—
Grammar—Problems, exercises, etc.   I. Title.
PE1112.M64   1997
428.2—dc20   96-26020
                                                             CIP

1 3 5 7 9 8 6 4 2

Printed in the United States of America
on acid-free paper

Contents

CHAPTER 6 CONSTRUCTING RELATIVE CLAUSES, 130

CHAPTER 7 REDUCING RELATIVE CLAUSES TO PHRASES, 155

CHAPTER 8 MAKING NOUN CLAUSES, GERUNDS, AND INFINITIVES, 181

CHAPTER 9 ADDING MODIFIERS TO SENTENCES, 212

CHAPTER 10 WHAT CAN YOU DO NOW THAT YOU CAN DO GRAMMAR? THE RHETORIC OF SENTENCES, 241

APPENDIX: SELECTED ANSWERS, 262

Preface

I doubt whether any school subject is so universally dreaded and loathed by students and remembered with so much discomfort by adults. The term *grammar* will generally make people grimace and snarl. When I want to free myself from a particularly obnoxious person at a cocktail party, all I have to do is tell him that I'm a grammarian. Without fail, he'll lower his head and sidle away, mumbling into his shirt collar, "I never did well at that in school." When I like the person and want to continue the conversation with her, I say I'm a linguist.

If you're one of those who would rather eat lint than do grammar, I know how you feel, because I hated grammar as a kid. I even failed eleventh-grade English because of my animosity for the subject. Grammar classes seemed an endless repetition of silly rules and mindless diagrams that took up a portion of every year from third grade to twelfth grade. The lessons never stuck in my mind because nothing about grammar ever seemed to make sense. Grammar was something you had to endure, like the awful tasting cough syrup that was supposed to be good for you.

It's odd that so many of us hate studying grammar. It's like cats hating to stalk prey. Or dolphins learning to dislike swimming. Humans are as much language animals as cats are stalking animals and dolphins are swimming animals. We are born to love language and everything associated with it—rhythm, rhyme, word meanings, grammar. If you want to make a three-year-old child roll on the floor laughing, just tell her a riddle, or alliterate words, or read her Dr. Seuss's lilting rhythms and rhymes about cats in hats or elephants who are "faithful, one hundred percent" or Sam I Am eating green eggs and ham on a boat with a goat. Listen to a child in a crib entertaining himself by repeating sounds and syllables, playing with language. Think about the games you played in kindergarten by creating strange words like Mary Poppins' supercalifragilisticexpialidotious. Keep a ten-year old entertained on a car trip by producing odd sentences in a "Mad Libs" game. Then ask an eighth grader what subject she hates most. The answer will invariably be grammar. We're born to love grammar. We are taught to hate it.

I was taught to hate it by well-meaning teachers who presented grammar as morality lessons of do's and don'ts. I learned only the most trivial lessons—that you shouldn't end sentences in prepositions or start sentences with conjunctions or write fragments. When I found professional writers who used fragments, who ended sentences with prepositions, or who began them with conjunctions, I was told that it's all right for professional writers to break the rules because they know them. Not a satisfactory answer. It made me disdain the subject even more.

Then in a junior-level grammar class at Florida State University, Kellogg Hunt introduced me to Paul Roberts's *English Sentences,* and I began to see grammar in a new way. Roberts said that grammar is "something that produces the sentences of a language." He went on to explain that grammar is a system which puts words into an understandable order. Roberts illustrated the point with a simple game. You put words on twenty-five cards, one word to a card, and place the cards in a hat. The words are **face, my, never, his, dog, usually, car, struck, the, liked, a, washed, window, sometimes, seldom, George, stroked, he, she, Annabelle, her, goldfish, often, Sam, touched**. If you pick the cards from the hat, one at a time, and place them in rows of five, you'll probably never come out with an English sentence. You'll get nonsense like **struck the she Sam touched.** But if you first arrange the cards into stacks following the pattern **Edith frequently ignored her son,** and pick them in order starting with the Edith stack, you'll always produce a five-word sentence like **George usually struck my goldfish** or **Annabelle sometimes touched her dog.** In fact, there are hundreds of such sentence in the hat.

What you've done by arranging the cards is to sort words into classes and then put the classes in order. If you play long enough with the sentences, you discover important facts about the ordering of words—that words make constituents, units like **his window, washed his window, seldom washed his window,** and **Sam seldom washed his window.** You find that a noun phrase can fit within a verb phrase, that the new verb phrase can pattern with another noun phrase to make a sentence: you've learned that constituents form hierarchies. You may also discover that some noun phrases can't function as subjects for some verb phrases and that some noun phrases can't function as objects with some verbs. **My window never stroked she** isn't an English sentence, though it follows the pattern noun phrase + adverb + verb + noun phrase. Roberts's game is a pretty simple idea. But it was a revelation: grammar is like a machine that fabricates sentences according to a set of discernible principles. When we speak or write, we don't throw words into sentences at random: we order them according to a GRAMMATICAL system. We build constituents and relate them to one another within hierarchical frameworks. Grammar made sense to me.

The next revelation was that you can take the simple sentences produced by such a grammar machine and put them together into new and different combinations, because the grammar of a language keeps recycling material, using the same constituents over and over in new combinations. In this way, grammar produces an infinite number of sentences from a small number of core constituents. To introduce beginning linguistics students to this idea, I ask them to combine two sentences into one in as many ways as they can. My favorite two sentences for this exercise are **It surprised me** and **Jane arrived late,** which my colleague Andy Kerek made up several years ago. If you try the exercise, remember that you can add words like **and,** or **when,** or **if,** and you can change the forms of words from **arrive** to **arriving** or **arrival,** for instance. Students will typically come to the next class with 50 or 60 combinations. The all-time champ was a mathematically inclined student who ran a factor analysis on the combinations and produced 467 new sentences, stopping, he said, not because he couldn't continue but because he finally got bored with the task.

Those two ideas, the grammar machine and the combining exercise, inform everything in the book. The first chapter introduces you to the core sentences—their constituents and how their constituents interact with verbs. The second chapter shows how the constituents fit together into hierarchies and how you can identify and label the parts. The third and fourth chapters expand the concepts of verb phrases and noun phrases. The fifth chapter shows how you can rearrange or compound components of the core sentences. The sixth chapter explains how you combine core sentences into relative clauses, while the seventh describes how to reduce those clauses to phrases. The eighth chapter demonstrates how you combine core sentences into substitutes for nouns—noun clauses, gerunds, and infinitives. The ninth explores ways you combine sentences into nonrestrictive modifiers. And the tenth shows that your knowledge of grammar can enhance your understanding of literary style and may even help you improve your writing.

Mastering the technical vocabulary and concepts in *Doing Grammar* demands the kind of studying you'd put into a science or math course. Go through the book slowly and methodically. Underline important concepts and write notes in the margins. Don't move ahead until you understand what you're reading. But don't be afraid of doing grammar, either. You already know more grammar than you suspect. You speak, write, and understand language without ever thinking about the identity and function of grammatical constituents. When you study grammar in school, you become conscious of how language operates to produce sentences. Grammar works by putting words, phrases, and clauses together into sentences. The grammarian's job is to take those structures apart, identify them, and explain how the parts relate to one another. Putting together is natural; taking apart and labeling are learned. The idea behind *Doing Grammar* is that, if you can see how you put sentences together, you can understand how to take them apart. It takes practice to learn grammatical analysis. So, besides the explanations, each chapter has lots of sentences for you to analyze. I hope you find them appealing as well as challenging. I've devoted a great deal of time and effort to finding example sentences that are interesting. Besides hating mindless grammar exercises, I always hated the sentences in grammar books because they were so lifeless that you could be sure they occurred nowhere else but in grammar books. The sentences in *Doing Grammar* are real sentences—vivid and detailed.

Doing Grammar is not tied to one ideology. Its terminology is traditional. It draws upon both traditional and generative grammars for its basic concepts. It is rooted in the traditional principles of Jespersen as well as in the contemporary formulations of Chomsky, with an admixture of Kenneth Pike's tagmemics and Robert Allen's sector analysis. It is nurtured through the textbook explanations of Paul Roberts and the language development research of Kellogg Hunt. When I have questions, I usually look for answers in Quirk, Greenbaum, Svartvik, and Leech (*A Comprehensive Grammar of the English Language*). These and other linguists and grammarians I've studied through the years form the book's academic credentials.

I have attempted to make the technical and obscure clear and sensible. The book assumes, loosely, that a small number of core sentences composed of basic classes of constituents can be rearranged or combined into new, more elaborate sentences. It also assumes that, if you learn to analyze the structures and relationships in the core sentences, you will be able to analyze the structures and relationships in the new combinations. After going through the book, you should be able to read and understand a traditional grammar text or be prepared to begin the study of linguistic theory. And you should be able to reflect more thoughtfully on how writers, including yourself, use language to create effects.

This second edition of *Doing Grammar* is larger and more detailed than the first edition. The book has grown from seven chapters to ten. I broke the first two chapters of the original book into four and expanded each of those. Then I added the tenth chapter, on style, usage, and punctuation. Though I originally aimed for a thin book, so that the explanations wouldn't become tedious and overwrought, I think this version, though thicker, is better because it's more complete. It answers most of the questions students and teachers have asked me about grammar in the last five years and didn't find answers to in the first edition. It addresses head on what sometimes the first edition only hinted at.

I can't promise that you will love grammatical analysis because you studied this book. But I think that you'll understand grammar after putting together and taking apart sentences. You learn grammar by doing grammar.

Oxford, Ohio   M.M.
September, 1996

Acknowledgments

It's not possible to properly acknowledge all the people who taught you, encouraged you, and helped you. I apologize to those I've missed.

Behind my own interest in language were lots of good teachers, and wonderful colleagues. Some stand out. I remember teachers from Miss Cole, my kindergarten teacher, to Fred Standley, the director of my dissertation. Of special import was Miss Cahill in second grade, who taught me to read. In a strange way, Jo Curto, though I failed her eleventh-grade English class at Miami Beach High, fueled my interest in literature and language. Len Singer, my first-year composition teacher at Miami-Dade Community College, made me believe I could write. Kellogg Hunt, at Florida State University, had limitless patience with a muddled graduate student in linguistics—and an ocean of T-units to analyze. My colleagues encouraged and supported me. Nancy Standley generously shared her classroom experience during my student-teaching days. Rich Wilson helped me get my first teaching job. Don Daiker and Andy Kerek taught me more about university politics and writing than I can acknowledge—and something about Bela Lugosi and Glenn Ford movies as well. Mary Fuller taught out of earlier versions of this book and encouraged me to complete it. Janet Ziegler's notes and observations on both editions were especially useful. Miami University's English Department gave me a semester off to write the first edition and reasonable teaching schedules so I could write the second edition. Thousands of students—from Leesburg (Florida) High School, Florida State University, the University of South Alabama, and Miami University—taught me to value young minds. Students in my introductory grammar classes responded to earlier drafts. Because of them, I could write with real students in mind.

The editors and production people at OUP have helped in various ways. Karen Shapiro and Tony English were thoughtful and patient editors. It must be hell to work with a grammarian who procrastinates as readily as he parses. Finally, Phil Leininger, when he was at OUP, reminded me I had promised him a grammar book that students would enjoy and learn something from. I've tried twice to keep my promise.

CHAPTER 1 | *Identifying Verb Types*

Preview

This chapter defines grammar and identifies six verb types. These six verb types produce a core of sentences that are basic to the structure of the English language. The core sentences contain fundamental components and relationships. The core sentences can be rearranged to produce questions, commands, and other sentence types, and they can be combined to produce more complex sentences. The six core sentence types are like malleable building blocks.

The core sentences form the basis of the grammar system. I believe that if you learn the basic structures and functions within core sentences and understand how to build larger, more complex sentences by rearranging constituents and combining these core sentences in various ways, you will see how our language is structured and organized. And you'll understand how to take sentences apart and identify their parts.

Building sentences and taking sentences apart (analyzing them)— these are the two processes that underlie most of the discussions in this book. Normally, doing grammar is all about analyzing sentences—naming the parts and identifying their relationships. Analyzing sentences is called PARSING; grammarians parse sentences by taking them apart, naming their structures, and identifying the relationships among the structures. Grammar is a system that puts sentences together; grammarians are analysts who take sentences apart (they parse sentences), just as

1

botanists take plants apart or physicists take atoms and molecules apart.

Grammarians don't analyze sentences just for the sake of analyzing sentences, any more than botanists analyze plants just to analyze plants or physicists analyze atoms just to analyze atoms. Grammarians analyze sentences in order to understand how language works. Grammarians use that knowledge in various ways. Some grammarians study how the mind produces language. Some grammarians study how languages change over time. Some grammarians study how people use language within social contexts. Some grammarians study how people speak and write.

Here are the points we'll cover in the first chapter:

- Grammar is the system that puts words together into meaningful units.

- Sentences are the basic building blocks of language.

- At the heart of any sentence is a verb.

- There are six core verb types: intransitive, linking, transitive, Vg, Vc, and BE.

- We classify verbs according to the structures that immediately follow them.

- A verb, its subject, and the other slots associated with it form a sentence nucleus.

- We define a function by how a structure relates to a verb.

What Is Grammar?

As a graduate student at Florida State University, I had to demonstrate proficiency in two foreign languages. So, for several years, I took courses in French and German that were specifically set up to teach graduate students enough of those languages to pass a reading knowledge test. I appeared for the German exam one Saturday morning with a graduate-student friend of mine, Joe Smith. After several hours of translating German, Joe and I left the exam room together for the short walk home. "Wasn't that a funny paragraph about the Virgin Mary in the monastery?" he asked as we stepped out into the bright Florida sunshine. The exam had taxed my knowledge of German, and I didn't remember anything funny about it, certainly not the paragraph about a fire in a medieval monastery, with the monks scurrying about trying to save various statues and religious objects as they worked to put out the fire. "No," I replied. "What do you mean funny?" Joe looked at me, hoping I would verify his interpretation of the passage. "Wasn't the Virgin Mary running around setting fires in the monastery?" he asked. "No, I don't think so, Joe," I replied. "One monk was carrying a statue of Mary while he ran around trying to put out the fires." Obviously, Joe had misread something. He had the statue performing an action, not simply being carried around.

If you've studied a foreign language in school, you've probably been in situations similar to Joe's, where you've known the meaning of the words in a sentence and still misinterpreted the sentence. When you know the meanings of the words and don't know what a sentence says, it's because you don't know the GRAMMAR of the sentence, the structural system that puts words together into meaningful units and indicates the relationships between the units. Put another way, the grammar of a sentence tells you who does what to whom. It tells you who is setting fires and what is being carried around by someone dousing the fires.

Let's take a look at an English example to emphasize this definition of grammar as **the system that puts words together into meaningful units**. In English, you can say

The cat chased the mouse.

Or you can say

The mouse chased the cat.

The sentences have the exact same words, but they mean different things. English grammar normally puts the doer of an action before the verb and the person or thing to which something is done after the verb. So you know in the first sentence that the cat is doing the chasing and the mouse is being chased. You know that in the second sentence the situation is reversed, with the mouse doing the chasing, because the noun phrase **the mouse** precedes the verb **chased** and the noun phrase **the cat** follows the verb. But if you were not a speaker of English and you had only a dictionary to translate the words into your own language, you might not be able to tell the difference between the actions in the first and second sentences. Knowing the words without knowing the grammar might give you as strange an interpretation of English as Joe got for German.

The Implications of How We Define Grammar

Grammar is a system that puts words together into meaningful units. This definition implies that we will study grammar in order to analyze the sentences in our language so that we may understand how they are put together. In brief, we're going to learn how our language is structured.

Not every grammar book defines grammar as a system that puts words together into meaningful units and that indicates relationships between units; and not every grammar book claims that the goal of studying grammar is to learn how a language is structured. One of the earliest English grammar books, Robert Lowth's *A Short Introduction to English Grammar*, published in 1762, said that the purpose of grammar was to teach us to "express ourselves with propriety" and "judge of every phrase and form of construction whether it be right or not." Many grammar texts have followed Lowth's goals—to teach students to express themselves in socially acceptable ways and to make judgments about correct and incorrect usage. Grammar books concerned with "right" and "wrong" usage spend a lot of time telling you that "he don't eat salads" or "between you and I" are "ungrammatical" because they don't meet certain standards of acceptable usage. This definition is often extended to writing, so that "proper" spelling and punctuation are also considered grammatical skills.

Doing Grammar has no such goals. It is not concerned with making you a "correct" speaker or writer; it is concerned with making you aware of the structure of the English language. It takes the view that grammar is the structured system that underlies our language and that the basic unit of structure is the sentence. For us, then, doing grammar means studying the structured system that allows speakers and writers to create sentences in the English language and that allows listeners and readers to understand those sentences. You study grammar, in the view taken in this book, in order to understand how language systems work, just as you study biology to understand how living systems work.

It's important to remember what our purpose is and what it is not.

We are concerned with describing and understanding how our language is structured, not with prescribing ways of speaking and writing as correct or incorrect. In the last chapter, we will look at how we can use our knowledge of English structure to better understand how language functions in literary works and in our own writing so that we can become more thoughtful writers and readers and perhaps more knowledgeable teachers of writing and reading. But first we'll look at grammar—the system that puts words together into meaningful units.

Verbs Are Central to Sentence Structure

When you study grammar, you learn to "take language apart" so that you can understand how the parts function together. Grammar is an analytic science, just like botany, or chemistry, or anthropology. Instead of identifying the components of plants, chemical compounds, or human communities, grammarians identify the components of language—like words, phrases, and clauses—in order to show how those components interact with one another within sentences. Grammarians consider sentences the basic building blocks of language, in the way that biologists consider DNA molecules the basic building blocks of life. So we'll begin our analysis of language by studying how sentences are put together. That brings us immediately to verbs.

Sentences are put together around verbs. Said another way, verbs are central to the construction of sentences. Verbs determine the other components in sentences and define the relationships among those components. Verbs tell you that certain noun phrases function as subjects and that others function as objects or as complements. The six verb types explained in this chapter will help you identify all the structures and relationships in English sentences, no matter how long or complicated those sentences may become.

A verb is followed immediately by either a noun, an adjective, or an adverb; or it is followed by nothing (some verbs end sentences). You normally categorize a verb according to two criteria: the structure that follows it and the relationship this structure has with the verb; or, in the case of an intransitive verb, by what does not follow it. The rest of this chapter explains in detail how to categorize verbs according to the structures and relationships that follow them.

Intransitive Verbs

The first verb category we'll look at is called INTRANSITIVE. We define intransitive verbs by what they don't do that other verbs must do. All other verbs must be followed immediately by either noun phrases or adjectives. Intransitive verbs don't need nouns or adjectives immediately to their right. They can end sentences or they can be followed by adverbs. For instance, in the sentence

The mayor spoke,

the verb **spoke** is intransitive. So is **slept** in

Margaret slept.

Both **spoke** and **slept** are intransitive because they are not followed by other words: the two verbs end sentences. Here are a few more examples of verbs that are intransitive because they end sentences:

Birds fly.

The yeast rose.

The window broke.

Intransitive verbs can end sentences, but they don't have to. Intransitive verbs may be followed by adverbs—words and phrases that answer questions like how? where? why? when? and how often? In the sentences

The baby panda cried softly

and

Toni Morrison writes exquisitely,

the intransitive verb **cried** is followed by the single-word adverb *softly*, and **writes** is followed by the adverb *exquisitely*. In the next set of sentences, the intransitive verbs (**sank, jumped, apologized, replied,** and **erupted**) are all followed by adverb phrases.

The Titanic **sank** in 1912.

The stuntman **jumped** from the third-floor balcony.

Shaquille **apologized** after the game.

Bryant Gumbel **replied** faster than Willard Scott.

The volcano **erupted** with the destructive force of an atomic bomb.

To summarize, intransitive verbs may end sentences or they may be followed immediately by adverbs.

Linking Verbs

LINKING VERBS, in contrast to intransitives, cannot end sentences, nor can they be followed immediately by adverbs. They must be followed by either nouns or adjectives; those nouns or adjectives may be single words or multiple-word phrases. Linking verbs are a small class of probably no more than a dozen or so verbs, including **seem, become, remain,** and the verbs of the senses, such as **taste, smell, sound, look,** and **feel.** Both **looked** and **tasted** are linking verbs in the following examples because they are followed by adjectives—**weary** and **scrumptious.**

The president **looked** weary.

The lasagna **tasted** scrumptious.

The linking verbs **remained** and **became** in the next sentences are followed by a noun phrase, **an honest man,** and a noun, **Superman.**

Silas **remained** an honest man.

Clark Kent **became** Superman.

Adjectives and nouns that follow linking verbs are closely associated with their subject noun phrases. An adjective that follows a linking verb generally summarizes some characteristic of the subject noun. In the above example, weariness is a characteristic of the president; that's why other people perceive him to be weary (he **looks** weary). Scrumptiousness is a characteristic of the lasagna; that's why it **tastes** scrumptious. A noun that follows a linking verb refers to the same person or thing that its subject noun refers to. Clark Kent and Superman are the same person and so are Silas and an honest man. Adjectives that follow linking verbs function as PREDICATE ADJECTIVES; nouns that follow linking verbs function as PREDICATE NOUNS.

Predicate adjectives are often multi-word phrases, just as predicate nouns are. A common way to make adjectives into phrases is by adding adverbs called INTENSIFIERS to them. Intensifiers are words like **very**, **pretty**, **terribly**, **incredibly**, and **damned**. Typically, you use them to amplify the impact of adjectives.

> The condom issue **turned** damned nasty.

> The jury **seemed** incredibly bored.

In brief, linking verbs are followed by nouns or adjectives that function as predicate nouns and predicate adjectives.

Transitive Verbs

TRANSITIVE VERBS must be followed by nouns or noun phrases. But unlike the nouns that follow linking verbs, the nouns that follow transitive verbs do not rename their subjects; they are not predicate nouns but DIRECT OBJECTS. Often the object of a transitive verb has something "done" to it by the subject, as in the following examples, in which the letter is **typed**, the Milk-Bone is **crushed**, and the health care bill is **supported**.

> The secretary **typed** the letter.

> Jamal's Doberman **crushed** the Milk-Bone.

> President Clinton **supported** the health care bill.

Here's a fact about transitive verbs that can often help you identify them. Sentences with transitive verbs can usually be turned into PASSIVE SENTENCES. Passive sentences, like the second of each pair below, invert subjects and objects.

> **Coyotes** destroyed **the carcass.**
> ↓
> **The carcass** was destroyed by **coyotes.**

> **Satellites** monitor **the Arabian pipeline.**
> ↓
> **The Arabian pipeline** is monitored by **satellites.**

> The fans applauded **Magic's decision.**
>
> $\downarrow$
>
> **Magic's decision** was applauded by **the fans.**

If a sentence can be made into a passive, you can be sure the verb is transitive.

To summarize, transitive verbs are followed by noun phrases that function as direct objects. Sentences with transitive verbs can usually be inverted to form passive sentences.

Two-Place Transitive Verbs

There are two more types of transitive verbs; they are both called TWO-PLACE TRANSITIVES. These verbs are transitive because they are followed by noun phrases that function as direct objects. But they are different from simple transitive verbs. The first two-place transitive we'll look at is followed either by two noun phrases (one after the other) or by a noun phrase and then a prepositional phrase introduced by **to** or **for**. The other two-place transitive is followed either by two noun phrases, by a noun phrase and then an adjective phrase, or by a noun phrase and then an infinitive phrase.

Two-Place Transitives: Vg Verbs

You can generally identify the first two-place transitive by the fact that it is like the verb **give** in the following sentence:

> The school board **gave** the teachers a raise

or like the verb **buy** in

> Donald **bought** Marla a diamond necklace.

We'll call this first type of two-place transitive Vg (vee gee) for short (in order to remember that it is often like the verb **give**). When Vg verbs are followed immediately by two noun phrases, as in the previous examples, the first noun functions as an INDIRECT OBJECT, the second as a DIRECT OBJECT.

> The school board gave **the teachers   a raise.**
>   IObj   DObj

Donald bought **Marla**   **a diamond necklace.**
              IObj   DObj

Indirect objects are almost always receivers of something. (They "receive" the noun that is the direct object.) In the examples, the teachers receive a raise and Marla receives a diamond necklace. Indirect objects have one other important characteristic: with few exceptions, they can **per**ceive as well as **re**ceive. In order to perceive, indirect objects are almost always animate; usually they are human.

Sentences with Vg verbs have an alternative form. You can often rearrange the noun phrases in a sentence with a Vg verb, placing the indirect object into a prepositional phrase introduced by **to** or **for**.

The school board gave **the teachers** a raise.
↓
The school board gave a raise **to the teachers**.

Donald bought **Marla** a diamond necklace.
↓
Donald bought a diamond necklace **for Marla**.

Notice that the nouns in these prepositional phrases remain the receivers of the nouns in the direct object positions. Vg verbs must always have both direct and indirect objects, whether those indirect objects are noun phrases placed directly after the verbs or noun phrases in **to** or **for** prepositional phrases. We'll say that the **to** or **for** in such prepositional phrases mark the indirect objects. In the following sentences, **fed** and **wrote** are Vg verbs because the **to** and **for** mark the indirect objects **the rats** and **Henry Miller**:

Researchers **fed** a noncaloric goo **to the rats**.

Anaïs Nin **wrote** the stories **for Henry Miller**.

Not all **to** and **for** prepositional phrases contain indirect objects. In the following sentence, **sent** is a Vg verb because the prepositional phrase **to her husband** contains the indirect object **her husband** and **to** marks that indirect object (which receives and perceives).

The florist **sent** the roses **to her husband**.

In the next sentence,

> The florist **sent** the roses to Cincinnati,

to Cincinnati is a prepositional phrase that functions as an adverb of place. Unless you personify Cincinnati, making it humanlike, it is simply a location, a city along the Ohio River. Because **to Cincinnati** is an adverb of place, the verb **sent** is a one-place transitive verb in this sentence, not a Vg verb.

You can usually test whether a word or phrase is an adverb by asking such questions about it as where? when? how? or how often? When the **to** or **for** phrase contains an indirect object, you have to ask "to whom?" or "for whom?" For instance, you can ask about the first florist sentence, "To whom did the florist send the roses?" **Her husband** is the answer. You can ask about the second florist sentence, "Where did the florist send the roses?" **To Cincinnati** is the answer. Determine whether the next two sentences are transitive or Vg verbs.

> Thomas Jefferson **left** a marvelous legacy for Americans.

> The truck **delivered** the bricks to the building site.

Since you can ask of the first sentence, "For whom did Thomas Jefferson leave a marvelous legacy?" and answer **Americans**, **Americans** is an indirect object and **left** is a Vg verb. But you must ask of the second sentence, "Where did the truck deliver the bricks?" **To the building site** is the proper reply. So **to the building site** is a prepositional phrase that indicates place, and **delivered** is a transitive verb.

Occasionally a Vg verb will have an inanimate indirect object, as in

> Siskel and Ebert **gave** two thumbs up to *Schindler's List*.

But asking the right question should still get you the correct answer. If you asked, "Where did Siskel and Ebert give two thumbs up?" you wouldn't expect the answer to be "to *Schindler's List*." If you asked, "To what movie did Siskel and Ebert give two thumbs up?" the answer would be "*Schindler's List*." Because it does not answer a question about place, the prepositional phrase **to *Schindler's List*** does not function as an adverb of place. The noun phrase ***Schindler's List*** does function as an indirect object, even though it is not animate.

Vg verbs are one type of two-place transitives; they must be followed by both an indirect object and a direct object, whether the indirect object is in a **to** or **for** prepositional phrase, or whether it sits next to the verb.

Two-Place Transitives: Vc Verbs

Vc verbs (pronounced vee cee) are also two-place transitives. But they are followed first by a noun phrase that functions as a direct object, then another noun phrase, an adjective, or an infinitive phrase. These phrases function as COMPLEMENTS. Vc verbs are like the verb **consider** as it occurs in either

> Republicans **consider** Democrats big spenders.

> or

> Some rock fans **consider** the Rolling Stones old-fashioned.

> or

> Thomas Jefferson **considered** the Missouri Compromise to be the death of the nation.

In the first example, **consider** is followed by the direct object **Democrats**, which in turn is followed by **big spenders**, a noun phrase complement. In the second example, **the Rolling Stones** is the direct object and the adjective **old-fashioned** is the complement. In the third example, the **Missouri Compromise** is the direct object; the infinitive phrase **to be the death of the nation** is the complement.

The term "complement" in grammar usually refers to a structure that completes a phrase or clause. In this sense, Republicans, in the example above, don't simply consider Democrats. They consider Democrats **big spenders**. Similarly, rock fans don't consider the Rolling Stones. They consider the Rolling Stones **old-fashioned**. Nor did Jefferson consider the Missouri Compromise. He considered it **to be the death of the nation**. Complements to objects in sentences with Vc verbs, are called OBJECT COMPLEMENTS. Here are some more sentences with Vc verbs followed by object complements:

> The sexual revolution **makes** some people **uncomfortable**.

> Many historians **believe** FDR **to be our most effective president**.

Ad agencies **call** young people **Generation X-ers.**

The second point to help you identify complements to Vc verbs is that object complements have some of the same characteristics as the predicate nouns and predicate adjectives that follow linking verbs. Noun object complements refer to the same person or thing as their objects, just as predicate nouns refer to the same person or thing as their subjects. In the examples, **big spenders** renames **Democrats** and **our most effective president** renames **FDR.** Adjectives that are object complements give characteristics of their direct objects. So, if some rock fans are correct, the Rolling Stones are **old fashioned** and some people can be **uncomfortable** because of the sexual revolution.

Vc verbs are two-place transitive verbs whose direct objects are followed by nouns, adjectives, or infinitive phrases, all of which function as object complements.

The Verb Be

Many grammar books include the verb BE with the linking verbs because it is like the linking verbs in several ways. But for reasons that will become apparent in later chapters, it is more efficient to list BE as a separate verb category. For one thing, listing BE as a separate category will simplify many of the statements that we make about verbs: we won't need to make as many exceptions.

It's easy to recognize the verb BE; all you have to do is remember that BE has eight different forms: *be, is, am, are, was, were, been,* and *being.* Like the linking verbs, BE can be followed by nouns or adjectives. And these nouns and adjectives function as predicate nouns and predicate adjectives, as in

The programmer **is** a math whiz.

Marilyn Monroe **was** insecure.

BE is unlike the linking verbs because it can be followed immediately by an adverb of place, as in

My mother **was** in the next room.

The post office **is** down the road.

An adverb that follows BE is sometimes called A PREDICATE ADVERB. Grammarians often classify the adjectives, nouns, and adverbs that follow BE as SUBJECTIVE COMPLEMENT.

Summary of Verb Types

The following chart summarizes the six verb types. The structures around the verbs are also identified in terms of their relationships. Parentheses around a structure means that it may or may not occur. So, parentheses around the adverb following an intransitive verb says that an intransitive may be followed by an adverb but that an adverb does not have to occur after the verb. Brackets around several structures mean that one or the other must occur. In this way, brackets around the adjective phrase and noun phrase following a linking verb means that a linking verb must be followed by either an adjective phrase or a noun phrase; one or the other of them must follow a linking verb. Relationships are defined after colons. So, **Noun Ph: DObj** says that a structure is a noun phrase that functions as a direct object.

1. Noun Ph: Subj + **Intransitive Verb (Adverb)**

2. Noun Ph: Subj + **Linking Verb** + $\begin{bmatrix} \textbf{Adjective Ph: Pred Adj} \\ \textbf{Noun Ph: PredN} \end{bmatrix}$

3. Noun Ph: Subj + **Transitive Verb** + **Noun Ph: DObj**

4. Noun Ph: Subj + **Vg** + $\begin{bmatrix} \textbf{Noun Ph: IObj + Noun Ph: DObj} \\ \textbf{Noun Ph: DObj} + \begin{Bmatrix} \textbf{to} \\ \textbf{for} \end{Bmatrix} \textbf{Noun Ph: IObj} \end{bmatrix}$

5. Noun Ph: Subj + **Vc** + **NP: DObj** + $\begin{bmatrix} \textbf{Adjective Ph: Obj Comp} \\ \textbf{Noun Ph: Obj Comp} \\ \textbf{Infinitive Ph: Obj Comp} \end{bmatrix}$

6. Noun Ph: Subj + **BE** + $\begin{bmatrix} \textbf{Adjective Ph: PredAdj} \\ \textbf{Noun Ph: PredN} \\ \textbf{Adverb of Place: Pred Adv} \end{bmatrix}$

Verbs and Slots and Nuclei

You can think of sentences as being composed of verbs and slots (positions) that have to be filled by specific structures; in turn, each of these structures has a function. Looked at in this way, a linking verb is followed by a slot that must be filled by an adjective functioning as a predicate adjective or by a noun functioning as a predicate noun; a transitive verb is followed by a slot that must be filled by a noun functioning as a direct object; a Vg verb is followed by two slots; and so on. Verbs are also preceded by noun phrase subject slots.

The six core verbs and the slots shown on the chart are sometimes referred to as SENTENCE NUCLEI. You can add other kinds of structures to any nucleus. We often add adverbs to sentence nuclei, for instance. So a sentence with a transitive verb may continue beyond the noun phrase direct object, as in

Lee Harvey Oswald shot JFK **from a window overlooking the motorcade route**.

From a window overlooking the motorcade route is a prepositional phrase functioning as an adverb of place (it tells you where the action took place). The point here is that, no matter how many other structures you add to the sentence, the nucleus contains a transitive verb, **shot**, that is followed immediately by a noun phrase functioning as a direct object. Adding other structures to a sentence nucleus does not change the essential relationships within the nucleus. The structures and functions within the nucleus determine the verb type.

We'll see in later chapters that these six verb types form a core of sentences that are the building blocks of the language. But in this chapter, we're concerned with identifying verbs and the slots associated with them within a sentence nucleus.

Verbs Can Change Categories

One important point to remember in identifying verbs is that, because they are defined by what immediately follows them, verbs fall into different categories when they are in different environments. So an individual word is not necessarily always a linking verb, or an intransitive verb, or a transitive verb. It may be one or another of those at different times. Suppose, for instance, instead of occurring in the sentence

> The president **looked** weary,

where it is a linking verb because it is followed by an adjective, **looked** occurred in the sentence

> The president **looked** at the reporters.

Then **looked** would be intransitive, not linking, because **at the reporters** is an adverb phrase that tells where the president looked. In the sentence

> Toni Morrison **writes** exquisitely,

the verb **writes** is intransitive, followed by an adverb telling how she writes. In the sentence

> Toni Morrison **writes** lyrical novels,

the verb **writes** is transitive, followed by a noun phrase object, **lyrical novels**. In the sentence

> GM **makes** the dream yours,

which appeared in a car ad, **makes** is a two-place transitive Vc verb, followed by a noun phrase object, **the dream**, and a noun phrase complement, **yours**. But in the sentence

> GM **makes** cars and trucks,

makes is a single-place transitive, followed only by a noun phrase object, **cars and trucks**.

The point is that because verbs are defined by what follows them, the same word can fit into several different verb categories.

More Patterns and Some References

Differentiating sentences into patterns is both a convenient and a practical way of classifying and subclassifying verbs. The six verb types presented in this chapter account for a large number of the verbs you're likely to come across. If you can distinguish these verbs, you should be able to analyze most English sentences, though perhaps not every one. After all, this book is an introduction to the system of English grammar, not an encyclopedic reference grammar. A more complete grammar would have to include several other verb classes and subclasses. And it would quickly become bogged down in minute and overwhelming details.

For instance, the explanation of verbs and sentence nuclei does not mention SEMI-TRANSITIVE verbs like **have, cost, resemble,** and **weigh,** which have some of the characteristics of transitive verbs. They are followed by noun phrase objects; but they can't be rearranged into passives. Sentences with semi-transitive verbs, such as

Emilio Estevez resembles Martin Sheen

and

Roseanne and Dan Connors weigh a ton,

do not have passive counterparts. You cannot say

*Martin Sheen is resembled by Emilio Estevez

or

*A ton is weighed by Roseanne and Dan Connors.

Nor does this chapter differentiate subclasses of two-place transitive Vg verbs. The sentence

The senator asked Ruth Bader Ginsburg a question

contains a verb with an indirect object (**Ruth Bader Ginsburg**) and a direct object (**a question**). But, unlike the indirect objects we looked at earlier, this indirect object will only move into an **of** prepositional phrase.

The senator asked a question of Ruth Bader Ginsburg.

---

*An asterisk in front of a sentence indicates that the sentence cannot occur in the language.

There are also sentences with **of** phrases, like

> United States policy deprived Native Americans *of their*
> *ancestral lands.*

While you cannot move the indirect object out of the prepositional phrase, nevertheless, the verb is still Vg.

Don't worry that you don't know everything. What you do know will allow you to analyze most of the subpatterns and relationships you haven't yet studied. If you can identify *Ruth Bader Ginsburg* and *a question* as noun phrases in the example, you know that the verb **asked** must be a two-place transitive. Though the first noun phrase following the verb moves into an **of** prepositional phrase rather than a **to** or **for** phrase, you can probably guess that the noun phrase *Ruth Bader Ginsburg* is an indirect object (Judge Ginsburg both receives and perceives the question) and that **asked** is a Vg verb. If you can see that *Native Americans* and *of their ancestral lands* are separate phrases, you can probably recognize *their ancestral lands* as an indirect object and **deprived** as a two-place transitive. In the same way if you are able to identify the noun phrases after **resemble** and **weigh** as objects rather than predicate nouns, you will know that the verbs are transitive rather than linking.

When you're ready for more grammatical information than this introductory text can offer, the following books provide excellent and copious reference material. Quirk, Greenbaum, Leech, and Svartvik's *Contemporary Grammar* is the latest and best one-volume grammar of English.

Curme, George O. *A Grammar of the English Language, I–II*. New York: D. C. Heath, 1931–1935; rpt. Essex, CT: Verbatim, 1977.

Jespersen, Otto. *A Modern English Grammar on Historical Principles*, I–IV. Copenhagen: Munksgaard, 1909–1949.

Quirk, Randolph and Sidney Greenbaum. *A Concise Grammar of Contemporary English*. New York: Harcourt, 1973.

Quirk, Randolph, Sidney Greenbaum, Geoffrey Leech, and Jan Svartvik. *A Contemporary Grammar of the English Language*. New York: Longman, 1985.

Summary

Knowing the six core verbs gives you a solid beginning for learning how to identify all the parts of a sentence nucleus. If you know, for instance, that in the sentence

> Dracula **remains** a popular literary character,

the verb **remains** is a linking verb, you know that the phrase **a popular literary character** must be either an adjective phrase or a noun phrase. Those are the only structures that can immediately follow a linking verb. Since **Dracula** and **a popular literary character** refer to the same person, you can identify **a popular literary character** as a noun phrase functioning as a predicate noun.

If you can identify the verb, you know what slot(s) must follow it. If you can identify the structure and function of the words in the slot(s) following a verb, you know the kind of verb. For instance, in the sentence

> Billy Joel **sang** "The Star-Spangled Banner,"

the phrase **"The Star-Spangled Banner"** is a noun phrase; thus the verb **sang** must be either a transitive verb, a linking verb, or a form of BE; only those three kinds of verbs can precede a single noun phrase. If you're unsure of which of the three it is, you can determine the answer by a process of elimination. Since you know that **sang** is not a form of BE, you can immediately narrow your choices to linking verb or transitive verb. Since **Billy Joel** and **"The Star-Spangled Banner"** do not refer to the same person or thing, you can be sure that **sang** is not a linking verb. It must be transitive. If you want more evidence, turn the sentence into a passive.

> "The Star-Spangled Banner" **was sung** by Billy Joel.

Everything that you know about verbs and the structures that follow them tells you that **sang** is transitive and that **"The Star-Spangled Banner"** is a direct object noun phrase.

To review, these are the main points of the chapter:

- Grammar is the system that puts words together into meaningful units.
- Sentences are the basic building blocks of language.
- At the heart of any sentence is a verb.
- There are six core verb types: intransitive, linking, transitive, Vg, Vc, and BE.
- We classify verbs according to the structures that immediately follow them.

- A verb, its subject, and the other slots associated with it form a sentence nucleus.
- We define a function by how a structure relates to a verb.

EXERCISES

I. WRITING DEFINITIONS

Define the following terms as completely as you can, giving examples wherever possible:

Parsing	Core verbs	Subjective complement
Transitive verb	Grammar	Predicate adjective
Linking verb	BE verb	Predicate noun
Indirect object	Vg verb	Predicate adverb
Direct object	Vc verb	
Intransitive verb	Complement	
Object complement	Intensifier	
Sentence nucleus		

II. IDENTIFYING VERB TYPES

Identify the verbs in the following sentences, and label the parts that follow the verbs. Explain how you decided that a verb was intransitive, linking, transitive, Vg, Vc, or a form of BE.

EXAMPLE

The umpire awarded Williams first base.

Explanation. In this sentence, I'm sure the verb **awarded** is a two-place transitive Vg. For one thing, it is followed by two noun phrases, **Williams** and **first base**. Since **Williams** can both perceive and receive the object, **first base**, **Williams** must be the indirect object. Another way I know that **awarded** is a Vg verb is that I can move the indirect object, **Williams**, into a **to** phrase, like this: The umpire **awarded** first base **to Williams**.

Sentences

1. Seat belts save lives.
2. War is a dangerous business.

3. Disney World offers visitors family entertainment.
4. Cancer frustrates microbiologists.
5. Roosevelt named Eisenhower Supreme Allied Commander.
6. Computer spreadsheets make business analysis easy.
7. Murphy's Law exists in our folklore.
8. Yellowstone is a national treasure.
9. Chris Evert demonstrated uncommon grace.
10. University officials suspended the fraternity.
11. The city council bought Saturns for the police department.
12. Women's colleges prepare students to be independent thinkers.
13. The cocaine supply seems limitless.
14. The audience remained absolutely silent.
15. Dad signed my report card.
16. Paranoids think themselves important.
17. Toxic waste threatens our habitat.
18. The state of Florida executed Theodore Bundy.
19. Social problems make law enforcement difficult.
20. Narcotics imitate the body's natural reward system.
21. Psychologist Stanley Coren calls border collies the smartest dogs.
22. Mutual funds provide investors high yields.
23. The first graders walked around the fire station.
24. God rested on the seventh day.
25. Cadillac's seating system acts like a shock absorber.
26. Some rebellious teens become runaways.
27. Alcoholism remains a major social problem.
28. The losing pitcher trudged to the locker room.
29. Beagle puppies are lovable.
30. Rattlesnakes scare most people.
31. A glade is a forest clearing.
32. American crocodiles are endangered.
33. My neighbor planted her perennials with care.
34. The Cordillero Sarmiento Mountains are in Chile.
35. A German submarine sank the *Lusitania*.
36. The *Lusitania* lies in 295 feet of water.
37. Sophie survived a concentration camp.
38. A brilliant moon paints the icebergs a fuchsia pink.
39. Libertarians oppose big government.
40. A steel band's sound is incredibly hypnotic.
41. Rubinstein became a concert pianist.
42. School resumes Monday.

43. Lincoln signed the Emancipation Proclamation.
44. Geraldo found Oprah an interesting guest.
45. The doorman found Oprah a cab.
46. Crack changed the drug scene.
47. The professor shouted.
48. Racism remains inexplicable.
49. Racism remains in our society.
50. Autism is a mystery.

CHAPTER 2 | *Analyzing Sentences*

Preview

In the first chapter, we classified verbs into six core types. In this chapter, we'll begin to analyze sentences into constituents. The first constituents we'll look at are noun phrase subjects and verb phrase predicates; then we'll consider the adverbs you can add to core sentence types; we'll examine prepositional phrases and multi-word verbs; and finally, we'll explore the principles of constituency and hierarchy.

The central fact to remember in analyzing sentences is that **grammar is a system**: parts of sentences aren't just strewn about helter skelter in any order. When you understand how the separate parts fit together systematically to form larger units, you understand how grammar works. Here are the points we'll cover in this chapter:

- Sentences break into two main parts—noun phrases and verb phrases (subjects and predicates).

- You can look at sentence parts as either structures (the classes they fall into) or functions (their relationships with other sentence parts).

- This book will sometimes show sentences analyzed into phrase structure diagrams. But no diagraming system can substitute for your being able to identify sentence parts and knowing how to label them as structures and relationships. Diagrams can help you visualize the analysis of a sentence; they are not the goal of sentence analysis.

- Words that work together as single units are called constituents.
- Sentence constituents are always nouns, verbs, adjectives, and adverbs; these appear as single words, phrases, or clauses.
- All constituents are constructed as hierarchies.
- Phrases have heads around which attributes cluster.

Two Main Sentence Parts

A sentence is composed of two main constituents—a NOUN PHRASE that functions as a SUBJECT and a VERB PHRASE that functions as a PREDICATE. In terms of meaning, a subject generally defines a topic and a predicate generally makes a comment about the topic. In terms of syntax, a subject occurs before a predicate.

To analyze sentences, you identify sentence components both by the class they fall into (their STRUCTURE) and by how they relate to one another (their FUNCTION). It is always important to differentiate structures from functions. Here are examples of the six core sentence types, with spaces separating subjects from predicates. Notice that when we analyze sentences, we will always label a component by both its structure (before the colon) and its function (after the colon), as in NP: Subj and VP: Pred.

1. Geraldo   **screamed**.
   NP: Subj   VP: Pred
2. The golfers   **seemed** frustrated.
   NP: Subj   VP: Pred
3. John Wayne Gacy   **disputed** the jury's decision.
   NP: Subj   VP: Pred
4. The police officer   **wrote** the mayor a ticket.
   NP: Subj   VP: Pred
5. Big city cops   **feel** themselves outgunned.
   NP: Subj   VP: Pred
6. *Citizen Kane*   **is** the best American movie.
   NP: Subj   VP: Pred

Finding Subjects and Predicates

Before we analyze the structures within predicates more closely, let's look at one method that many students find helpful for identifying subjects and predicates. This method is based on two facts about sentences. The first fact is that most sentences make statements, like

> The president will visit Moscow in June.
>
> American priorities have changed since the collapse of the Soviet Union.
>
> The researchers who discovered the oncogene are working on a new drug for cancer.

The second fact is that you can change a statement into a question that someone can answer with a "yes" or a "no." Here are the three statements again, turned into questions:

> The president will visit Moscow in June.
>
> Will the president visit Moscow in June?
>
> American priorities have changed since the collapse of the Soviet Union.
>
> Have American priorities changed since the collapse of the Soviet Union?
>
> The researchers who discovered the oncogene are working on a new drug for cancer.
>
> Are the researchers who discovered the oncogene working on a new drug for cancer?

To make a statement into a yes/no question, you move a word to the front of the sentence. As in the above examples, you often have words like **will**, **have**, and **are** to move; these are auxiliary words (you might know them as "helping verbs"). Auxiliary words signal the beginning of the predicate. The word or phrase that you move them around to form a question is the subject. So the above examples break into subjects and predicates in the following way:

Subject	*Predicate*
The president	**will** visit Moscow in June.
American priorities	**have** changed since the collapse of the Soviet Union.
The researchers who discovered the oncogene	**are** working on a new drug for cancer.

Verb phrases don't always contain a word like **will, have,** or **are** to move around the subject; often they begin with a verb alone, as in

Harriet's mother works at Wal-Mart.

If the predicate does not begin with an auxiliary word like **will, have,** or **are,** but with a verb, you make a yes/no question by putting **do, did,** or **does** at the beginning of the sentence.

Harriet's mother works at Wal-Mart.
↓
Does Harriet's mother work at Wal-Mart?

In this situation, you can test for subjects and predicates by going in the other direction: first put the **do** word at the beginning of the sentence; then move it to make the sentence an emphatic statement.

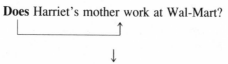

↓
Harriet's mother does work at Wal-Mart.

The subject is the phrase you move the **do** word around; the predicate begins at the word you move the **do** word next to, a verb. In the example, **Harriet's mother** is the subject of the original statement; **work(s) at Wal-Mart** is the predicate. This yes/no question test to find subjects and predicates is almost foolproof, whether you're working with short simple sentences or long complex sentences. The yes/no question test should help you get started identifying subjects and predicates.

Constituents and the Colonel

Noun phrases and verb phrases that function as subjects and predicates are the two main CONSTITUENTS of sentences, but they are far from the only constituents. Constituents are those words that work together as single units. For instance, noun phrase constituents work together as if they were single nouns; they may function as subjects, direct objects, indirect objects, complements—anything that nouns can function as. Verb phrase constituents work together to function either as predicates, as infinitive phrases, or as other constructions we'll meet in later chapters. Adverb constituents work together as adverbs (to show place, time, manner, etc.), and adjective constituents work as adjectives.

In its simplest sense, grammar consists only of noun, verb, adjective, and adverb constituents, and some "little" words like articles and conjunctions that essentially hold the noun, verb, adjective, and adverb constituents together and relate them to one another. Constituents can be single words, phrases several words long, or clauses dozens of words long.

Since sentences are composed of constituents that either sit next to one another or exist within one another, grammatical analysis is a little like cutting a chicken into parts. If you do it correctly, each part will be a recognizable component—a wing, a breast, a thigh, a leg.

The chicken metaphor points to the essence of the issue. Some years ago, KFC ran a TV commercial that showed customers of another chicken restaurant dismayed when they looked into their buckets to find unrecognizable parts counted as complete pieces of chicken—legs cut in two, for instance. When they questioned the clerk, he replied brashly, "pieces is pieces." When the scene switched to a KFC store, the customers happily looked into their buckets to find parts they recognized as proper constituents of chickens—complete legs, thighs, and other parts.

Like the KFC customers, you'll find only recognizable constituents when you do grammatical analysis—nouns, verbs, adjectives, and adverbs. No strange-looking parts cut in half. Grammatical constituents will always be nouns, verbs, adjectives, and adverbs. They may be single words, multiple-word phrases, or clauses. They may get very long and very complicated. But they'll always be recognizable parts. In grammatical analysis, as in chicken cutting, it's not true that "pieces is pieces." Pieces are constituents. Recognizable constituents. This is important to the structural system of language.

Some people find it helpful when they're doing grammatical analysis to show the constituents and their relationships visually on diagrams. Here are the first six example sentences diagramed to reflect all the structural and functional information discussed so far:

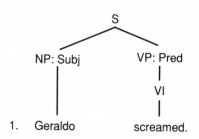

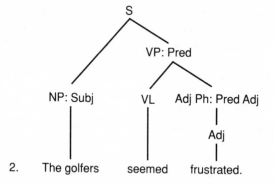

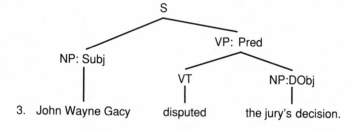

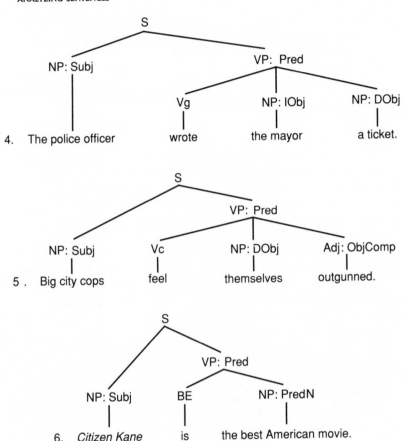

4.
S
NP: Subj — VP: Pred
The police officer

VP: Pred — Vg / NP: IObj / NP: DObj
wrote / the mayor / a ticket.

5.
S
NP: Subj — VP: Pred
Big city cops

VP: Pred — Vc / NP: DObj / Adj: ObjComp
feel / themselves / outgunned.

6.
S
NP: Subj — VP: Pred
Citizen Kane

VP: Pred — BE / NP: PredN
is / the best American movie.

The diagrams show that the sentences are each composed of a noun phrase plus a verb phrase. The verb phrases in turn are composed of either a verb alone (as in the case of the intransitive) or a verb followed by various structures. Because they show sentences broken down into their structural patterns, diagrams such as these can help you to understand the relationships among the constituents.

The last diagram above, for instance, shows that the noun phrase constituent *Citizen Kane* and the verb phrase constituent **is the best American movie** function as the two main components of the sentence, the subject and the predicate. It also shows that the noun phrase constituent **the best American movie**, since it follows the verb **is** and is part of the verb phrase, functions as the predicate noun. It is important to determine constituency when you analyze sentences; it is the most important issue in grammatical analysis. You have to understand which words work together as units before you can establish relationships among the units.

Hierarchies

The large constituents like clauses (sentences are independent clauses; independent clauses can stand alone), noun phrases, and verb phrases break down into smaller constituents. This fact that larger constituents contain smaller constituents points to the major structural pattern of language: the HIERARCHY. A hierarchy is a pattern in which structures fit within structures. Hierarchies define the basic structural principle of clauses and phrases.

We've already seen that clause constituents break down into subjects and predicates. Phrase constituents break down into heads and attributes. ATTRIBUTES are words that "cluster around" or "aggregate around" heads. The HEAD of a phrase constituent is central to the phrase. It is always a word that the constituent structure is named for: the head of a noun phrase is a noun, the head of a verb phrase is a verb, the head of an adjective phrase is an adjective. You get the picture. In sentence 6 above, the head of the noun phrase that functions as the predicate noun, **the best American movie**, is the noun **movie**. The attributes **American**, **best**, and **the** all cluster around the noun **movie** in constituents within constituents. Here is a more complete diagram to show how the noun phrase **the best American movie** is constructed:

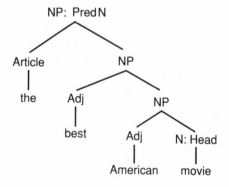

When attributes cluster around heads, they form HIERARCHIES. They don't simply clump around heads in any order; they make structures that fit within structures, as the diagram of the noun phrase **the best American movie** indicates.

Constituency, heads, and how attributes cluster around heads in hierarchical configurations are central issues in grammatical analysis. We'll be discussing them in more detail as they become important in other chapters. For the rest of this chapter, we'll be concerned with showing how to analyze sentences into their major constituents. In later chapters, when we discuss in more detail the various components of sentences, we'll break those constituents into smaller and smaller pieces, but always into recognizable pieces—into constituents.

This section on hierarchies can be summarized in simple terms. The hierarchy is the major structural principle of grammar: smaller constituents fit within larger constituents. Just as clauses are composed of subjects and predicates, phrases are composed of heads and attributes.

You can liken this hierarchical system of language to the nested boxes you might have played with as a child. When you opened one box, there was a smaller, exact duplicate within it, and so on until you reached the last one. That's the way with sentences. No matter how large or complicated they become, if you take them apart one piece at a time, you'll find familiar constituents fitting inside one another. It sounds complicated, but when you understand this basic structural principle of language, you'll be able to do any kind of grammatical analysis. In fact, when you get stuck, you might want to re-read these sections on constituency and hierarchies.

Diagraming and a Ride on the Author's Hobbyhorse

There are several ways to diagram sentences. The examples in the previous section are called TREE DIAGRAMS because they show constituents "branching off" from one another. Tree diagrams clearly illustrate the structure of constituents and how constituents relate to one another. You can show exactly the same information with IMMEDIATE CONSTITUENT DIAGRAMS, which are rather like tree diagrams turned upside down.

disputed	the jury's decision.
VT	NP: DObj

John Wayne Gacy

NP: Subj   VP: Pred

You can also diagram sentences by enclosing constituents in LABELED BRACKETS, one inside the other.

[[John Wayne Gacy]   [[disputed]   [the jury's decision]]]
        NP:Subj   VT   NP: DObj
           S   VP: Pred

You can draw traditional diagrams, with lines going off in all directions.

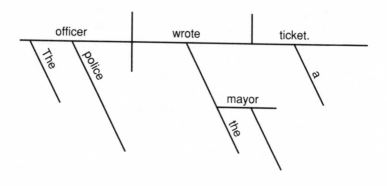

Or you can diagram as I do in the Appendix by naming constituents and drawing lines beneath them:

John Wayne Gacy   disputed   the jury's decision.
—— NP:Subj ——   —VT—   ——NP:DObj ——
                 ————————VP:Pred————————

How often you diagram, what kind of diagrams you should use, or how detailed you should make your diagrams depends on how helpful you find diagraming. Because they capture the relationships between constituents and reflect hierarchies in the structure of constituents, tree diagrams will often be used in this book to illustrate how sentences are analyzed. You have to keep in mind that we're working with fairly simple sentence structures in these first few chapters. Any diagraming system works to some extent with such sentences. When sentences become long and complicated, any diagraming system falls apart, becomes too complicated to give you much help.

Hanging on a wall in my office is a poster that diagrams a "sentence," a 958-word stretch of text from Proust's *Cities of the Plain*. The label on the poster claims it is the longest sentence. The poster is wrong; the 958 words from Proust do not make "the longest sentence." It's not the longest sentence anyone has written; nor is it the longest sentence anyone could write. But that's another issue.

The issue we're concerned with is the usefulness of the diagram. It's not very useful, but it is much admired. The traditional diagram that outlines the "sentence," with lines going off every which way to fill the 3' × 5' poster, is marvelled at by almost everyone who comes into my office for the first time. "Wonderful," some say, or "I wish I could do that." They're wrong to value the diagram so much. It doesn't seem to have helped the diagrammer understand that he or she was diagraming a long fragment, though the diagrammer did know when to draw lines horizontally, when to draw them vertically, when to draw whole lines, and when to draw dotted lines. The diagram on the poster has so many lines coming off it in so many different ways that it is useless as a visual aid. The monster diagram is what it is: an interesting conversation piece in a grammarian's office. It is absolutely useless for any other purpose that I can figure out. It certainly wouldn't help anyone to understand the structure of the Proust sentence: the diagram is complicated and daunting.

The point to remember about diagraming is simple: if it helps you to visualize the structure and function of constituents, use diagrams. But don't get too caught up in them; no diagraming system will help when sentences become much more involved than those we're analyzing in these first few chapters. And diagraming is neither a virtue nor a central goal of grammatical analysis. Diagraming is at best a tool that can sometimes help you visualize constituents and their relationships. Diagrams are tools, not goals.

Prepositional Phrases

PREPOSITIONS seem to occur everywhere in speaking and writing. You probably can't write or speak more than a sentence or so without using a preposition. Prepositions relate sentence parts. You may have learned in elementary school that prepositions show what an airplane can do to a cloud: the plane can fly **through** the cloud, **into** the cloud, **over** the cloud, **under** the cloud, **around** the cloud, **toward** the cloud, or **by** the cloud. Actually, prepositions are much more diverse than the airplane-cloud mnemonic device suggests. Among other things, they tell us when (**after** the dance), how long (**for** the summer), why (**because of** the stock market collapse), how (**like** a sailor), or what condition (**despite** his disability). Prepositions are usually one word, like **out**, **on**, or **with**. But they can sometimes be two or or even more words long, like **except for**, **as for**, **with regard to**, or **in spite of**.

As their name implies, prepositions are **pre**-positions. They precede the noun phrases with which they form constituents. A noun phrase that follows a preposition functions as an OBJECT OF A PREPOSITION; sometimes objects of prepositions are called OBLIQUE OBJECTS, to differentiate them from objects of verbs, direct objects. A preposition along with its noun phrase object constitutes a PREPOSITIONAL PHRASE. Prepositional phrases often function as adverbs. Here is a sentence with a prepositional phrase, **through the Danish Straits**, that functions as an adverb of place:

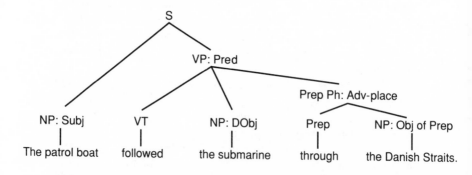

The next sentence contains a prepositional phrase that functions as an adverb that shows a cause (the coal smoke caused the stinging):

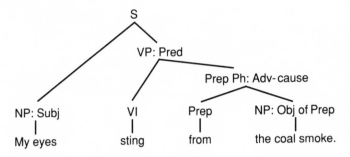

Adverbs Explained, Sort Of

You can expand any sentence nucleus by adding ADVERBS to it. Adding adverbs does not change the verb type.

> The baby cried loudly **all night long.** (VI)
>
> The Soviet Union remained our enemy **throughout the cold war.** (VL)
>
> Marge was the best real estate agent **in this town.** (BE)
>
> The new outfielder hit two homers **to prove his value.** (VT)
>
> L.L. Bean sent the package to Mom **by mistake.** (Vg)
>
> Perot called the president foolish **when the White House proposed the trade agreement.** (Vc)

Often you can add two, three, or even more adverbs to the nucleus of a sentence.

> L.L. Bean sent the package to Mom **[in Tucson] [by mistake].**
>
> The new outfielder hit two homers **[into the red seats] [before the fourth inning] [to prove his value].**

Among other things, adverbs tell you how, when, where, why, through what means, to what extent, how often, how far, under what condition. By giving you such information, adverbs specify relationships and help to orient readers and listeners. Adverbs usually put the content of a sentence into the proper context, like time, place, manner, reason, condition, extent.

In his recent book on the relationship of linguistics to school grammar texts, Brock Haussamen calls adverbs "one of the most complex and slippery categories in all of grammar."[1] Haussamen suggests introducing students to the concept of adverbs with a definition he cites from a book by Shuan-Fan Huang: "'Adverbs may be described as the principal ways in which the language user characterizes the conditions and circumstances, the hows and wherefores of actions and events.'" Haussamen continues that the important point to convey to students is "the great range of descriptive possibilities that the adverb provides." I like Haussamen's suggestions because they are close to my own sense of the subject. Adverbs are complex and slippery. You should remember that they put the content of a sentence into the proper context (my definition) or, if it makes more sense to you, that they are the principal means by which a writer or speaker "characterizes the conditions and circumstances . . . of actions and events" (Shuan-Fan Huang's definition).

Now let's look at some of the ideas adverbs can convey and the variety of forms they can assume (don't worry about all the forms yet; you won't have to identify adverbial infinitive phrases or adverb clauses, for instance, until several chapters down the road). Take a look at the example sentences above. In the first sentence, **loudly** is an adverb of manner; it's a single word that tells how. In the second, **throughout the cold war** is an adverb of duration; it's a prepositional phrase that tells how long. **To prove his value** is an adverb of reason (or purpose); it's an infinitive phrase that explains why. **By mistake** is an adverb of cause; it's a prepositional phrase that tells the motive (or cause). And **when the White House proposed the trade agreement** is an adverb of time; it's a clause that tells when. There are also adverbs of

instrument (The carpenter hit the nail **with a hammer**),

means (The firefighter reached the second floor **by the stairs**),

agency (The tree was trimmed **by the gardener**),

association (The senator votes **with the Democrats**),

---

[1]*Revising the Rules: Traditional Grammar and Modern Linguistics.* Dubuque, IA: Kendall/ Hunt, 1993.

frequency (Justine listens to the news **every so often**),

condition (The health care bill would go nowhere **without Hillary**),

extent (Ruth hit the ball **as far as possible**).

These are the most common adverbial relationships, but they do not exhaust all the possibilities.

Adverbs are difficult to define and sometimes difficult to identify. They are difficult to define because they show so many different kinds of relationships; they are difficult to identify because they are "realized" by so many different kinds of structures. Here are some examples of the kinds of structures you will most frequently find as adverbs. We commonly make adverbs out of adjectives by adding **-ly**.

> loud → loudly
>
> bright → brightly
>
> frequent → frequently
>
> quick → quickly
>
> hasty → hastily

We sometimes use nouns and noun phrases as adverbs.

> last summer
>
> the day before yesterday
>
> Tuesday

We often use prepositional phrases as adverbs.

> in the middle
>
> by the bridge
>
> with the British
>
> because of his disability
>
> during the game

We use whole clauses as adverbs.

because Koresh refused to surrender

after the attorney general accepted blame

although the plumber guaranteed his work

in case it rains

if the Republicans continue to filibuster

And we use other structures as adverbs as well, structures like participles, absolute phrases, and infinitives; we'll talk about these in later chapters.

Try not to let all this confuse you. There are lots of different structures that can function as adverbs, and there are lots of different kinds of adverbial relationships. But as you learn more and more about grammatical analysis, you'll see that the system of grammar makes sense because all the parts fit together into a whole. And while it is true that adverbs can be dismaying, it is also true that most of the time they're simple and straightforward. As you work through the book, you'll discover how adverbs fit into the overall picture.

Multiple-Word Verbs

So far we've discussed only one-word verbs. But it is common in English for two or more words to function as a single verb constituent. The key word here is "constituent," indicating words that function together as single units. In the following sentences, for instance, the two-word phrases **picked up** and **bawled out** function as single constituents; they are two-word transitive verbs.

Edward Albee **picked up** a third Pulitzer Prize in 1994.

Tony La Russo **bawled out** the umpire.

To test whether **picked up** and **bawled out** are transitive verbs, you can make the sentences passive, moving the subject noun phrases into **by** phrases and the object noun phrases into the first positions.

Edward Albee picked up **a third Pulitzer Prize** in 1994.
↓
A third Pulitzer Prize was picked up **by Edward Albee** in 1994.

Tony La Russo bawled out **the umpire**.
↓
The umpire was bawled out **by Tony La Russo**.

When multiple-word verbs are transitive, you can often move the VERB PARTICLES—the words like **up, down,** and **out** that form constituents with the verbs—around the object noun phrases.

David Letterman **pulled off** the scam.
↓
David Letterman **pulled** the scam **off**.

The librarian **looked up** the author in *Who's Who*.
↓
The librarian **looked** the author **up** in *Who's Who*.

In fact, if the object of a multiple-word transitive verb is a pronoun, the particle must occur after it.

David Letterman **pulled** it **off**.

The librarian **looked** it **up** in *Who's Who*.

You can't say

*David Letterman **pulled off** it.

*The librarian **looked up** it in *Who's Who*.

Multiple-word verbs are not always transitive; they can be intransitive as well. In the next examples, **blew up, played around,** and **broke down** are intransitive verbs.

The silo **blew up**.

George **played around** before his marriage.

The defendant **broke down** after the verdict.

In those intransitive verb examples, **up, around,** and **down** are not adverbs telling places. They form constituents with **blew, played,** and **broke**—verb constituents.

Constituency is the issue. Verb particles are often confused with prepositions. They differ from prepositions, though, because they make constituents with verbs, not with noun phrases. Notice the difference between the following two sentences:

> The secretary of state **called up** the president.

> The secretary of state **called** up the stairs.

To begin with, when you read them aloud, you say them differently because of their different constituency. In the first, you pause slightly before the noun phrase **the president**. In the second, you pause before **up**. That's because **up the stairs** makes a single constituent in the second sentence; it is a prepositional phrase that functions as an adverb of place. **Up the stairs** answers the question, "Where did the secretary of state call?" So **call** is an intransitive verb followed by an adverb of place. And **up** is a preposition, forming a constituent with the noun phrase **the stairs**. In the first sentence, **called up** is a single constituent, a two-word transitive verb followed by a noun phrase direct object, **the president**. **Up** is a verb particle because it forms a constituent with the verb, not with the following noun phrase. As a further test that **called up** is a transitive verb constituent in the first sentence, you can turn that sentence into a passive.

> The secretary of state **called up** the president.
> ↓
> The president was **called up** by the secretary of state.

If you diagram the two sentences, you would diagram them differently to show their different constituencies.

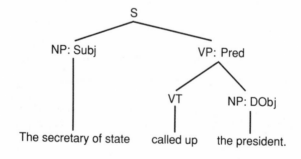

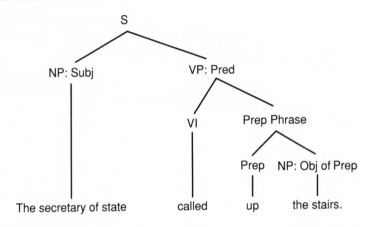

When you consider the differences between multiple-word verbs, verbs that form constituents with particles, and prepositional phrases, prepositions that form constituents with noun phrases, you can see why constituency is such a central principle in grammatical analysis.

Summary

Like math and science, grammar is a cumulative subject. That is, what you learn in one chapter affects what you learn in the next. You have to remember the information about verb types from chapter 1 in order to successfully navigate through the beginning lessons on analyzing sentences in chapter 2. And you'll need the information and skills you acquire in chapters 1 and 2 to make it through chapter 3, and so on. To make it through chapter 10, you'll have to know all the information in the previous nine chapters.

So learning the information is important, very important. But information alone won't make you proficient. You'll need to do more than read the chapters in this book and memorize patterns and definitions in order to master grammatical analysis. If you know the old joke about the Midwestern tourist who gets lost in Manhattan and stops an old woman on the street to ask for directions to Carnegie Hall, you know what more you'll need to do. Here's the joke for those who aren't familiar with it:

"How do you get to Carnegie Hall?" asks the Midwesterner. The old woman looks sternly at the young man, shakes her umbrella in his direction, and says (in an ethnic dialect of your choice), "Young man, you have to Practice! Practice! Practice!"

Like a lot of old jokes that pass from generation to generation, there's a lesson to be learned from this one. Practice will make you proficient at grammatical analysis as well as get you to Carnegie Hall. To encourage you to "get to Carnegie Hall" grammatically, each chapter in the book has lots of exercises for you to test your knowledge and try out your new skills. So Practice! Practice! Practice! Knowledge and practice together are the essence of doing grammar.

The following are the main points of chapter 2:

- Sentences break into two main parts—noun phrases and verb phrases (subjects and predicates); you begin to analyze sentences by identifying those two parts.
- You can look at sentence parts either as structures (the classes they fall into) or as functions (their relationships with other sentence parts).
- This book will sometimes show sentences analyzed into phrase structure diagrams. But no diagraming system can substitute for your being able to identify sentence parts and knowing how to label their structures and relationships. Diagrams can help you visualize the analysis of a sentence; they are not the goal of sentence analysis.
- Words that function together as single units are called constituents.
- Sentence constituents are always nouns, verbs, adjectives, and adverbs; these appear as single words, phrases, or clauses.
- All constituents are structured as hierarchies.
- Phrases have heads around which attributes cluster.

EXERCISES

I. WRITING DEFINITIONS

Define the following words and phrases as completely as you can, giving examples whenever possible:

Noun phrase	Verb phrase
Structure	Function
Subject	Predicate

Constituent	Head
Hierarchies	Prepositional phrase
Adverb	Multi-word verb
Particle	Attribute

II. IDENTIFYING SENTENCE CONSTITUENTS

First, identify the verb types in the following sentences. Then analyze the sentences as far as you are able, labelling both structures and functions. Identify, as well, heads of constituents. If it helps your analysis, diagram the sentences. When appropriate, comment on how you came to decisions about constituents or labels.

EXAMPLE

Oncology nurses care for dying patients.

Explanation. Only six words but a tough sentence. **Oncology nurses** is the noun phrase subject. The yes/no question test assures me of that. I can make the sentence into a question by adding **do: Do** oncology nurses care for dying patients? And I can move the **do** around **oncology nurses**, to produce Oncology nurses **do** care for dying patients. So **care for dying patients** is the verb phrase predicate. Now comes the tough part. The verb is either a two-word transitive, **care for**, or a single-word intransitive, **care**, followed by a prepositional phrase, **for dying patients**, which functions as an adverb. I'll choose **care for** as a two-word transitive verb. For one thing, I say "**care for**" as a single unit, without pausing between the words. For another thing, I can turn the sentence into a passive: **Dying patients are cared for by oncology nurses.** Here is the sentence diagramed:

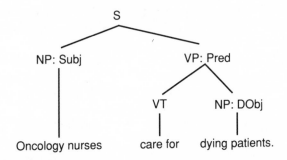

Sentences

1. The boiler exploded with a loud bang.
2. A dancer's body is her living voice.
3. Americans love informal dining.
4. The aircraft commander behaved prudently.
5. Sagebrush carpets western terrain.
6. Dr. Jekyll became a different person after his experiment.
7. The groom showed up in a brocade tux.
8. Stephen King gives readers scary stories.
9. Our local yards turned brown because of the winter frost.
10. Literary historians call many nineteenth-century American writers regionalists.
11. The International Olympic Committee returned Jim Thorpe's medals to his family in 1983.
12. Holocaust Museum visitors find their experience unsettling.
13. Amelia Earhart disappeared in 1937 during an around-the-world flight.
14. Spring is hiking season in Idaho.
15. The chef made the anniversary couple a mango-basil soup.
16. The Senate came up with a compromise bill despite White House opposition.
17. AIDS was a big-city plague until the '90s.
18. The 1948 Chrysler Town and Country convertible makes an unforgettable impression at antique car shows.
19. George Washington named this West Virginia town Bath for its warm springs.
20. American voters remain skeptical about politicians' sincerity.
21. Jell-O sales plummeted during the '70s.
22. Thomas Jefferson left Americans a marvelous legacy.
23. Huck is an unreliable narrator.
24. Many Midwesterners moved to California after World War II.
25. A peaceful new world order proved a fleeting dream in the cold war's aftermath.
26. Oberlin's three-year degree program reduces college tuition by one-fourth.
27. Cowhands consider the Calgary Stampede a rip-roaring party.
28. *Hamlet* ends in a bloody melee.
29. Gardening clothes became fashionable during the '80s.

30. Thoreau offered advice to young people in *Walden*.
31. South Africans elected Mandela their first president.
32. Soviet economic policy was ineffective in the technological age.
33. The Mets gave up three runs in the fifth inning.
34. A human being breathes 500 million times during an average lifetime.
35. General Grant's determination made him victorious.
36. Leadville, Colorado, is America's highest city.
37. Distance comes from a balanced golf swing.
38. The shuttle *Columbia* carried *Star Trek* creator Gene Rodenberry's ashes into space.
39. TV broadcasts the Super Bowl throughout the world.
40. Lead-based paint remains a danger in older housing projects.
41. The Appalachian Center looks out for eastern Kentucky's image.
42. One fitness guru dubbed couch potatoes vidiots.
43. Orlando is the world's biggest tourist attraction.
44. The Supreme Court gave women an option with the *Roe* vs. *Wade* decision.
45. IRS sends taxpayers their refunds within six weeks.
46. The Tagua Palm grows in the Ecuadorean rain forest.
47. Bosnia's situation turned nightmarish after Yugoslavia's dissolution.
48. Fifteen million Americans suffer from carpal tunnel syndrome.
49. A great burger is great because of its prime beef.
50. Many elderly people see their lifestyles diminished after retirement.

CHAPTER 3

Expanding Verb Phrases

Preview

In this chapter, we'll look closely at the components of the MAIN VERB—the verb phrase constituent which contains the verb, along with the elements that mark the categories TENSE, MODALITY, and ASPECT. These three categories indicate the STATUS of a verb. Many grammar books lump the three into one category that they call tense, and then these books equate tense with real-world time. In contrast, we'll look at tense, modality, and aspect as separate but closely related grammatical concepts that overlap with real-world time but aren't always the same thing. We'll also take a close look at the constituents that make up tense, modality, and aspect: modal auxiliaries, the auxiliary markers HAVE and BE, verb past participle forms, and verb present participle forms.

If you keep an open mind to the idea of separating the three concepts into distinct but closely related categories that differ from each other in both form and meaning, you should find the ideas in the chapter interesting and enlightening. I think you'll find it's actually much simpler to look at the status of a verb as composed of three concepts rather than one. I hope you'll agree once you've worked your way through the chapter.

Here are the main points in the chapter:

- The verb and its tense, modality, and aspect markers make up the main verb.

- Tense, modality, and aspect are three separate grammatical categories indicating the status of a verb.
- Tense in English has two forms—past and present.
- Tense determines the physical shape of the first word in the main verb, only the first word. The rest of the words in the main verb will take a different form, a different principal part.
- Modality, or mood, relates to the purpose of a sentence—whether it makes a statement, asks a question, gives an order, or indicates possibility. Modality is indicated by a change in the form of a sentence.
- Conditional mood, which essentially refers to possibility or probability, is formed by the addition of a modal auxiliary (helping verb) to the verb phrase.
- Aspect, which indicates that the action of a verb is either completed or ongoing, occurs in two forms—perfect and progressive.
- Most verbs in English are regular; this means that they form their past tense with a -d or -ed and that their past tense forms are the same as their past participle forms.
- Verbs have five principal parts: base (infinitive), present tense, past tense, present participle, and past participle.

Verb Status

When they categorize the three concepts tense, modality, and aspect under the single cover term tense, grammar books conjugate verbs into such categories as past tense (played), future tense (will play), past conditional tense (might play), present perfect tense (has played) or present progressive tense (is playing). Then they ask you to memorize their long, complicated conjugation lists. Lots of grammarians, myself included, don't think that it's correct to dump all three concepts into one large category called tense; nor do I think it's useful to memorize long lists.

Defining tense as one large category that includes tense, modality, and aspect and that corresponds exactly to real-world time, obscures certain basic characteristics of verb phrases. Making students memorize lists of conjugations wastes time and energy: any native English speaker already knows how to conjugate the verbs in her own language. And she can learn to name the various concepts if she understands how the system works to create verb status.

Let's look at why it's more productive to think of tense, modality, and aspect as three separate grammatical categories indicating the STATUS of a verb. The main reason to think of them as separate categories is that tense, modality, and aspect occur as distinct forms: they are marked in three different ways. Here, for instance, is how the verb **play** changes form to show tense, modality, and aspect. The past tense form of **play** is shown by the -**ed** ending in **played**. The condition or modality of the verb is revealed by the word **might** in **might play** or by **will** in **will play**. The perfective aspect is expressed in the phrase **has played** by the word **has** plus the verb form **played**. And the progressive aspect is shown by the word **is** along with the verb form **playing** in the phrase **is playing**. Underlying these changes from tense to mood (modality) to aspect is a system that works in a regular manner for all but a small set of verbs in the language (the key words here are **system** and **regular**).

Just as tense, modality, and aspect should be thought of as different from each other because they are realized by different forms, the three concepts should be thought of as different from the real-world time concepts, which they correspond with only partially. Though they sometimes overlap with our sense of time in the real world, tense, mood, and aspect are grammatical concepts not exactly bound to real time.

The verb, along with the forms that show its tense, modality, and aspect, is called the main verb. The forms that show tense, modality, and aspect (the **might** or **will**, **has**, and **is** in the example above) constitute the AUXILIARY elements of the main verb.

In the sections that follow, we'll explain separately the auxiliary elements that create tense, modality, and aspect; then we'll look at how these auxiliary elements can fit together into larger patterns.

Tense

Tense determines the form of a verb. This point is important to note because, for reasons buried in the history of our language, English verbs exhibit only two tense forms — PAST and PRESENT. (Remember that we're talking about the grammatical concept tense, not real-world time, and we're focusing on the form changing characteristic of tense. The English language has perfectly adequate ways to show future time and other real-world time concepts.) Don't let the names past and present confuse you; the two verb forms could just as easily be called Form 1 and Form 2 (this discussion would probably be less confusing if that were the case). The past tense form more clearly relates to past time than the present tense form relates to present time. This explanation may be a bit different from the way you usually think of tense, but it's easy enough to demonstrate.

The two tense forms relate to time in different ways. If you were asked, "What did your neighbor do last night?" you could answer

My neighbor **walked** her dog.

The past tense form **walked** clearly indicates the action took place in the past. But the present tense form, either **walks** or **walk**, does not necessarily mean that the action of the verb is taking place at the present time. It often means that the action of the verb is a common practice, that it is something that happens habitually. For instance, if you were asked, "What does your neighbor do for exercise?" You'd probably answer with the present tense form **walks**, as in

My neighbor **walks** her dog.

By using the present tense form, you state that it is a common practice for your neighbor to walk her dog for exercise. She might not be out walking her dog at the present moment; nonetheless, she walks the dog frequently enough that you consider it routine for her to do so. So the present tense form can mean that an action takes place habitually.

Here's another example of how the present tense doesn't have to relate to present time. If we say,

Superman **defeats** Lex Luther again and again,

the verb **defeats** is officially in present tense form. Yet we might be using the present tense form to mean a past time idea, as the following sentences illustrate:

In early comic books, Superman **defeats** villain after villain. But in this new book-length comic, a villain kills Superman.

It's even possible to use the present tense form to indicate future time. Imagine being asked, "When does your plane leave?" You would likely answer with a present tense:

My plane **leaves** in three hours.

Here are diagrams to show how you indicate the main verb constituent and its tense:

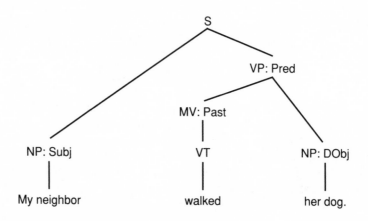

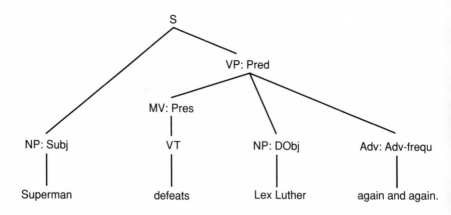

Tense and the Predicate

Tense is the only one of the three auxiliary concepts that *must* occur in the verb phrase predicate of a sentence. In fact, without tense, a verb phrase can't be a predicate. Because tense is necessary for a verb phrase to be a predicate, we can now expand our definition of a sentence from the first two chapters. A sentence is not simply a noun phrase subject plus a verb phrase; it is a noun phrase subject plus a verb phrase that contains tense.

Remember, if there is no tense, there is no predicate, and therefore there is no sentence. A verb that exhibits tense is said to be FINITE. In contrast, a verb that does not show a tense form is called an INFINITIVE because it is nonfinite. Some grammarians call a nonfinite form the BASE FORM rather than the infinitive.

Mood, a Brief Definition

We often classify sentences according to their purpose. Sentences generally make statements (Polynesians ruled Hawaii until 1788). They can ask questions (Why does cancer frustrate microbiologists?). They can order or command (Turn in your homework by noon Friday). Or sentences can indicate possibility or eventuality (Women athletes can compete against men in most sports). These notions about purpose—to make statements, to ask questions, to issue commands, or to indicate possibility—are called MOOD, or MODALITY. When a sentence makes a statement, it is in the INDICATIVE mood: this is the normal (unmarked) mood. When it asks a question, it is in the INTERROGATIVE mood. When it gives a command, it is in the IMPERATIVE mood. And when it indicates possibility, it is in the CONDITIONAL mood.

Modal Auxiliaries and Conditional Mood

Modal Auxiliaries

The mood, or purpose, of a sentence is related to its form. In this section, we're interested in how to construct the **conditional** mood. Normally, we make sentences conditional by adding a word like **may**, **should**, or **must** to the main verb. These words are called MODAL AUX-ILIARIES or simply MODALS. Some books call them HELPING VERBS. The most common modal auxiliaries are

Base/Present Form	*Past Form*
can	could
shall	should
will	would
may	might
	must

Ought to, used to, dare to, seem to, need to, happen to, want to, and **have to** can also act as modal auxiliaries; they are sometimes called SEMI-MODALS.

When they occur in a sentence, modal auxiliaries (or semi-modals) always occur at the beginning of the main verb constituent, as in

> Photography promotes visual awareness.
> ↓
> Photography **might** promote visual awareness.

> The president's speech reassured the Republicans.
> ↓
> The president's speech **has to** reassure the Republicans.

Notice that modals exhibit tense (since they occur first in the main verb). They are either past or present in form. **Could** is the past form of **can**; **should** is the past form of **shall**; **might** is the past form of **may**; and **would** is the past form of **will**. **Must** has no present form. So the first example sentence is in the *past* conditional mood; the second sentence is in the *present* conditional. **Might promote** and **has to reassure** are the main verbs of these sentences, as you can see in the diagrams.

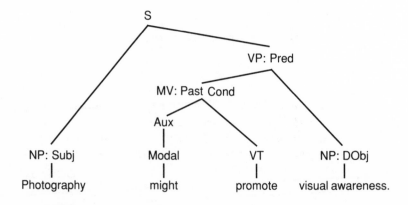

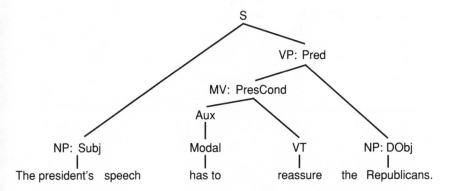

Conditional Mood and Future Time

The conditional moods concerns possibility (and the related notions of certainty, obligation, desire, necessity, promise, and even threat). Look at the example sentences again. The first notes the possibility that photography promotes visual awareness (it **might**). The second indicates the necessity that the president's speech reassure the Republicans (it **has to**).

Because they are related to possibility, conditional concepts concern events in the future. After all, something that is possible or necessary would have to happen at some point in time down the road. Since the concepts expressed by the conditional mood overlap the real-world concept of futurity, modals are sometimes said to express futurity. The next example may be viewed as a promise of some future engagement by the singer.

Mary Chapin Carpenter **will** perform in the civic auditorium.

The actual time for the performance is unspecified (just a vague promise) unless you add an adverb that indicates time more exactly. In the next sentence, the prepositional phrase **on Friday** functions as the adverb of time that specifies when Mary Chapin Carpenter will perform.

Mary Chapin Carpenter **will** perform in the civic auditorium **on Friday**.

This sentence does indicate future time, but it does so with an adverb.

Before we leave the conditional mood, we should note one more fact about its structure. The verb following a modal auxiliary is always in its nonfinite form, as are **promote, reassure,** and **perform** in the previous examples. Tense changes the form of only one word in a main verb, of the first word. This is an extremely important concept to remember when you have to identify the principal parts of words in the main verb. Since tense changes only the first word in a main verb to past or present form, the verb following a model is in its nonfinite form.

What Happened to Future Tense?

It's probably worthwhile addressing the question about future tense more than once in this chapter, since this question troubles some students and frequently arises in class. I haven't manipulated the language to rid it of future tense. The idea that there are only two tense forms in English—past and present—is not a new idea. For more than 150 years, grammarians who study the history of the language have noted that one of the differences between Germanic languages and other Indo-European languages is that Germanic languages exhibit only two tense forms (English is a Germanic language, like modern German, Dutch, and Swedish, among others). Grammarians from every school of grammar—traditional to tagmemic—readily acknowledge the fact that English has only past and present tense forms. The key word here is **form.** Tense in English is a form as well as an idea.

In short, that English has two tense forms is an old idea and well accepted in grammatical studies (except in some high school and junior high textbooks). The idea of two tenses takes nothing away from the language. Speakers of English can indicate future time easily enough. Generally we indicate future time, as the previous section indicates, by making the main verb conditional and by adding an adverb of time to the sentence, like this:

> *Gourmet Magazine* **will publish** ten chocolate cake recipes **next month.**

If it takes nothing away from our language, acknowledging the two-tense structure of main verbs doesn't complicate our grammatical system either. In fact, it probably simplifies the way we can explain the relationships between tense, modality, and aspect. In essence, recognizing that English has two tense forms allows us to look at verb phrases in a more analytic way than some textbooks present them.

Aspect

The relationship between tense and aspect can be complex. For our purposes it will do to say that ASPECT indicates that the action of a verb is either completed or continuing. Aspect occurs in two varieties—PERFECT and PROGRESSIVE.

Perfect Aspect

Perfect aspect indicates that the action of a verb is completed. Perfect aspect is shown by the auxiliary HAVE followed by a PAST PARTICIPLE (**had predicted**, **have unraveled** in the examples below).

The astrologist **had predicted** an earthquake on the sixteenth of the month.

Political relationships **have unraveled** on almost every continent.

Because the auxiliary **have** in the first example is in the past tense form, **had predicted** is past perfect, while **have unraveled** in the second example is present perfect. Don't let the terms past perfect and present perfect confuse you. Remember that both versions of the perfect aspect relate to completed action. The past and present designations refer only to the tense form of the auxiliary HAVE. Here are the two sentences diagramed:

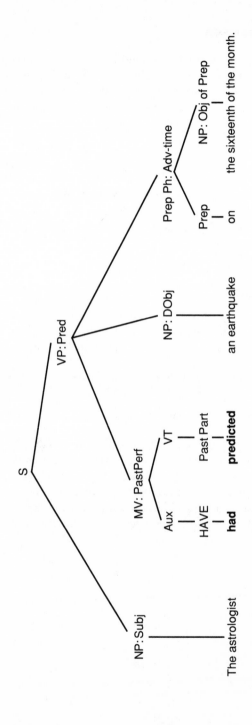

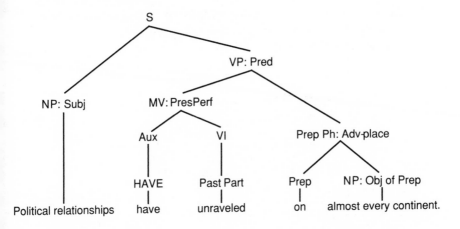

Past Participles

This is a good place to stop and talk about past participles before moving on to progressive aspect. The word **past** in *past participle* does not refer to time. It refers only to a verb's form, as *past* does in *past tense*. A past participle is the form of a verb that can follow **have**. The past participle of a regular verb is the same as the past tense form of the verb, as **predicted** or **unraveled** in the examples above. The past participle for irregular verbs vary with the verbs. Some add **-n** or **-en** to the basic form:

drive → driven

wrote → written

Some change a vowel.

drink → drunk

sing → sung

Others don't change pronunciation from their base form.

become → become

However complicated the variations from basic form to past participle may seem, verb forms are so fundamental to the language that you can pretty much depend on your knowledge of English to find the past participle of a verb, whether it's regular or irregular. Simply fill in the blank after **have** or **has** in the following frames with a verb.

> I (you, we, they) **have** _____ .
>
> He (she, it) **has** _____ .
>
> > or
>
> I (you, we, they) **have** _____ (it, them).
>
> He (she, it) **has** _____ (it, them).

For the vast majority of verbs in English, you'll know the past participle, the word that fills in the blank after **have** or **has**. Try this test for yourself. What, for instance, are the past participles for **type, swallow, bite, find,** or **sleep**? If you answered **typed, swallowed, bitten, found,** and **slept**, you're correct, as the test-frame shows.

> I have **typed** the paper
>
> They have **swallowed** the soup.
>
> She has **bitten** the bullet.
>
> He has **found** Barbara's jacket.
>
> They **have** slept.

For a very few verbs, probably no more than a half dozen or so that are in the process of changing their forms—like *swim* (**swum**), *dive* (**dove**), *wake* (**waked**), or *strive* (**strived** or **striven**)— you might have to look up the correct past participle.

Progressive Aspect

Just as the perfect aspect denotes completed action, the progressive aspect refers to continuing action. Progressive aspect is composed of a form of BE used as an auxiliary, followed by a PRESENT PARTICIPLE, as in

> John Travolta **was dancing** at a Brooklyn ballroom.
>
> Beth **is crying**.

Because the auxiliary **was** in the first example is in the past tense form, **was dancing** is past progressive, while **is crying** in the second example is present progressive. The past and present designations refer only to the tense form of the auxiliary BE, just as "past" and "present" refer to the tense form of the auxiliary HAVE in the perfect aspect. The present participle, by the way, is always the -ing form of the verb. There are no exceptions.

$$develop \rightarrow developing$$

$$provide \rightarrow providing$$

$$respond \rightarrow responding$$

$$throw \rightarrow throwing$$

Here are the two example progressive sentences diagramed:

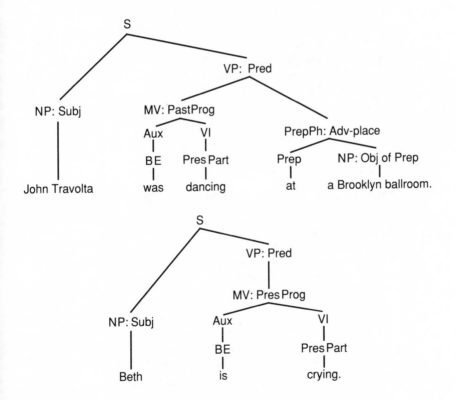

Differentiating Participles from Adjectives

You should be aware that, though a present participle is always an **-ing** form, not every word ending in **-ing** is a present participle. In the following sentence, for instance, the word **charming** is an adjective, a predicate adjective; it is preceded by the past tense form of the verb BE. In this example Princess Di seems charming to the reporters. "Charmingness" thus is a characteristic of Princess Di, an adjective.

> Princess Di was **charming** to the reporters.

Contrast the adjective **charming** in the above example with the present participle **charming** in the next:

> The pope was **charming** his American audience.

In the second example, the pope is doing something to the American audience— entertaining them (charming them). Since **charming** in the second example is a transitive verb, the phrase **was charming** is an instance of the past progressive aspect (the past tense form of the auxiliary BE plus the present participle form of the verb).

The fact that **charming** can be an adjective in one circumstance and a present participle in a different circumstance is simply another instance of a word changing from one category to another. It's a common occurrence in grammar, as we've already seen.

Putting Tense, Modality, and Aspect Together

You've already seen that tense is shown by the verb itself or by either the modal (conditional mood), HAVE (perfect aspect), or BE (progressive aspect) when they occur together with the verb. Conditional mood, perfect aspect, and progressive aspect can occur separately or in various combinations with one another. Here are several examples:

> William C. Ferris **directed** the Institute of Southern Culture. (past tense)

> You **can catch** Lyme disease from ticks. (present conditional)

> The president **might have changed** his position before the Senate vote. (past perfect conditional)

Mick Jagger **has been dabbling** in real estate for years.
(present perfect progressive)

The Russians **should have been deploying** their forces along
the road to Grozny. (past perfect progressive conditional)

Notice that tense appears only once in any individual predicate (this
is a particularly important point to remember); tense appears in the first
word of the main verb— whether the word is a verb, a modal auxiliary,
the auxiliary BE, or the auxiliary HAVE. The fact that it appears in the
first word in the main verb means that tense changes the form of the
first word in the main verb. In the first example above, the verb **directed**
is in the past tense form; in the second example, the modal **can** is in the
present tense form; in the third, the modal **might** is in the past tense
form; in the fourth, the auxiliary **has** is in the present tense form; in the
fifth, the modal **should** is in the past tense form. All the words in the
main verb except the first word are in one or another nonfinite form—
infinitive, past participle, or present participle. It's worth repeating in
order to summarize the central idea in this paragraph: only the first word
in the main verb shows tense; the rest of the words in the main verb are
nonfinite forms. We'll go over this point again after discussing principal parts later in the chapter.

When the main verb contains more than one concept, your diagram
or explanation must include all the components. Here is a diagram of
the main verb of the Mick Jagger sentence from the examples above:

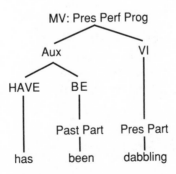

Though the constituents occur in a main verb in the order **tense +
modality + perfective aspect + progressive aspect**, you always describe status beginning with the tense form of the first word of the main

verb, then the perfect aspect (if it occurs), then the progressive (if it occurs), then the modality (if a modal occurs or if the mood is imperative or interrogative). We typically don't mention the mood if it is indicative (though you can, if you wish to). That's why you say "past perfect conditional" when you describe the status of the Russian example above.

Here is a schematic of the possible combinations of tense modality and aspect within the main verb (parentheses indicate a construction is optional; it may or may not occur):

tense + (modal) + (perfect) + (progressive) + verb

To emphasize that tense must occur in the main verb, the schematic shows tense as a freestanding unit, though tense actually becomes part of the modal, HAVE, BE, or verb that is the first word of the main verb. The schematic should help you remember the ways to expand a main verb. It indicates that a main verb must contain a verb as well as a tense. A main verb may have, in various combinations, a modal, perfect aspect, or progressive aspect. Remember that tense occurs only once in the main verb constituent; it changes the form of the first word in the main verb.

The schematic says in brief that a main verb may be expanded in the following eight ways:

1. tense + verb
2. tense + modal + verb
3. tense + perfect + verb
4. tense + progressive + verb
5. tense + modal + perfect + verb
6. tense + modal + progressive + verb
7. tense + perfect + progressive + verb
8. tense + modal + perfect + progressive + verb

Principal Parts of Verbs

Most verbs in English are REGULAR verbs, which means both that their past tense forms end in **-d** or **-ed** and that their past participle forms are the same as their past tense forms. Here are some examples of regular verbs:

Base/Infinitive		Past Tense		Past Participle
accept	→	accepted	→	accepted
call	→	called	→	called
formulate	→	formulated	→	formulated
render	→	rendered	→	rendered
slow	→	slowed	→	slowed
grieve	→	grieved	→	grieved
rave	→	raved	→	raved

A verb that either does not form its past tense with **-d** or **-ed** or that has a past participle that is not the same as its past tense is called IRREGULAR. There are only about 100 irregular verbs in English. Here are some examples:

Base/Infinitive		Past Tense		Past Participle
choose	→	chose	→	chosen
drive	→	drove	→	driven
fight	→	fought	→	fought
be	→	was/were	→	been
bring	→	brought	→	brought
swim	→	swam	→	swum
sit	→	sat	→	sat

As you have seen, every verb has five forms: infinitive (or base), past tense, present tense, present participle, and past participle. These five forms are often called PRINCIPAL PARTS. Some grammar books give long lists of verbs with their principal parts and instruct readers to memorize those lists. Just as you don't have to memorize lists of past participles, you shouldn't have to memorize long lists of verbs and their principal parts. You should be able to make your own list of the principal parts of every verb in the language if you remember just the following six facts about verb forms:

1. The base form of a verb does not show tense (often, though, it looks exactly like the present tense form that takes a plural subject).
2. The present tense form that takes a singular third-person subject (like he/she/it) ends in **-s** or **-es** for just about every verb in the language, regular or irregular.
3. The past tense form for most regular verbs ends in **-d** or **-ed**.
4. The present participial form always ends in **-ing**. This is true for regular or irregular verbs.

5. The past participial form of regular verbs is the same as their past tense form.

6. You can "test" for past participles by putting any verb after **have**. Past participles can always follow **have**, as in I(They) **have/has** —––––––– (it). The form of the verb that can fill the blank is the past participle.

Here are some verbs and their principal parts:

Base/Infinitive	write	use	float	sing	remember
Present Tense	write(s)	use(s)	float(s)	sing(s)	remember(s)
Past Tense	wrote	used	floated	sang	remembered
Present Participle	writing	using	floating	singing	remembering
Past Participle	written	used	floated	sung	remembered

Now, with this information about principal parts, let's look again at the main verb constituent. We've noted that tense changes the form of the first word in the main verb, only the first word. The rest of the words in the main verb are in different forms (one of the other principal parts). Here, for instance, is a sentence in which the status of the main verb is past perfect progressive conditional:

The president's staff **should have been planning** more than one campaign strategy.

The modal **should** is in the past tense form. **Have** is in the base (infinitive) form. **Been** is in the past participle form. And **planning** is in the present participle form.

Summary

We've examined the components of the MAIN VERB—the verb phrase constituent that contains the verb along with the elements that mark the categories TENSE, MODALITY, and ASPECT. These three categories indicate the STATUS of a verb. We've explained tense, modality, and aspect as separate but closely related grammatical concepts that overlap real-world time but aren't always the same thing. We've looked at the constituents that make up tense, modality, and aspect: modal auxiliaries, the auxiliary markers HAVE and BE, verb past participle forms, and verb present participle forms. And we've considered the five principal parts of verbs.

Here are the main points of chapter 3:

- The verb, together with its tense, modality, and aspect markers, make up the main verb.
- Tense, modality, and aspect are three separate grammatical categories indicating the status of a verb.
- Tense in English has two forms—past and present.
- Tense determines the physical shape of the first word in the main verb, only the first word. The rest of the words in the main verb will take a different form, a different principal part.
- Modality, or mood, relates to the purpose of a sentence—whether it makes a statement, asks a question, gives an order, or indicates possibility. Modality is indicated by a change in the form of a sentence.
- Conditional mood, which essentially refers to possibility or probability, is formed by the addition of a modal auxiliary (helping verb) to the verb phrase.
- Aspect, which indicates that the action of a verb is either completed or ongoing, occurs in two forms—perfect and progressive.
- Most verbs in English are regular; this means that they form their past tense with a -d or -ed and that their past tense forms are the same as their past participle forms.
- Verbs have five principal parts: base (infinitive), present tense, past tense, present participle, and past participle.

EXERCISES

I. WRITING DEFINITIONS

Define the following terms as completely as you can, giving examples wherever possible:

Status	Modal auxiliaries (modals)
Auxiliary	Aspect
Tense	Perfect aspect
Past and present	Progressive aspect

Mood (modality)	Past participle
Indicative	Present participle
Interrogative	Regular verb
Imperative	Irregular verb
Conditional	Principal parts

II. CHANGING MAIN-VERB FORMS

Make the main verbs of the following sentences into the forms indicated in parentheses:

EXAMPLE

Police battle against the odds. (present progressive)
↓
Police are battling against the odds.

1. Ovophiles switch to egg substitutes to avoid cholesterol. (present progressive)
2. Richard Gere is shy. (present conditional)
3. Mercedes Benz is the epitome of luxury. (past perfect)
4. The weather forecaster predicted rain for the area next week. (present progressive conditional)
5. The dollar's rise had been worrying the White House. (past indicative)

III. IDENTIFYING VERB STATUS AND ANALYZING SENTENCES

Identify the status of the main verbs in the following sentences and label the other constituents in the sentences, both their structures and functions. Explain how you identified the status of the main verbs.

EXAMPLE

The truce has unraveled between the two Balkan nations.

Explanation. In this sentence, **has unraveled** is the main verb. **Has** is the marker of perfect aspect, and **unraveled** is a past participle. Since **has** is in the present tense form, the status of the main verb is present perfect. **The truce** is a noun phrase subject. **Has unraveled between the two Balkan nations** is a verb phrase functioning as the predicate.

The verb **unraveled** is intransitive; it is followed by a prepositional phrase, **between the two Balkan nations**, which functions as an adverb of place. **Between** is a preposition, and **the two Balkan nations** is a noun phrase functioning as the object of the preposition.

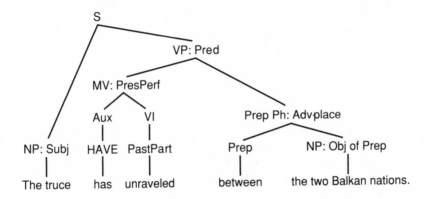

Sentences

1. The state legislature might offer parents school vouchers next year.
2. The student senate denied funding to the gay rights organization.
3. Females are initiating dates nowadays.
4. Garland College will have three science buildings by 2008.
5. Springfield would have built a police station with the federal grant.
6. The Navy can finance your college education.
7. Edna Buchanan has focused her stories on the Miami street scene.
8. Winston Churchill was a complicated giant on the world stage.
9. Franklin Roosevelt had understood the Nazi threat before World War II.
10. Elvis may be the century's biggest star.
11. My history class is reading *The Diary of Anne Frank*.
12. Stingrays could have been cruising near the beach.
13. The prince may complete his education at Harvard.
14. Paul Simon's lyrics have become political.
15. The environment will suffer during the next decade.
16. The silo might have blown up.
17. Lawsuits can cripple medical practices.
18. My roommate's nervousness was becoming a burden.

19. Eddie Murphy was being vulgar during the interview.
20. A poor Christmas season could shut down several department stores.
21. Miami Beach has traded in its dowdy image.
22. Cable TV companies may compete with traditional communications organizations for telephone service contracts within the decade.
23, The architecture students have to come up with a functional home design.
24. Education can be a potent weapon.
25. Rhino Records is working on a "Monkees Greatest Hits" disc.
26. Concert tickets will be available at the Coliseum tonight.
27. The Japanese have rebuilt their cities several time this century.
28. Kennedy had faced down Khrushchev during the Cuban Missile Crisis.
29. The primatologist may be gambling away her welcome among the chimp family.
30. The Reds fans were screaming for a hit in the ninth inning.
31. Humidity can make my dog uncomfortable.
32. The prizefighter had come to after the knockout.
33. Communism seems to be dying around the world.
34. Superman was fighting the Axis during World War II.
35. The Weather Bureau had been playing Chicken Little with the coastal residents.
36. Raskolnikov could hear the murdered man's voice in his dreams.
37. Brad Pitt was wearing a buckskin outfit through most of the movie.
38. Congress has made problems for the president since the election.
39. Joseph Conrad had become fluent in English.
40. Portfolios can document your writing ability.
41. Mary Cassatt seems to have given financial assistance to an important French art dealer.
42. Some women are using the word "babe" in a new way.
43. Washington ought to downsize before the next election.
44. Another Hemingway may be waiting in the wings.
45. Newman's blue eyes can make older women mushy.
46. The committee had been examining our undergraduate program.
47. Language has been Chomsky's passion.
48. Orville wanted to make the design public.
49. O.J. had denied guilt.
50. A banjo player was sitting in front of Woolworth's.

| CHAPTER 4 | *Exploring*
Noun
Phrases |

Preview

In this chapter, we'll look closely at nouns and pronouns, as well as the components of noun phrases, like determiners and genitive constructions.

Here are the main points in the chapter:

- Nouns can be classified in various ways, but we'll be especially concerned with how to differentiate between proper and common nouns.
- Determiners are structure words that pattern with nouns and include such words as articles, demonstratives, numbers, possessive pronouns, and pre-articles.
- Genitive constructions come in two types—inflective and phrasal.
- Besides the possessive pronouns, we also have personal, reflexive, and indefinite pronouns.

Types of Nouns

Grammarians classify nouns in various ways, as common (**pope**) or proper (**John XXIII**), concrete (**teacher**) or abstract (**pedagogy**), countable (**soda**) or noncountable (**water**), collective (**team**) or noncollective (**quarterback**). Noun classes often overlap. So a noun like **team** might be at the same time common, concrete, countable, and collective, as in

The **team** met to watch the game films.

Since there is so much overlap among the classes, noun classification schemes can quickly become too complicated to be useful for beginning students. You should be aware of the different noun classes, though the only ones we'll be concerned with in any detail are proper and common.

Proper or Common

Perhaps the most obvious way to differentiate noun types is to look at them as PROPER or COMMON. Proper nouns refer to unique people, places, or things; they are sets of one and typically name something or someone, like **God, the Statue of Liberty, Maryland, Chicago, Dustin Hoffman, Cheerios, Miami Beach High School, President Truman**, or *Moby-Dick*. Proper nouns are often two or more words long, like **the Louvre, the Empire State Building, the Rio Grande**, and many proper nouns include the definite article **the**. Typically, we capitalize proper nouns. By their nature, proper nouns are singular, but there are situations that allow you to make proper nouns plural, especially when you use a proper noun to indicate a whole class:

If there were more **Trumans** in national politics, Americans might have a higher regard for politicians.

There don't seem to be any *Moby-Dicks* on the literary horizon.

All the nouns that are not proper are common, like **divine being, statue, state, city, movie star, cereal, high school**, and **former president**. You don't need special situations to make common nouns plural: **divine beings, statues, states, cities, movie stars, cereals, high schools, former presidents**.

Determiners

Most noun phrases consist of a noun alone or a noun together with an ARTICLE, a POSSESSIVE, a DEMONSTRATIVE, a NUMBER or a PRE-ARTICLE. These structures belong to a larger category called DETERMINERS. The determiners occur so routinely with nouns that you can often use them to test whether a word is a noun: if a determiner makes a constituent with a word or phrase, you can be sure that constituent is a noun. Determiners are so closely identified with nouns that they can even make other kinds of words into nouns. Perhaps the most famous literary example of that is the title of Stendahl's novel *The Red and the Black*, in which the article **the** makes the adjectives **red** and **black** into nouns. Articles, possessives, demonstratives, numbers, and pre-articles are so frequently a part of noun phrases that it's easy to overlook their significance.

The Difference between Determiners and Adjectives

Some grammar books consider determiners to be adjectives because adjectives and determiners both make constituents with nouns. But determiners are not adjectives. Adjectives are CONTENT WORDS, like nouns, verbs, and adverbs. Determiners are STRUCTURE WORDS, like prepositions, pronouns, and conjunctions. Content words are OPEN CLASSES; they freely admit new words. You can create new nouns, verbs, adjectives, and adverbs, as Lewis Carroll did in his poem "Jabberwocky." One stanza from the poem is repeated here with the content words boldfaced:

'Twas **brillig** and the **slithy toves**
Did **gyre** and **gimble** in the **wabe**
All **mimsy** were the **borogoves**
And the **mome raths outgabe**.

Structure words are CLOSED CLASSES. They do not allow new members. You can't make up new determiners, conjunctions, pronouns, or prepositions. Look back at "Jabberwocky" and notice how the structure words are common English, articles (**the**), conjunctions (**and**), and prepositions (**in**). The verb BE and the auxiliary **do** are closed as well.

Another way to tell adjectives from determiners is that adjectives can usually be compared (this is a **thinner** board than that; my dog is the **most handsome** animal on our block) and intensified with adverbs like **pretty** and **very** (the new restaurant makes a **pretty good** pizza; the 747 is a **very large** plane). Adjectives can also follow linking verbs, especially **seem**: this drawer seems **warped**.

The difference between structure words and content words is basic to language. In any language, structure words make up a small set. There aren't many of them, though they occur frequently.

Articles

The articles are **a, an,** and **the. The** is DEFINITE, while the two other articles are INDEFINITE. The difference between definite and indefinite refers to whether the information in the noun phrase is shared by the speaker (writer) and the listener (reader). The definite article indicates that the speaker and listener share information. In some grammar books, SHARED INFORMATION is called OLD INFORMATION. Indefinite articles do not indicate shared information.

Let's take a closer look at this idea of shared information. Imagine that your friend Jamal called and asked you to his apartment for dinner. He might add, "Would you bring the chair with you? We don't have enough seating." If he made the request that way, with the noun phrase "the chair," he would be indicating that you know what chair he is referring to; in other words, you and he share information about a chair. Otherwise he couldn't use the definite article **the** in the phrase. By using **the,** Jamal shows that he expects you to bring a particular chair that you and he both know about. Since the chair is known to both of you, old, or shared, information, he uses the definite articles.

In contrast, notice what would happen if Jamal made a similar request but used an indefinite article. "Would you bring a chair with you? We don't have enough seating," he might say. If he made the request that way, with the noun phrase "a chair," he would be indicating with the indefinite article **a** that you could bring any chair you wanted to bring. Since he's not making reference to a chair you and he both know about, he uses the indefinite article.

Here are diagrams of noun phrases with articles; the diagrams show how articles form constituents with nouns:

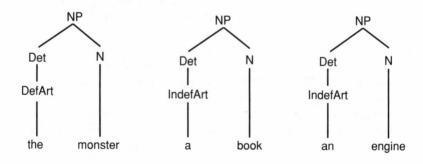

Demonstratives

This, **that**, **these**, and **those** are DEMONSTRATIVES. Like definite articles, demonstratives indicate old information. But they do something more as well. They also point to things: **this** computer, **that** telephone, **these** books, **those** marbles. You can hardly say a noun phrase that includes a demonstrative without trying to point. The grammatical concept of pointing is called DEIXIS. **This** and **these** point to things that are near; **that** and **those** point to things that are farther away. **This** and **that** are singular; **these** and **those** are plural.

Possessive Pronouns

Some POSSESSIVE PRONOUNS are determiners; they form phrases with the nouns they precede. Some possessive pronouns are independent; they pattern just like nouns. Here are the eight determiner-possessive pronouns, followed by diagrams to show how they pattern:

Singular	*Plural*
my	**our**
your	**your**
his, her, its	**their**

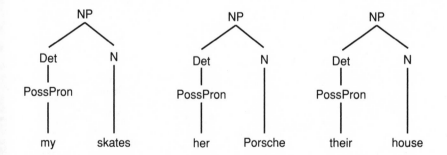

Independent possessive pronouns are not determiners; they stand alone in noun phrases. They're introduced here with the determiners because they are related to the determiner-possessive pronouns. The eight independent possessive pronouns follow:

Singular	*Plural*
mine	**ours**
yours	**yours**
his, hers, its	**theirs**

These independent possessive pronouns derive from the determiner-posssessive pronouns. **My** adds an **n** sound (**my** → **mine**); **her, our, your,** and **their** add an **s** (**her** → **hers, our** → **ours, your** → **yours,** and **their** → **theirs**); **his** and **its** do not change form. Independent possessive pronouns fill noun phrase slots. In the first two examples below, **hers** and **yours** function as predicate nouns, **ours** functions as a subject.

This locker is **hers**. That's **yours**.

The Smith's house was destroyed by the hurricane. **Ours** remained standing.

Here is a diagram of the first example.

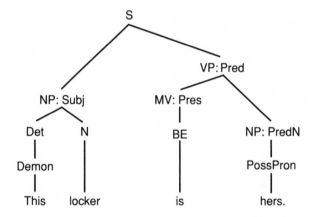

Numbers

NUMBERS are considered determiners when they precede nouns, as in *ten* **giraffes** or **mom's** *first* **balloon trip**. Numbers fall into one of two classes: CARDINAL (**one, two, three** . . .) or ORDINAL (**first, second, third** . . . **next, last**). Ordinal numbers generally follow articles or possessives.

his **third** date

the **next** explosion

The following diagrams show how numbers pattern with nouns and articles or possessives to form noun phrases. Notice how the word closest to the head noun forms a constituent with the head (**third date, next explosion**) before the next word to the left forms with those two as a larger constituent (**his third date, the next explosion**).

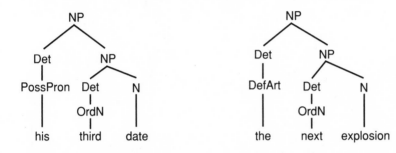

Numbers that do not precede nouns are generally considered nouns themselves, as in

My granddad will be **seventy-five** on his next birthday,

where **seventy-five** is a noun that functions as a predicate noun.

Pre-articles

Several word classes can precede articles, including PARTITIVES, QUANTIFIERS, and MULTIPLIERS. In order to simplify the discussion, we'll classify the partitives, quantifiers, and multipliers all under one category called PRE-ARTICLES, since they can all occur before articles. Here is a list of some of the quantifiers and partitives:

all (of)	a lot of
any (of)	many (of)
both (of)	neither (of)
a bowl of	no
each (of)	none (of)

either (of)	plenty (of)
every	a pound of
(a) few (of)	a quart of
a good deal of	several (of)
half (of)	a slice of
an item of	a small quantity of
a jar of	some (of)
(a) little (of)	

Here are three diagrams to show how pre-articles pattern with nouns.

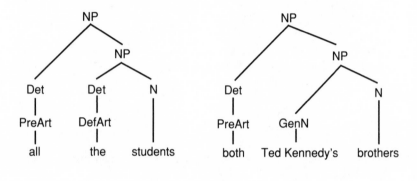

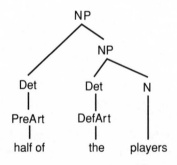

Notice that when the word **of** appears with a pre-article, it forms a constituent with the pre-article, not with the following noun. So **of** with a pre-article is not strictly a preposition. This is a point worth noticing because it is part of the difference between phrases composed of pre-articles plus nouns and phrases composed of nouns and phrasal genitives, which we'll look at in a page or so. Here are diagrams of three more noun phrases with pre-articles. Two of the pre-articles include **of**; look carefully at how they form constituents with their pre-articles, not with the following nouns.

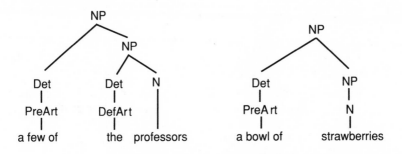

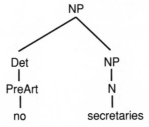

The last pre-articles we'll examine are the multipliers and the fractions. Multipliers include such words and phrases as

> once (a, every, each)
>
> twice (a, every, each)
>
> three times (a, every, each).

The words **a, every**, and **each** that may follow multipliers are determiners that form constituents with the following nouns. The **a** is, of course, an indefinite article; we'll consider **each** and **every** unspecified determiners in order to avoid the sticky issue of whether **each** and **every** are determiners or adjectives. Many grammarians classify them as adjectives. Some grammarians even fudge and call them semi-adjectives.

Since they act more like structure words than content words, I think it's more consistent to include **each** and **every** among determiners and leave it at that.

When fractions, like the other pre-articles, include **of**, they form constituents with **of**. Here, too, **of** is not a preposition:

a third (of)

two-thirds (of)

three-fifths (of)

Here are some multipliers and fractions diagramed. Following the practice to simplify the classification of pre-articles, I've labelled them as pre-articles.

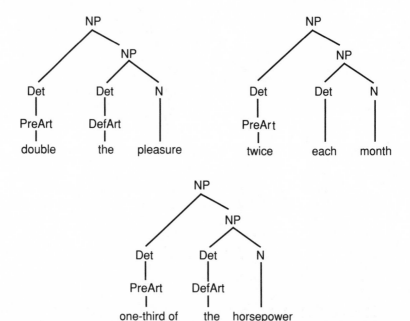

To keep pre-articles straight, just remember that they are among the structure words, the closed classes. The pre-articles include words and phrases that are often listed separately as quantifiers, partitives, multipliers, and fractions. We're listing them all together under the single category pre-article and placing that category within the determiner system. When prepositions occur with pre-articles, the prepositions form constituents with them, not with the following nouns.

Post-noun Modifiers

All and **both**, among others, can occur after nouns as well as before them. When they occur after nouns, such words become post-noun modifiers, no longer part of the determiner system.

> The students **all** participated in the election.

> Ted Kennedy's brothers **both** were assassinated.

Here is how post-nouns look diagramed:

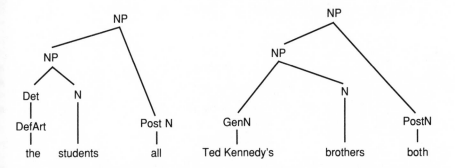

Genitive Nouns (*a.k.a.* Possessive Nouns)

Though possessive nouns are not determiners, they act like possessive pronouns; so I've included them at the end of the section about determiners. Possessive nouns come in two varieties, inflected and phrasal. Inflected possessive nouns always end in **'s**, as in the following examples:

> **The reporter's** assignment was inner-city gangs.

> Mark Twain tells a **boy's story** in *Tom Sawyer.*

Phrasal possessives always include the preposition **of**. They are prepositional phrases.

> General MacArthur defied the authority **of President Truman**.

> The music **of Bach** heralds the modern age.

Phrasal possessives can usually be turned into inflected forms. For instance, you can change the prepositional phrases **of President Truman** and **of Bach** into inflected nouns.

> General MacArthur defied **President Truman's** authority.

> **Bach's** music heralds the modern age.

Sometimes you can't turn possessive nouns back and forth from phrasal to inflective or from inflective to phrasal: you can't make **my mom's new car** into **the new car of my mom**. And sometimes when you move a noun from the prepositional phrase to the front of the head noun, the moved noun won't inflect.

patterns of **behavior**
↓
behavior patterns

a network of **computers**
↓
a **computer** network

Because possessive nouns are not exactly determiners and because they don't all pattern alike, some grammar books label possessive nouns, whether phrasal or inflective, as adjectives.

We'll call the inflected and phrasal nouns GENITIVES; genitive is the old term for the case of the noun indicated by the **'s** or the **of** phrase. Similarly, what we've called a possessive pronoun is often called a genitive pronoun. Genitive is a more accurate term than possessive for these structures (since we started using the term possessive for pronouns, we'll continue to use the term for pronouns but switch to genitive for nouns). The term genitive indicates that a noun with either the **'s** form or the **of** phrase may show more relationships than simple possession. After all, the phrase **Anne Rice's book** may denote a book that belongs to the author Anne Rice but which she did not write, as in

That dictionary is Anne Rice's book.

Or it may denote a book that she wrote but does not possess, as

Interview with the Vampire is Anne Rice's book.

In the same way, **the destruction of Warsaw** (or **Warsaw's destruction**) in the next example is not in any way a destruction that belonged to the city but a destruction that was levied against Warsaw, as in the following, where Warsaw is actually the object of **destroyed** (or **destruction**), as the following indicates.

The German air force destroyed Warsaw.
↓
the destruction of Warsaw

or

Warsaw's destruction

Look at the next examples. Her parents do the consenting in the genitive forms as well as in the underlying sentence, where the noun phrase **her parents** functions as the subject. But in no way do they "possess" the consent.

Her parents consented.
↓
the consent of her parents

or

her parents' consent

Sometimes the genitive phrase can be unclear about who performs an action and who is acted upon. In a sentence like

The shooting of the hunters bothered the townspeople,

we can't be sure whether the hunters had done the shooting or had been shot. When you identify noun phrases with inflective genitives, you treat the genitives much as you would possessive pronouns, though you don't include them under determiners. The following diagrams indicate the correct analysis of noun phrases with inflective genitives.

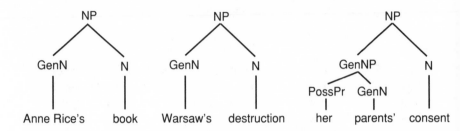

Phrasal genitives are prepositional phrases; the prepositions form constituents with the following noun phrases (You might want to look back at the discussion of pre-articles to see how prepositions are treated there.) When you parse phrasal genitives, you should indicate both their structure (Prep Ph) and function (Gen). If you draw diagrams, you should also show that the phrasal genitive makes an NP constituent first with the noun head before this NP makes a larger NP constituent with an article.

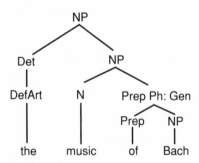

Other Types of Pronouns

There are several different kinds of pronouns in addition to the possessive pronouns we've already looked at. The pronouns you encounter most frequently are PERSONAL PRONOUNS, INDEFINITE PRONOUNS, and REFLEXIVE PRONOUNS.

Personal Pronouns

The personal pronouns include the following:

Subject Forms	Object Forms
I	me
you	you
he, she, it	him, her, it
we	us
you	you
they	them

In general, the personal pronouns refer to previously mentioned nouns.

The president had a bad day with congressional leaders. **He** couldn't get **them** to support his foreign aid package.

The senator voted against the bill to close thirteen military bases across the country. **She** especially wanted to protect jobs in her own state.

Reflexive Pronouns

Reflexive pronouns refer to the subject of the clause they are in, as

The football players sat by **themselves** in the corner of the cafeteria.

The graduating seniors threw **themselves** a party.

We recognize eight reflexive pronouns. They end in **-self** or **-selves**.

Singular Forms	Plural Forms
myself	ourselves
yourself	yourselves
himself, herself, itself	themselves

Reflexive pronouns can fill any noun position except subject. When they are in the direct object slot of a sentence, you will not be able to turn the sentence into a passive in order to test for a transitive verb. You cannot, for instance, make

Hitchcock often put **himself** into his movies

into

*Himself was often put by Hitchcock into his movies.

You can't make sentences with reflexive pronouns into passive sentences because of a principle that is true in all languages—the CROSSOVER PRINCIPLE. The crossover principle will not allow nouns with the same referent to cross each other when you rearrange the parts of a sentence. To make the example sentence into a passive, you would have to let **himself** and **Hitchcock** pass by each other. That's a no no!

Indefinite Pronouns

Unlike the personal and reflexive pronouns, the indefinite pronouns don't refer to specific nouns. As their name suggests, their meaning is indefinite or general. The most common indefinite pronouns are

somebody	something	someone
anybody	anything	anyone
everybody	everything	everyone
nobody	nothing	no one

Summary

We've looked not only at the types of nouns and pronouns but also at the components of noun phrases, such as determiners and genitive constructions.

Here are the main points in the chapter:

- Nouns can be classified in various ways, but we especially differentiate between proper and common nouns.

- Determiners are structure words that pattern with nouns and include such words as articles, demonstratives, numbers, possessive pronouns, and pre-articles.

- Genitive constructions come in two types—inflective and phrasal.

- Besides the possessive pronouns, we also have personal, reflexive, and indefinite pronouns.

EXERCISES

I. WRITING DEFINITIONS

Define the following terms as completely as you can, giving examples wherever possible:

Proper nouns	Common nouns
Articles	Possessive pronouns
Demonstratives	Number
Pre-articles	Determiner
Content words	Structure words
Open classes	Closed classes
Definite article	Indefinite articles
Old information	Shared information
Demonstratives	Deixis
Ordinal numbers	Cardinal numbers
Post-noun modifiers	Personal pronouns
Reflexive pronouns	Indefinite pronouns
Crossover principle	

II. IDENTIFYING NOUN CONSTITUENTS AND ANALYZING SENTENCES

Identify the noun constituents in the following sentences and label the other constituents in the sentences, both their structures and functions. Identify the status of the MV constituents as well. Sentences with personal pronouns are presented in pairs or triplets in order to make them more natural; analyze the two or three sentences in the unit. Some noun phrases include adjectives or other structures that function as adjectives, like **hospital** in the example, a noun functioning as an adjective. It's not necessary to identify these yet. Simply label a constituent like **hospital visit** as a noun phrase; we'll discuss these structures in the seventh chapter. Concentrate on the noun phrase and verb phrase constituents we've covered so far.

EXAMPLE

Shaquille will autograph the kids' casts during his hospital visit.

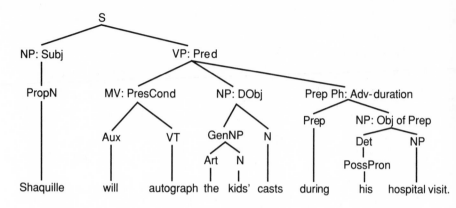

Explanation. In this sentence, **will autograph** is the main verb. **Will** is a modal in the present tense form. So the status of **will autograph** is present conditional. **Shaquille** is a proper noun, functioning as the subject of the sentence. **The kids' casts** is a noun phrase composed of the genitive noun phrase **the kids'** along with a common noun **casts**. **During his hospital visit** is a prepositional phrase that functions as an adverb of duration. The noun phrase **his hospital visit** functions as the object of the preposition **during**. **His** is a possessive pronoun, and **hospital visit** is a noun phrase.

Sentences

1. Bruce Wayne will turn 70 in 2009.
2. The torte recipe required a cup of almonds.
3. Kwanza celebrates the heritage of African Americans.
4. Compact discs outsell all other media now. (**Other** is simply a determiner; **all** is a pre-article.)
5. The class liked *The Sun Also Rises*. It describes the lives of young Americans after World War I.
6. Movie reviewers praise Tarantino's directing skills.
7. The oil industry's misjudgments have scarred Alaska deeply.
8. Stephen J. Gould's books address the question of evolution.
9. Umpires must administer the rules of the game fairly.
10. Dad's surgeon plopped herself into a plastic chair. She had listened to his complaints for 15 minutes.

11. Anti-smoking activists are dancing on the Marlboro Man's grave.
12. No one answered the phone at your house last night. I called four times.
13. Americans consumed 640 billion cigarettes in 1981. They smoked 500 billion cigarettes in 1995.
14. Napoleon crowned himself emperor of France in 1804.
15. Pep rallies serve several purposes. They give teams support. They give students a sense of togetherness.
16. Longwood Gardens unfolds in 4 miles of paths.
17. One Japanese honeysuckle may produce 30 feet of vine in a single year.
18. The "Baby Jessica" case symbolizes the perils of modern adoption.
19. Anti-adoption advocates have been attacking the concept of adoption.
20. Lisa Henson was the first woman president of the *Harvard Lampoon*.
21. The modern study of grammar began with Noam Chomsky's *Syntactic Structures* in 1957.
22. Computers perpetuate a two-tiered system of education in our country.
23. Most of the country was rain-free last month.
24. Lack of money fuels divorce.
25. Boredom is contagious. It can cause a chain reaction in a dorm.
26. Forty-two percent of the nation's entrepreneurs are women.
27. China's economic growth is outstripping its development of infrastructure.
28. A good poem can change direction swiftly.
29. The new drug may increase a patient's risk of arthritis.
30. Ireland kept European culture alive during the Dark Ages.
31. A beef brisket can be the star of a Passover meal.
32. The Watergate investigation motivated President Nixon's resignation.
33. Cray's supercomputer can perform 60 billion calculations per second.
34. John Amos transforms himself into a parade of characters in *Halley's Comet*.
35. The manufacture of U.S. weapons is in the hands of a few giant corporations.
36. Today's circuses preserve the excitement of the Big Top.

37. Teachers often label hyperactive children troublemakers.
38. Edgar Allan Poe's work inspired Stephen King.
39. Pam Tillis left country music at 19. She returned at 35.
40. Charleston puts on a pretty face for its visitors.
41. Men's fashions are returning to an elegant look.
42. Calvin Klein's world is a world of subdued chic.
43. "Dark Star" was the Grateful Dead's signature song for twenty-five years.
44. Ted Turner built the family billboard company into an entertainment colossus.
45. Ad agencies call Nike's Winged Victory symbol "THE SWOOSH."
46. Michael Tilson Thomas became the music director of the San Francisco Symphony in 1995. He is a charismatic orchestra director.
47. Goya ranks behind Picasso as Spain's greatest artist.
48. Weight-related illnesses kill 300,000 Americans every year.
49. The federal government is reconsidering the economic decisions of the last five decades.
50. Stephen Steinberg's *Turning Back* confronts the legacy of slavery.

| CHAPTER 5 | *Rearranging and Compounding* |

The six core sentence patterns defined in the earlier chapters form the basis of all the other sentences in the language. This is an important point; it shapes everything else we will do in this book. You may combine the core sentences into larger, more complex sentences; or you may change them in several other ways to produce varied sentence structures. Think of the six core sentences as grammatical Lego Blocks that you can use to build all the other sentences of the language. Not only can you put these building blocks together in various ways, but you can also change their shape and make them into new kinds of blocks. The grammar system uses a small number of parts to build an infinite number of structures. That is, there is no end to the number of sentences you can build by rearranging and combining the core sentences. Mathematicians call a system like grammar a DISCRETE COMBINATORIAL SYSTEM.

That's a fancy way of saying that a small number of structures and operations will produce all the sentences in the language, no matter how long or complex. Chapters 5 through 9 explain how grammar builds sentences by rearranging and combining core sentences. Since little sentences grow into big sentences, big sentences can be viewed as combinations of little sentences. When you can apply this basic principle to analyze the structure of sentences, you're well on your way to becoming a grammarian.

Preview

From this point on, we'll be working with the original core sentences as building blocks. In this chapter, we'll look both at how to change the shape of our blocks by rearranging constituents and how to put the blocks together into new, larger structures by compounding. In later chapters, we'll look at other ways to change the core sentences and to put them together in order to form larger, more complex sentences.

Here are the main points in the chapter:

- Constituents of the six core sentence patterns can be rearranged and compounded.
- To make a sentence negative, you add the negative marker **not**.
- There are two types of question sentences—yes/no questions and Wh-questions.
- Core sentences with transitive verbs (VT, Vg, Vc) can be made into passive sentences.
- Certain core sentences with BE can be rearranged into existential-there sentences.
- To make a core sentence imperative, you delete both **you** and **will**.
- One way to make sentences longer is by compounding structures within them.
- Typically, you use commas and conjunctions in order to link compound constituents. But you may also use punctuation and compounding to create various effects within and between your sentences.
- Conjunctive adverbs connect clauses but mark the discourse differently from conjunctions.

Rearranging

You can create new sentences out of the six core sentence types by rearranging their constituents. By rearranging constituents, you can make positive sentences negative, turn statements into questions, convert active sentences into passives, change certain kinds of sentences which have BE as the main verb into existential-there sentences, and render conditional remarks into commands.

Negative Sentences

One way to vary the core sentence patterns is to change sentences from positive to negative. All the sentence patterns so far have been positive. You make positive sentences negative simply by inserting the NEGATIVE WORD **not** into the auxiliary component of the main verb. If the status of the main verb is conditional, you insert **not** after the modal but still under the auxiliary constituent. In other words, **not** makes a constituent with a modal.

> Many high school students can locate Australia on a map.
> ↓
> Many high school students can**not** locate Australia on a map.

The diagram of the new sentence is on the next page.

Of course, you can contract the **not** with the modal to make **cannot** into **can't**.

> Many high school students can't locate Australia on a map.

If the status of the main verb is progressive aspect or perfective aspect, then you make the sentence negative by inserting **not** after the auxiliary HAVE or BE. Just as it does with a modal, **not** makes an auxiliary constituent with HAVE or BE. Here are some examples; the diagrams are on the following pages.

> Suburban voters are supporting the proposed tax levy.
> ↓
> Suburban voters are **not** supporting the proposed tax levy.

> or

> Suburban voters are**n't** supporting the proposed tax levy.

> Russian industries have kept up with Western technology.
> ↓
> Russian industries have **not** kept up with Western technology.

> OR

> Russian industries have**n't** kept up with Western technology.

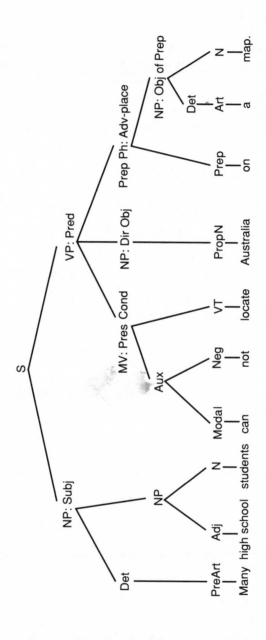

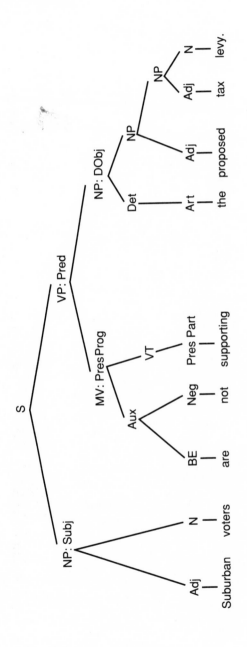

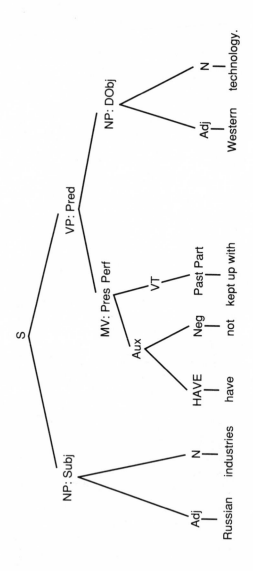

When the main verb of the sentence is the copula BE, you make the sentence negative by placing **not** after the BE.

Loons are graceful on land.
↓
Loons are **not** graceful on land.

or

Loons are**n't** graceful on land.

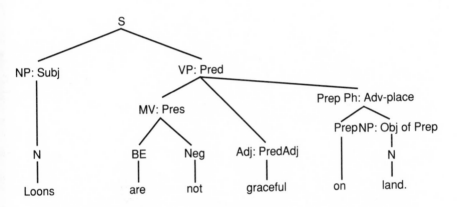

If the main verb of the sentence is a verb other than BE and the main verb constituent exhibits neither conditional mood nor aspect, then you make the sentence negative by inserting DO along with **not** into the auxiliary constituent. Notice that DO will always exhibit the same tense as the verb of the original sentence and that the verb after you insert DO will be in its base (nonfinite) form. In a sense, the DO acts like a modal, and the verb acts just as it would if it followed a modal; the DO holds tense, and the verb is nonfinite. Not and DO form an auxiliary constituent.

The Senate approved the president's cabinet appointment.
↓
The Senate **did not** approve the president's cabinet appointment.

or

The Senate **didn't** approve the president's cabinet appointment.

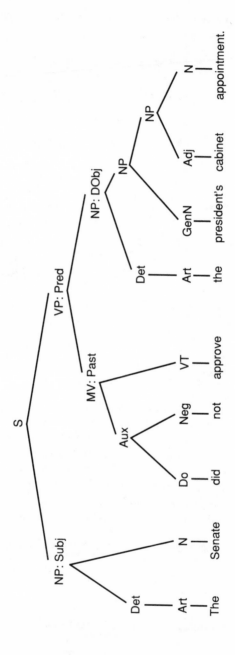

Except in the case of the copula BE, when the negative marker follows BE and becomes a component of the main verb itself, **neg** is always a part of the auxiliary.

Questions

The core sentences are all STATEMENTS; they make assertions. But you can change statements into questions. The two most common question sentences are called YES/NO QUESTIONS and WH-QUESTIONS.

Yes/No Questions

Yes/no questions, quite simply, are questions that you can answer with yes or no, like "Did Mary go to the movies last night?" or "Can the new pitcher throw a curve ball?" To turn a core sentence into a yes/no question, you have to move a part of the main verb to the front of the sentence. If the main verb contains a modal, HAVE, or BE, then you move the modal, HAVE, or BE. It does not matter whether the BE comes originally from the auxiliary, as in "Toxic wastes **are** threatening animal populations," or whether it is the copula BE from MV (main verb). In either case, you move BE to the front of the sentence. Here are several statements turned into yes/no questions.

> Nightmares **can** reveal psychotic states.
> ↓
> **Can** nightmares reveal psychotic states?

> Social problems **have** made police work difficult.
> ↓
> **Have** social problems made police work difficult?

> Toxic wastes **are** threatening animal populations.
> ↓
> **Are** toxic wastes threatening animal populations?

Bill Gates's brainstorm **was** MS DOS.

↓

Was Bill Gates's brainstorm MS DOS?

The diagram on the next page indicates that you disjoin part of the MV when you make a yes/no question: you move the first component of Aux.

Notice that this disjunction (the movement of HAVE to the front of the sentence) does not change any functional relationships. The subject, the predicate, the direct object, and the object complement remain in exactly the same relationships. Even the MV is still HAVE ... **made**, with the ellipsis indicating the fact that HAVE has been moved around the subject noun phrase. The constituents in a yes/no question keep their core relationships.

If the MV contains a verb other than BE and if it does not exhibit aspect or the conditional mood (if it has no modal, HAVE, or BE), then, just as you add DO to make a negative sentence, you must add DO to make a yes/no question.

Citizen patrols stop crime in high-risk neighborhoods.

↓

Do citizen patrols stop crime in high-risk neighborhoods?

The DO acts like a modal (see diagram on p. 100). That is, it takes the tense form, in this case present tense. And the verb shifts to its base form. These changes are easier to see when the verb is in past tense form and when it is irregular, as in:

The police department bought six Jeep Cherokees.

↓

Did the police department buy six Jeep Cherokees?

Wh-Questions

Wh-question sentences query a content phrase, generally a noun phrase or an adverb phrase. To make a core sentences into a Wh-question, you have to replace a noun phrase with an interrogative pronoun (**what, who,** or **whom**) or an adverb phrase with an interrogative pro-adverb (**where, when, why, how, how often**). Sometimes you query only a determiner with **whose, which,** or **what**. Here is an example of a core sentence

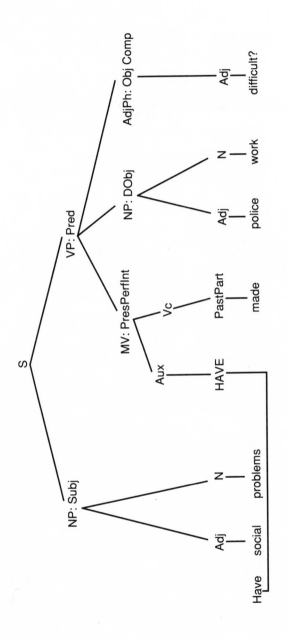

100

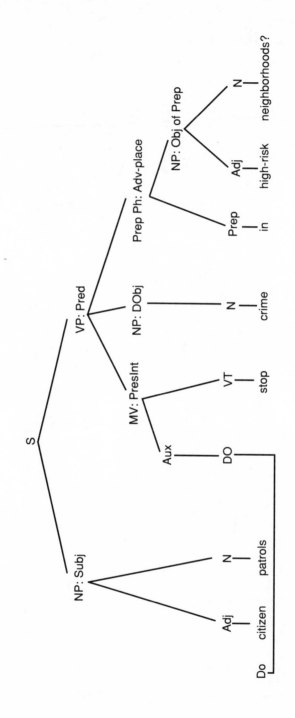

changed into a Wh-question when its subject noun phrase is replaced by **who**:

> **Who**
> ~~The GOP frontrunner~~ joked with the reporters during yesterday's press conference.

$$\downarrow$$

Who joked with the reporters during yesterday's press conference?

Since the noun phrase replaced by **who** is the subject of the sentence, you don't have to move it or move other sentence constituents. Generally, after you replace the noun phrase, determiner, or adverb phrase, you have to move the phrase to the front of the sentence. Moving a phrase to make a Wh-question sentence demands that you also move a modal, HAVE, or BE, just as you do when you make a yes/no question:

> **how**
> Business leaders **can** stimulate school reform ~~by investing in education~~.

$$\downarrow$$

How can business leaders stimulate school reform?

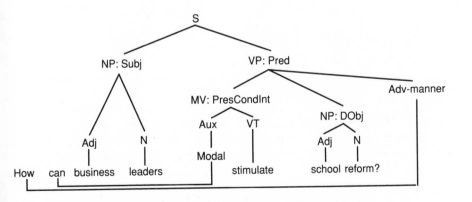

Just as the relationships remain the same between constituents when you disjoin them to make a yes/no question, the relationships remain the same between the constituents when you disjoin them to make a

Wh-question. In the example above, the MV remains **can ... stimulate**; the interrogative pro-adverb **how** is still an adverb of manner. In
the next example, the direct object noun phrase, **the Serbian troop
movements**, is replaced by **what** and moved to the front of the sentence. But it remains the direct object of the sentence. **Had** is moved
out of the normal auxiliary position, but **had ... worried about** is still
the MV, just as **worried about** is still a two-word transitive verb, though
its object has been moved to the front of the sentence:

what

The U.N. officers had worried about ~~the Serbian troop movements.~~

↓

What had the U.N. officers worried about?

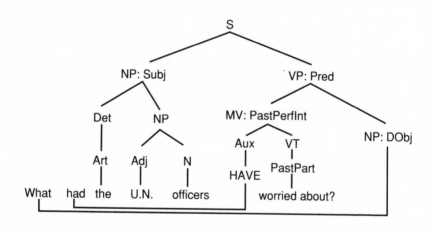

If the core sentence contains no auxiliary element, then you may have
to add the auxiliary DO to the sentence in order to make it into a Wh-
question. Here is a sentence with the verb **provided** as the only component of the MV:

> The satellite pictures of Venus provided the scientists new
> geological information.

Since the core MV has no auxiliary word, you have to add DO to Aux
in order to complete the question sentence. Notice that, as with nega-

tive sentences in which you add DO, the DO takes on the tense form and the verb changes to the infinitive form. The relationships between the constituents remain the same. **Provide** is a Vg verb. **What** replaces the direct object NP. **The scientists** is the indirect object. And **do . . . provide** is the MV. See the diagram on the next page.

what

The satellite pictures of Venus provided the scientists ~~new geological~~
~~information~~.

↓

What did the satellite pictures of Venus provide the scientists?

When you question a determiner or a genitive noun in a noun phrase, you move the whole noun phrase to the front of the sentence, not simply the genitive noun, as the next example and the diagram on the next page show.

whose

The vandals trashed ~~Sally's car~~ last night.

↓

Whose car did the vandals trash last night?

which

The House Democrats voted ~~this~~ **way** on the education bill.

Which way did the House Democrats vote on the education bill?

Passive Sentences

The most common rearranged sentence pattern is called a PASSIVE. The rearrangement into a passive sentence demands that you introduce BE into the auxiliary, add a prepositional phrase, change the verb into its past participial form, and move both the subject and object noun phrase. Here is a core sentence rearranged as a passive:

Congress funded the cleanup.

↓

The cleanup was funded by Congress.

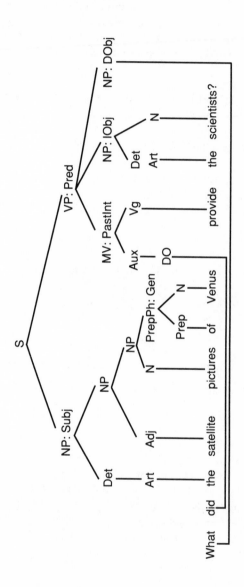

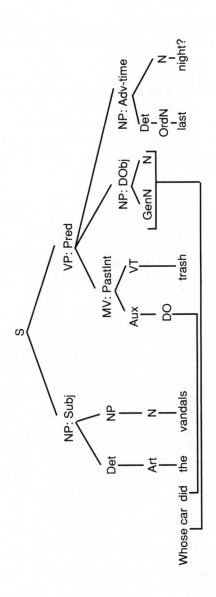

The Structure of Passives

Passives can only be made from sentences with transitive verbs, one-place or two-place transitives (VT, Vg, or Vc). The passive is closely linked with transitive verbs; as you remember, the passive was originally introduced as a test for whether a verb was transitive. You make a sentence passive by taking the core object and moving it to the front of the verb; then you put the core subject into a prepositional phrase headed by the preposition **by**; finally, you change the core verb into its past participial form and add BE—either **is, was,** or **were**—to the auxiliary constituent. Here is another passive, with the movements shown in schematic form:

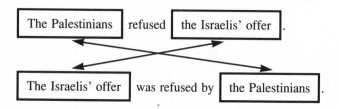

Since the original core object noun phrase (**the Israelis' offer**) sits in the normal subject position before the verb, it is called a GRAMMATICAL SUBJECT (the original object noun phrase occupies the grammatical space that a subject normally occupies); the core subject (**the Palestinians**), now the object of a preposition (by **the Palestinians**), is called a LOGICAL SUBJECT (semantically, the core subject still does what a subject normally does: it performs an action). At the same time that it functions as the logical subject, the noun phrase you've moved into the prepositional phrase functions as the object of a preposition. The **by** prepositional phrase itself functions as an adverb of agency. Agency in this sense refers to "performing the action," what the subject of a transitive verb normally does. So calling the prepositional phrase an adverb of agency is just another way of saying that the noun phrase object of the preposition relates to the verb just as a subject noun phrase normally relates to a transitive verb, as an agent or performer of the action. Since the object of the preposition is the original subject, you would expect it to retain this role as performer of the action. Here is the passive example diagramed:

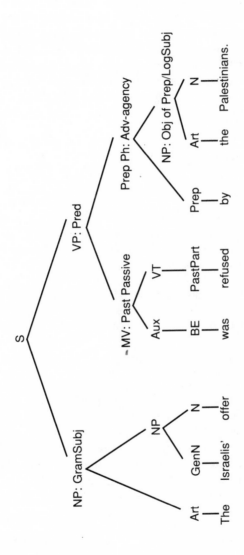

Deleting By Phrases

Under certain circumstances, you may delete the **by** phrase from passive sentences. You may delete it if the information in the **by** phrase is available from other sources in the general context, like a previous sentence in the paragraph; or you may delete the **by** phrase if the information in it is general knowledge. If, for example, you were writing a story about police and gangs in Los Angeles, you might have already written that it is the new gangs in town who are challenging the police. So you wouldn't have to repeat **by the new gangs** in the following sentence:

> The police are challenged ~~by the new gangs~~ in several
> neighborhoods.
> ↓
> The police are challenged in several neighborhoods.

Or if you were writing an article for a gardening magazine, you might assume that the readers understand it is gardeners who grow hostas for their foliage. So you wouldn't have to include the phrase **by gardeners** in the following sentence:

> Hostas are grown ~~by gardeners~~ for their handsome foliage.
> ↓
> Hostas are grown for their handsome foliage.

Where Have All the Constituents Gone?

The constituents haven't exactly gone to graveyards, as the old Peter, Paul, and Mary song said about the flowers. But they have moved around in passive sentences. So sometimes their functions seem buried under six feet of earth. The best way to clarify for yourself what the sentence constituents are and what their functions are is to put the constituents back into their core arrangement. It's important, also, to remember that only a transitive verb (VT, Vc, or Vg) can be made into a passive and that the verb remains transitive even after it is made passive. Let's look at a few examples. In the passive sentence

> The Russian royal family was executed in June, 1917,

the agent phrase has been deleted. It would be something like **by Soviet soldiers**, or more vaguely **by someone**. So if you were unclear about relationships in the passive and wanted to rebuild the core sentence, you would have to put either **Soviet soldiers** or **someone** in as the subject.

Soviet soldiers executed the Russian royal family in June, 1917.

If you put the passive and active forms back to back, you should be able to see clearly what is going on in the passive. The verb is the transitive verb **executed**. It is transitive in the core sentence; it is transitive in the passive sentence, though its object noun phrase, **the Russian royal family**, has been moved to the grammatical subject position and its subject, **Soviet soldiers**, was moved into a **by** phrase and then deleted. Here's a bit more complicated example:

The GOP's tax plan was considered divisive.

Again, you have to reconstruct a deleted agent before you make the sentence active. **By reporters** seems reasonable; **by someone** would work. So, here is the rebuilt sentence:

Reporters considered the GOP's tax plan divisive.

Considered is the main verb of the reconstructed active sentence. It is a Vc verb. **The GOP's tax plan** functions as a direct object, and **divisive** is an adjective that functions as the object complement. Nothing new here. Having established the original relationships, you can determine the relationships in the passive sentence because they're the same. The main verb of the passive is **be considered**, with **considered** the head. **Considered** was a Vc verb in the active; it's a Vc in the passive. **Divisive** was an adjective functioning as an object complement in the active; it's an adjective functioning as an object complement in the passive. **The GOP's tax plan** was a direct object; now it's called a grammatical subject because it's the underlying direct object moved into the normal subject slot. If you keep in mind that the six core sentence types and their relationships underlie all the sentences in the language, no matter how much the parts are rearranged or added to, you can always go back to the originals to determine relationships. Remember that the core sentences are like blocks that you can use to build longer, more complicated sentences. They are at the core of rearranged and combined sentences in the language. You'll see this concept working more and more as we move through later chapters.

Adjectives or Past Participles?

There is a problem you'll face when you have to identify a passive with a deleted **by** phrase. A passive with a deleted agent can look like a core sentence that has BE as the main verb followed by a predicate adjective. This is because past participles and adjectives can look alike. Sometimes the difference between past participles and adjectives is obvious, as in

The characters on *M*A*S*H* were drunk by midnight. (Adjective)

The martinis were drunk by the characters on *M*A*S*H*. (past participle)

In the first example, **drunk** is clearly an adjective because no one would dream of **drunk** as the past participle of a verb in this context (you can't **drink** characters). In the second example, **drunk** is clearly the past participle of the verb because martinis can't be **drunk** unless someone **drinks** them. At other times the meaning of a sentence does not clearly differentiate an adjective from a past participle:

Lois is frustrated.

Lois may be frustrated **by Clark** (from **Clark frustrated Lois**), in which case the example sentence is passive (auxiliary BE plus a past participle). Or Lois may be in a state of frustration (verb BE plus an adjective). If you are given a sentence like the last example to analyze, with no contextual clues to help you decide whether **frustrated** is a past participle or an adjective, the best you can do is to indicate that you are aware of both possible analyses.

Passives with Get

Passive sentences normally imply that the logical subject (the core subject) caused something to happen to the grammatical subject (the core object). But passive sentences can also suggest a sense of "becoming." **Get** seems to suggest this sense of becoming stronger than BE. So sometimes you'll find **get** as the auxiliary in a passive sentence rather than BE, especially in informal language, in order to emphasize the sense of becoming, as in

The paper's TV critic panned the final episode of *Cheers*.

↓

The final episode of *Cheers* **was** panned by the paper's TV critic.

or

The final episode of *Cheers* **got** panned by the paper's TV critic.

Dad chewed out my little brother.
↓
My little brother **was** chewed out by Dad.

or

My little brother **got** chewed out by Dad.

Negatives and Questions in Passives

Once you turn a sentence into a passive, you can make it negative or change it into a question, just as if it were a core sentence with BE. Since the BE of a passive sentence is already in the Auxiliary, simply place the negative marker **not** after the BE in order to make a negative sentence. Move BE to the front of the sentence to make it a yes/no question, or move both BE and either a noun phrase or adverb phrase in order to make a Wh-question.

The communications satellite was recovered by the shuttle crew.
↓
The communications satellite was **not** recovered by the shuttle crew.

Billy the Kid **was** shot by Pat Garrett.
↓
Was Billy the Kid shot by Pat Garrett?

~~Billy the Kid~~ was shot by Pat Garrett.
↓
Who was shot by Pat Garrett?

MV Status in Passives

When you have to identify the status of the main verb of a passive sentence, you normally state that it is passive as the final comment. Here are some variations on a single sentence, with the status identified for each:

> The students **were attacked** by Chinese army troops in Beijing. (past passive)
>
> The students **may be attacked** by Chinese army troops in Beijing. (present conditional passive)
>
> The students **are being attacked** by Chinese army troops in Beijing. (present progressive passive)
>
> The students **had been attacked** by Chinese army troops in Beijing. (past perfect passive)
>
> The students **might have been attacked** by Chinese army troops in Beijing. (past perfect conditional passive)

Sentences with *There*

When a core sentence contains the verb BE followed by an adverb of place, you can sometimes add **there** and rearrange the constituents to produce a new sentence called an EXISTENTIAL-THERE SENTENCE. The name may sound imposing and difficult, but the rearrangement is straightforward. And the outcome is a common sentence type. Here are two examples:

> Millions of drug dealers are in the United States.
> ↓
> **There** are **millions of drug dealers** in the United States.

> Several first-class restaurants are in the new mall.
> ↓
> **There** are **several first-class restaurants** in the new mall.

To create the existential-there sentence, you move the original subject noun phrase around the verb BE and add **there** in the now empty core subject position. As in a passive sentence, the constituent in the original subject position is called the grammatical subject, while the original core subject, which has been moved to the right of the verb, is called the logical subject. The diagram on the next page shows the relationships in the first example sentence. The original subject noun phrase, **millions of drug dealers**, follows the verb BE as the logical subject; **there** fills the core subject position as the grammatical subject.

Some existential-**there** sentences don't seem to be rearrangements of core sentences; nonetheless, they have the other characteristics of rearranged sentences, including **there** as the grammatical subject sitting to the left of the verb BE, and a noun phrase functioning as the logical subject, following the verb, as in

There may be a labor shortage in a few years.

For such a sentence, **there** does not seem to be a core-sentence source like ***A labor shortage may be in a few years.**

Expletives

The **there** that functions as the grammatical subject in an existential-there sentence is called an EXPLETIVE. An expletive is a word that has a grammatical function in a sentence but has no meaning of its own. In the case of existential-there sentences, **there** replaces a noun and functions as a grammatical subject. But it is not a noun itself; nor is it a pronoun.

There are two other expletives in English: **do** and **it** in certain circumstances can be expletives. The **do** that occurs in the auxiliary of negative or question sentences to hold tense is an expletive. It has no other role but to show the tense form; it's sort of like a dummy modal. The **it** in the subject position of existential sentences like

It is raining

and

It's hot today

is also an expletive. The word **it** in such sentences is not a pronoun; it does not refer to a previous noun, as a pronoun would. The expletive **it** does perform a noun job, though. It functions as the subject of the sentence. In the chapter on noun clauses, we'll also look at rearranged sentences like

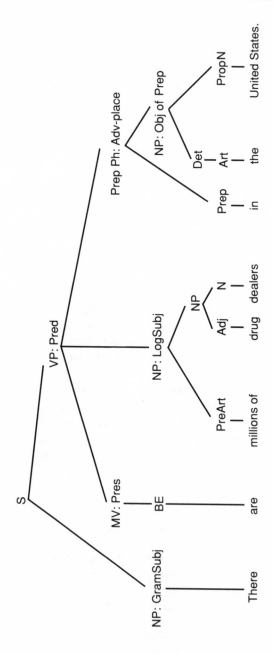

It seems that the Bulls will win the playoffs

and

It occurred to Andy that Barney needed help at the jail.

In these sentences, expletives function as grammatical subjects.

Imperative Sentences

IMPERATIVE SENTENCES are commands or instructions. They tell you to do something: clean your room, take the dog out, or erase the blackboard. Parents and teachers use a lot of imperative sentences. So do writers of cookbooks and other how-to books. Here are some imperative sentences:

Mix the herbs with the spices.

Stir the garnish into the soup.

Don't wear black to the dance.

Set the modem on 28,800 baud.

Insert tab A into flange B before assembling base.

Understood You in Imperative Sentences

You've probably learned that imperative sentences have an "understood you" as the subject. That is, you can understand **you** to be the subject of a sentence like **Stir the garnish into the soup**, though the word **you** does not occur in the sentence. It is the case that, in order to make a core sentence into an imperative form, you have to delete the pronoun **you** from the subject noun phrase. But it is the case that you have to delete a modal **will** along with the pronoun **you**. To demonstrate why this is so, we'll have to look first at how you make TAG QUESTIONS.

Tag questions repeat the subject and auxiliary of a sentence in a TAG PHRASE. So, to make a tag phrase, you take the first word in AUX, make it negative (if it is positive), and add the subject of the sentence; if the subject is a pronoun, simply copy the pronoun. Otherwise, turn the noun phrase subject into its pronoun form.

Congress will pass the new tax bill.
$$\downarrow$$
Congress will pass the new tax bill, **won't it**?

We have put too much money into the chemical weapons program.
$$\downarrow$$
We have put too much money into the chemical weapons program, **haven't we**?

Making tag questions is pretty straightforward. Now let's take a look at imperative sentences in relation to tags.

If you were given an imperative sentence like

Turn in the paper before class,

you could make the following tag:

Turn in the paper before class, **won't you**?

As this example shows, when you make tags for imperative sentences, you invariably use both the pronoun **you** and modal **will**. Most grammarians take this fact to be proof that both **will** and **you** exist in the underlying (core) structure of imperative sentences. In other words, both **you** and **will** are "understood."

Diagraming Imperatives

When you diagram imperative sentences, you can leave out the subject and modal, showing VP as the single constituent of S and the verb as the only constituent of MV.

The Status of Imperatives

Imperative is a mood, like indicative, interrogative, or conditional. You indicate that fact when you label the status of the main verb. The status of the example is simply **imperative** or **imperative mood**, if you wish. The main verb of an imperative has no tense. This is an interesting point about imperatives. Since you delete the modal **will** from an imperative sentence, you delete tense as well. The verb of an imperative is always in the infinitive form.

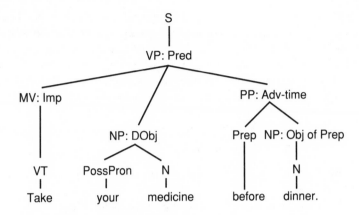

Imperatives and Negatives

The negative form of imperatives contains a **do not**, just like the negative of a sentence without an auxiliary constituent. If we build on the idea that imperatives delete **you** and **will**, then it follows that to make an imperative into a negative, you first insert **not** after **will**. Then, after you delete **you** and **will**, you insert an expletive **do** in order to "hold" the **not**. Otherwise, imperative sentences would sound like ***Not wear black to the dance**. But of course they don't. Here is how to derive a negative imperative:

You will wear black to the dance.
↓
You will not wear black to the dance.
↓
Not wear black to the dance.
↓
Don't wear black to the dance.

Compounding

The most common way to make sentences longer is to COMPOUND structures within them (the term "compound" is used interchangeably with

CONJOIN or COORDINATE). When you compound structures, you put them together into a single new constituent, usually with connective words and phrases called CONJUNCTIONS. If you compound more than two constituents, you usually need commas as well. You can compound any level of constituent—words, phrases, or clauses. Here are three nouns compounded:

> Edison suffered from dyslexia.
>
> Einstein suffered from dyslexia.
>
> Michelangelo suffered from dyslexia.
> ↓
> **Edison, Einstein, and Michelangelo** suffered from dyslexia.

On a diagram, you show compounded words or phrases first as single constituents, along with their unitary function, then you break the units down into their separate constituents. In the diagram on the next page, the nouns **Edison, Einstein,** and **Michelangelo** are first shown as a noun phrase, then the individual nouns are shown as separate noun phrases joined with the conjunction **and**. The three noun phrases put together this way make a single compound noun phrase constituent that functions as the subject of the sentence. Compound words and phrases together make constituents that can function wherever and however single words or phrases can function. Here are compound noun phrases functioning as direct objects:

Lorenzo steals **Shylock's daughter and a pile of Shylock's money.**

Columbus didn't find **India or Japan**.

Here are examples of different kinds of compound words and phrases:

> Fujicolor **freezes the action and gives you vibrant color.**
> (VP: Pred)
>
> Soviet leaders usually left office **in a coffin or in disgrace.**
> (Prep Ph: Adv-manner)
>
> Elephants are endangered **by poachers and by complacent governments**. (Prep Ph: Adv-agency)
>
> The Saturn was **designed and built** in North America. (V)

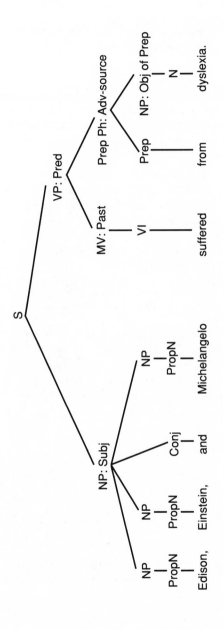

Here are compound sentences:

> **Hanna-Barbera introduced** *The Flintstones*, **and Disney**
> **gave us** *Pocahontas*.

Conjunctions

There are two types of conjunction, COORDINATE and CORRELATIVE. The coordinate conjunctions are the single words **and**, **but**, and **or**. The correlative conjunctions are pairs of words—**both** . . . **and**, **either** . . . **or**, **neither** . . . **nor**, and **not only** . . . **but also**. Correlative conjunctions are more emphatic than coordinate conjunctions because the first of the pair demands that you anticipate the coordinated word or phrase. Note the difference between the first example with the coordinate conjunction **or** and the second version with a correlative conjunction **either** . . . **or**:

> Those prehistoric idols supposedly produced fecundity in the
> marriage bed **or** the farm field.

> Those prehistoric idols supposedly produced fecundity in
> **either** the marriage bed **or** the farm field.

As you know, it's difficult to diagram disjoined constituents like correlative conjunctions. The last example is diagramed on the next page. The correlative conjunction **either** . . . **or** is shown as two words linked together into one disjoined constituent. In this reading, the conjunction is **either** . . . **or**, and the word **either** is moved to the left of the compound noun phrase **the marriage bed** . . . **the farm field**.

Punctuating Compounds

Normally when you conjoin only two words or phrases, you do not punctuate the compound.

> We celebrated the centennial of **Tootsie Rolls and Cracker Jack**
> in 1996.

When you conjoin more than two words or phrases, you generally put a conjunction before the final item in the compound and commas between the items.

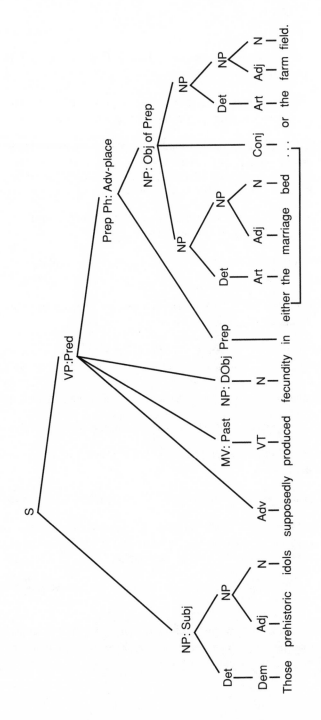

121

We celebrated the centennial of **Tootsie Rolls, Cracker Jack, and Michelob** in 1996.

When you use conjunctions to link sentences, you have several punctuation options. You can put a comma before the conjunction.

The French love Charlie Chaplin's subtle clowning**, but** they revere Jerry Lewis's brash antics.

You can put a semicolon before the conjunction.

The French love Charlie Chaplin's subtle clowning**; but** they revere Jerry Lewis's brash antics.

Or you can end the first sentence with a period and begin the next with a capital.

The French love Charlie Chaplin's subtle clowning**. But** they revere Jerry Lewis's brash antics.

When you need to produce a special effect with compounds, you can change the normal punctuation. In the following example, for instance, the adverb of frequency **again** is repeated with conjunctions and no punctuation in order to emphasize the way the children rode the carousel.

The preschoolers rode the carousel **again and again and again**.

There are also times when you might want to use commas but no conjunctions:

Our office copier not only copies but also **staples, stacks, collates**.

Without the commas, the series jumps from one verb to another, almost mimicking the movement of the copy machine. Notice how much smoother the movement is with a conjunction.

Our office copier not only copies but also **staples, stacks, and collates**.

In some cases—if they are brief—you can even connect sentences as you would phrases, either with commas alone, with commas and conjunctions, or with conjunctions only.

Winds howled, waves crashed, decks swayed.

or

Winds howled, waves crashed, and decks swayed.

or

Winds howled and waves crashed and decks swayed.

The more standard practice would separate the sentences with periods.

Winds howled. Waves crashed. And decks swayed.

But separating this series of sentences with periods would lose some of the sense of the turbulence of the storm.

So the way you punctuate coordinate structures can change the effect sentences have on readers. Be careful, to break standard punctuation practice only when it is important to make a special point. Otherwise hold to the standard practice. It's what readers expect. And readers don't normally want to have expectations broken unless they can see good reason for it.

Conjunctive Adverbs

Closely related to conjunctions are CONJUNCTIVE ADVERBS. They connect sentences, but they give a different kind of information about the relations between sentences than conjunctions do. Some grammarians call conjunctive adverbs DISCOURSE MARKERS. The reason is that conjunctive adverbs are in some sense the writer's or speaker's comments about how she wants her text read or understood; in that way, conjunctive adverbs mark the discourse. It's as if the writer is saying, "now I'm going to sum up"; or "Now I want the reader to understand what is happening in the meantime." The most common conjunctive adverbs are words and phrases like **besides, furthermore, first, for, finally, however, in the first place, in the meantime, likewise, moreover, nonetheless, notwithstanding, on the other hand, rather,** and **then.** When you punctuate, you typically use conjunctive adverbs along with periods.

Brand-name cereals are expensive. **Nonetheless,** they appeal to kids.

But you can just as readily use conjunctive adverbs with semicolons in order to show that you mean for the ideas in the two independent clauses to be more closely linked than a period would indicate.

Brand-name cereals are expensive; **nonetheless**, they appeal to kids.

Conjunctive adverbs do not have to introduce the second clause. You can generally move them to the middle or end of a clause.

Brand-name cereals are expensive; they **nonetheless** appeal to kids.

Brand-name cereals are expensive; they appeal to kids **nonetheless**.

Summary

In this chapter, we've looked both at how to change the shape of our building blocks (the core sentences) by rearranging constituents and how to put the blocks together into new, larger structures by compounding. This is the first chapter in which we've worked with the original core sentences as building blocks. That we can build and rearrange sentences to make new sentences out of old material makes grammar a discrete combinatorial system. In later chapters, we'll look at other ways to put the core sentences together in different ways to form larger, more complex sentences.

Here are the main points in the chapter:

- Constituents of the six core sentence patterns can be rearranged and compounded.
- To make a sentence negative, you add the negative marker **not**.
- There are two types of question sentences—yes/no questions and Wh-questions.
- Core sentences with transitive verbs can be made into passive sentences.
- Certain core sentences with BE can be rearranged into existential-there sentences.
- To make a core sentence imperative, you delete both **you** and **will**.
- One way to make sentences longer is by compounding structures within them.
- Typically, you use commas and conjunctions to link compound con-

stituents. But you may also use punctuation and compounding to create various effects within and between your sentences.

- Conjunctive adverbs connect clauses but mark the discourse differently from conjunctions.

EXERCISES

I. WRITING DEFINITIONS

Define the following terms as completely as you can, giving examples wherever possible:

Negative word	do
Statements	Yes/no questions
Wh-questions	Passive sentence
Logical subject	Grammatical subject
Existential-there sentence	Expletive
Imperative	Compound
Conjoin	Coordinate
Coordinate conjunction	Correlative conjunction
Conjunctive adverb	Discourse marker
Discrete combinatorial system	

II. REARRANGING AND COMPOUNDING SENTENCES

Change the following core sentences into the patterns indicated in parentheses:

EXAMPLE

Potato fields had been on Long Island before World War II.
  (There)

↓

There had been potato fields on Long Island before World War II.

1. Alfred Hitchcock directed *Psycho*. (Passive)
2. You will go to your room. (Imperative)
3. The Mafia is ripping off the government. (Yes/no question)
4. A kid can read something. (Wh-question with the object questioned)
5. No Saabs are in the school lot. (There)

6. The hospital threw out razor blades in safe ways.
   The hospital threw out hypodermic needles in safe ways. (Negative and compound NPs)

7. Hispanics have gained political clout during the last decade.
   Women have gained political clout during the last decade.
   African Americans have gained political clout during the last decade. (Use NPs from all three sentences to make one sentence with compound NPs; experiment with different ways of compounding and punctuating)

8. Saturns give you peace of mind.
   Saturns give you pride of ownership. (Compound with **not only . . . too**)

9. Whole wheat flour can turn your brownies into nutritional treats.
   Whole wheat flour can turn your cakes into nutritional treats.
   Whole wheat flour can turn your cookies into nutritional treats. (Compound NPs; experiment with different ways of compounding and punctuating)

10. Police officers have the highest suicide rate.
    Miners have the highest job-fatality rate. (Conjoin the sentences with either a conjunction or a conjunctive adverb)

III. ANALYZING SENTENCES

Analyze the following sentences, identifying the structures and their functions as far as you are able. If the constituents are rearranged from their core positions, be sure to note whether the subjects and objects are logical and grammatical. Be careful, also, to indicate whether any of the constituents are compounds; if they are, indicate how they are compounded—with conjunctions or conjunctive adverbs, or with punctuation alone. Feel free to diagram if you find that diagraming helps your analyses.

EXAMPLE

How can Washington stop the flow of drugs into the United States?

Explanation. **How can Washington stop the flow of drugs into the United States?** is a Wh-question sentence. It is derived from the statement **Washington can stop the flow of drugs into the United States**

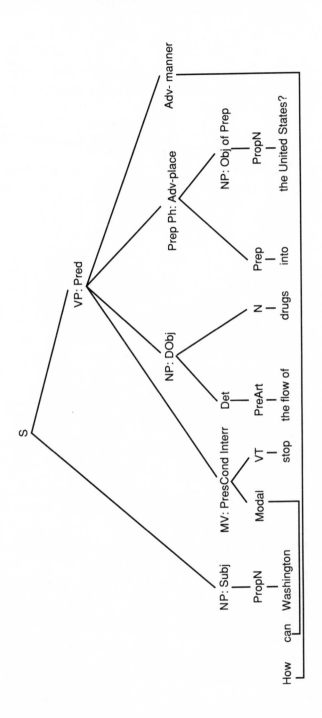

127

in some way. The modal **can** is moved to the front of the sentence; then the adverb of manner, the prepositional phrase **in some way**, is changed to the pro-adverb **how** and moved before the modal. The subject of the sentence is the proper noun Washington. The main verb is **can . . . stop**; its status is present conditional interrogative. The transitive verb **stop** is followed by the object noun phrase **the flow of drugs**. The noun phrase object is composed of the pre-article **the flow of** and the noun **drugs**. The prepositional phrase **into the United States**, which functions as an adverb of place, is composed of the preposition **into** and the noun phrase **the United States**.

Sentences

1. The sporty Jaguar is called the XJR.
2. The Blackhawks haven't eliminated Detroit.
3. Why do school buildings sit empty most of the day?
4. The Sox couldn't put together a rally in the fifth.
5. Fingernails are scrutinized by nutritionists for vitamin deficiencies.
6. The Marx Brothers were funny and progressive and creative.
7. The U.S. ski team carries a lot of prestige. But it doesn't carry American Express.
8. Paul Newman's performance captures the sadness and heroism of Cool Hand Luke.
9. One-third of American households sort their garbage now. So 40,000,000 tons of garbage is recycled yearly.
10. The senator should not have forgotten the concerns of her constituents.
11. What values are taught by our schools?
12. There is racism throughout the world.
13. Homeowners shouldn't keep firewood close to the house.
14. Could the pioneers and the Native Americans have co-existed without violence?
15. Julia Child's first TV show was called *The French Chef*. But she is neither French nor a chef.
16. Why didn't George Washington free his slaves after the Revolution?
17. How often has genocide reared its ugly head since the Holocaust?
18. Bake the mixture in the oven for 20 minutes.
19. Tokyo has not loosened trade restrictions.
20. The tarot cards were set out on the table by the fortuneteller.

21. Seafood is featured on the menu of the new Mexican restaurant.
22. Gunfire could be heard throughout Sarajevo.
23. Diet and exercise can lower cholesterol.
24. Boys don't read Nancy Drew.
25. Churchill, Stalin, and Roosevelt created modern Europe at Yalta in 1945.
26. Alzheimer's strips away mind and ideas.
27. There was no warning before the quake.
28. Does peace have a price?
29. Help the hungry in your community.
30. Can the wilderness heal an oil spill?
31. Martin Luther King called for liberty and justice.
32. There are raspberries and blackberries in the tart.
33. What would Thanksgiving be without the Macy's parade?
34. The beach was cleaned by Exxon workers.
35. Where can you escape from crowds, earphones, and fax machines?
36. Rap rhythms and gospel messages make Christian hip-hop a strange musical blend.
37. How do you capture the spirit of a book page on a computer monitor?
38. Modern poetry can be ironic, ambiguous, and complex.
39. There are many superb burgundies in California.
40. Why can't we afford good nursing care in America?
41. Americans love golf. But it is a cruel, inscrutable game.
42. There's big money in burger franchises.
43. The Balkan countries can't escape their bellicose history.
44. White teenage girls define beauty in terms of physical perfection. In contrast, black teenage girls define it in terms of the right attitude.
45. There are four outdoor concerts at the riverfront park this summer.
46. Pop spotted the overturned van and stopped our car.
47. Marine recruits are taught the values of the Corps by their drill instructors.
48. The women's movement won't fade away.
49. Walt Whitman's poetry was not appreciated in his day. Nonetheless, *Leaves of Grass* sings out fresh and vibrant today.
50. Most single-parent families don't happen by choice.

CHAPTER 6 | *Constructing Relative Clauses*

Preview

This chapter explains restrictive relative clauses; restrictive relative clauses are dependent clauses that function as adjectives within noun phrases. Here are the points to remember in the chapter:

- Clauses are either independent or dependent.
- Dependent clauses are either noun, adjective, or adverb constituents.
- The relative clauses in this chapter are embedded within noun phrases as adjective constituents; they are also called restrictive or bound.
- Relative clauses have the same two basic parts as other clauses: a noun phrase subject and a verb phrase predicate.
- You make a clause into a relative clause by replacing a noun phrase with a relative pronoun and, if it is not the subject, moving the relative pronoun to the front of the clause.
- The relative pronouns—**who**, **whom**, **which**, **that**, and **whose**—replace noun phrases.
- Fronted relative pronouns retain the relationships they had in their original clause positions.

Clauses

Clauses are either INDEPENDENT or DEPENDENT. All the clauses we've looked at so far are sentences. Sentences are independent clauses; that means they are not included within other clauses. Dependent clauses (which are also called SUBORDINATE clauses) are included within larger clauses; the grammatical term for included within is EMBEDDED. Subordinate clauses will always be either noun, adjective, or adverb constituents. In other words, they fill a noun, adjective, or adverb position (slot) in a larger clause. Whether they are dependent or independent, all clauses contain a noun phrase subject and a finite verb phrase predicate. Dependent clauses are built around the same six core verb types as independent clauses. You can expand their noun phrases and verb phrases. And you can rearrange and conjoin them. So the new subordinate clauses we'll meet in this and later chapters are structurally the same as the independent clauses we've looked at and analyzed in the previous chapters. They have all the same parts. Subordinate clauses just occur in different places: embedded within larger clauses.

When you embed a clause as a dependent clause, it's as if you took one sentence and combined it into another. When you analyze COMPLEX SENTENCES (sentences with at least one subordinate clause), you can reverse the combining process, separating the combined clauses into their original sentence forms. You create dependent clauses in your speech and writing with ease. You can as easily learn to recognize and parse them.

The dependent clauses we'll look at in this chapter are called RELATIVE CLAUSES. More specifically, they are RESTRICTIVE relative clauses, which is another way of saying that they function as adjectives.

Why Do You Combine Clauses?

Why do you combine clauses within larger structures when you speak and write? You don't have to, of course. You could simply string independent clauses together with **ands**, as small children frequently do. It wouldn't be unusual for a child to tell you about her trip to the store in this way: "I went to the store, and I bought some peanut butter, and I took it home, and I was gonna make a sandwich." But stringing clauses together that way is a terribly inefficient way to speak or write; as we grow older, we learn to combine clauses in order both to specify relationships between our ideas and to save words. So we'd probably make the child's sentence into something like, "When I went to the store, I bought some peanut butter, which I took home to make a sandwich." The new sentence is much more efficient; it contains fewer words and states more clearly the relationships between the events. If you read the original string of clauses and then the combined sentence aloud, you'll see how much more adult the combined sentence sounds. When the clauses are simply conjoined, you can almost hear a child's breathless outburst.

Relative Clauses

As you can see, building sentences by embedding clauses into one another is natural. If you were assigned a paper about labor relations at a factory in your town, you might write the following two statements.

> The labor arbitrators examined the problems.
>
> The problems had caused the strike.

Since both sentences contain the noun phrase **the problems**, you can combine the two sentences into one, making the second into the relative clause **that had caused the strike**.

The labor arbitrators examined the problems.

The problems had caused the strike.

↓

The labor arbitrators examined the problems **that had caused the strike**.

The Structure and Function of Relative Clauses

Where Relative Clauses Are Embedded

When you combine clauses, you follow the design that the language allows. You embed a relative clause into a noun phrase, nesting a constituent within a constituent to create a new, larger constituent. The second chapter indicates that the hierarchy is the basic structural principle of language and that all constituents are structured as hierarchies, boxes nested within boxes. When you embed a relative clause into the noun phrase of a larger clause, you follow that same principle: you nest it as a hierarchy. The diagram on the next page that illustrates the relationship between the dependent clause and the sentence in the above example about labor arbitrators and strikes.

The relative clause is embedded within the larger clause; the "larger clause" in the example happens to be a sentence. Like all restrictive relative clauses, the relative clause in our example is embedded within a noun phrase constituent, in this case the object noun phrase of the sentence. So the original direct object noun phrase, **the problems**, and the embedded clause, **that had caused the strike**, combine to make a new noun phrase constituent, **the problems that had caused the strike**. The expanded noun phrase, like the original one, **the problems**, is the direct object of the verb **examined**. This is an important point to understand. It's worth repeating: the original noun phrase and the embedded clause make a new noun phrase constituent. The new noun phrase is a single noun phrase constituent, and it functions as the direct object of the verb **examined**. Look again at the noun phrase **the problems that had caused the strike**. The original noun phrase **the problems** functions as the head of the new phrase. The relative clause functions as an adjective within the larger noun phrase. **The problems that had caused the strike** is a new constituent. It is a noun phrase, and it can be used anywhere that the original noun phrase could be used.

These two points are crucial to understanding what happens when clauses are embedded as restrictive relative clauses: (1) the relative clause and the noun phrase it is embedded into form a new noun phrase constituent, and (2) the relative clause functions as an adjective within the new noun phrase constituent.

The Structure of Relative Clauses: The Way It Was

Before we look at the structure of relative clauses, here's a story that might help you remember the main lesson. A TV commercial for the Bob Evans restaurant chain depicts customers enjoying their food in a relaxed, old-fashioned atmosphere; the visual message is that the restaurants bring back the service and the hearty food of bygone days. The voiceover, a resonant male voice, emphasizes the visual message with

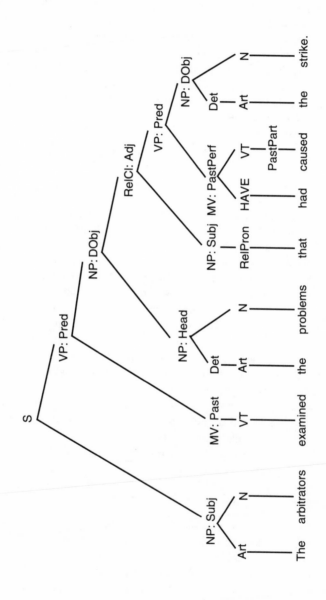

the statement, "The way it was is the way it is." It's a good theme for a restaurant chain that wants to make its customers feel comfortable in familiar surroundings; and it could be the theme for every chapter on dependent clauses. It's certainly the theme for this section on the structure of relative clauses. You should feel comfortable parsing relative clauses because there's something familiar and comfortable about them: the way it was is the way it is.

Now we can look more closely at relative clauses. The relative clause **that had caused the strike** has the same structure you've come to expect in a clause. Here's the relative clause constituent separated from the rest of the diagram:

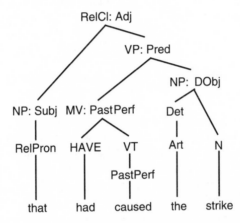

The relative clause has exactly the structure it had when it was a separate sentence, except that the RELATIVE PRONOUN **that** has replaced **the problems** as the subject noun phrase. **Had caused the strike** is the verb phrase that functions as the predicate of the clause. The verb **cause** is a transitive verb; **the strike** is a noun phrase that functions as its object. The status of the main verb **had caused** is past perfect. The major difference between this clause and the independent clauses you've already learned to parse is that it doesn't stand alone: it is embedded within another clause.

Everything else you know about the structure of independent clauses remains the same for relative clauses (or any other dependent clause). There are still six basic verb types. You can expand both the main verb constituents and the noun phrase constituents. You can rearrange and conjoin constituents as well. In Bob Evans restaurants or in dependent clauses, you're in familiar surroundings: the way it was IS the way it is.

The Relation of a Relative Clause to Its Matrix Clause

A dependent clause is embedded in a larger clause called a MATRIX CLAUSE. Dependent clauses are not combined haphazardly into matrix clauses but are placed into specific constituents. A relative clause, for instance, is embedded within a noun phrase of a matrix clause. It may be embedded within any noun phrase in a matrix clause—a subject, a direct object, an oblique object, an object complement, a predicate noun.

Relative clauses that are embedded within noun phrases—the relative clauses we look at in this chapter—function as adjectives; in other words, they are ADJECTIVE CLAUSES. Here's a relative clause embedded within the subject noun phrase of its matrix clause:

> **The senator *who co-sponsored the abortion bill* didn't attend the president's reception.**

The subject noun phrase of the matrix is **the senator who co-sponsored the abortion bill.** That noun phrase is composed of two constituents, a head NP **the senator** and a relative clause **who co-sponsored the abortion bill.** The diagram of the sentence, with the noun phrase subject highlighted by a rectangle, is on the next page. It's important to remember that the noun phrase subject is composed of a head NP and a relative clause and that the two constituents together make one single noun phrase constituent. Like all the relative clauses in this chapter, **who co-sponsored the abortion bill** is embedded in a noun phrase and functions as an adjective.

The matrix clauses we've looked at so far have been sentences, independent clauses. But a matrix clause may itself be embedded within another clause, as you've known since you were a little kid, when you embedded one relative clause after another to tell about the house that Jack built:

> This is the man who married the woman who owned the dog that chased the cat that ate the rat that stole the cheese that lived in the house that Jack built.

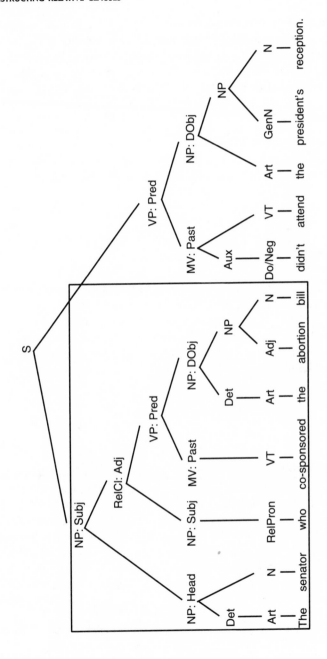

You wouldn't expect to find sentences as extreme as this, but embedding constituents in embedded constituents is common practice. It's one way we make sentences longer and more complex. Here's a less extreme example, with one relative clause (**who retired**) embedded in another relative clause (**that include stars who retired from the NBA**).

> The Globetrotters may play teams **that include former stars who retired from the NBA**.

Together, they make a single relative clause constituent. The diagram on the next page indicates all the relationships in the sentence:

Boxes are nested within boxes.

Constructing Relative Clauses

It's easy to construct relative clauses and embed them into larger clauses. You can take any independent clause and make it into a relative clause. First you have to change one of its noun phrases into a relative pronoun. In the following sentence, the subject noun phrase **computers** is replaced by the relative pronoun **that** to make the relative clause **that think like humans**.

that

~~Computers~~ think like humans.

↓

that think like humans

Relative pronouns must occur at the front of their own clauses. So if you make the subject noun phrase into a relative pronoun, as in the example, that's all you have to do to complete the relative clause; the subject noun phrase is already at the front of the relative clause. If you make any other noun phrase into a relative, you must also move the relative pronoun into the initial position, as in the next example, where the direct object **the program** is replaced by the relative **which**; then the relative pronoun is moved to the front of the clause.

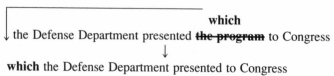

which

↓ the Defense Department presented ~~the program~~ to Congress

↓

which the Defense Department presented to Congress

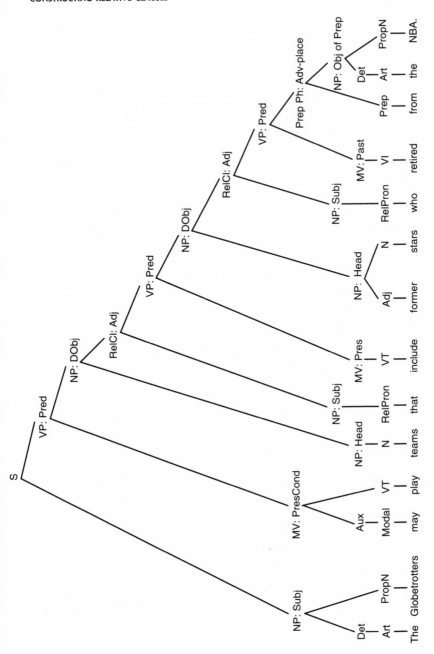

After you create a relative clause, you can embed it into a noun phrase in a matrix clause, as in the next example, where the relative clause is embedded into the matrix noun phrase **the program**.

The program will increase naval firepower dramatically.

   ┌──────────────────────────────**which**

   ↓ the Defense Department presented ~~the program~~ to Cogress
                      ↓

The program **which the Defense Department presented to Congress** will increase naval firepower drastically.

Here are some more examples. Notice how the second sentence in each example is made into a relative clause and then combined into a noun phrase in the first sentence to make a new, larger noun phrase.

We arrived in Denver after a breathtaking flight.

    that
~~The flight~~ ended in a smooth touchdown.
             ↓

We arrived in Denver after a breathtaking flight **that ended in a smooth touchdown**.

Dieters are culinary terrorists.

       who
~~Culinary terrorists~~ bring fear into your kitchen.
             ↓

Dieters are culinary terrorists **who bring fear into your kitchen**.

The bill bans aid to the rebel government.

   ┌──────────**that**
   ↓ Congress passed ~~the bill~~ yesterday.
             ↓

The bill **that Congress passed yesterday** bans aid to the rebel government.

Relatives

Choosing a Relative Pronoun

The RELATIVES, or RELATIVE PRONOUNS, are **who, whom, which, that,** and **whose**. The five relative pronouns replace different kinds of noun phrases in relative clauses. Both **who** and **whom** replace noun phrases that refer to humans; **who** replaces human noun phrases functioning as subjects, while **whom** replaces human noun phrases functioning as objects, either direct or oblique. For example, if you make

> The terrorist had threatened some female hostages.

into a relative clause, you can replace the subject noun phrase **the terrorist** with **who,** as in

> Police psychologists calmed the terrorist.

> **who**
> ~~The terrorist~~ had threatened some female hostages.
> ↓
> Police psychologists calmed the terrorist **who had threatened some female hostages**.

Or you can replace the object noun phrase **some female hostages** with **whom**, as in

> The female hostages escaped before the shootout.

> ┌─────────────────────────────── **whom**
> ↓ The terrorist had threatened ~~some female hostages~~.
> ↓
> The female hostages **whom the terrorist had threatened** escaped before the shootout.

Which replaces noun phrases that do not refer to humans, whether those noun phrases function as subjects or objects. So you can make

> Barley can clear cholesterol from the blood

into a relative clause by replacing the subject noun phrase **those grains** with **which**, as in

Barley is one of those grains.

which
~~Those grains~~ can clear cholesterol from the blood.
↓
Barley is one of those grains **which can clear cholesterol from the blood.**

Or you can make

The gang committed the violence in Central Park

into a relative clause by replacing the object noun phrase **the violence** with **which**, as in

New Yorkers were shocked by the violence.

┌──────────────── **which**
↓ The gang committed ~~the violence~~ in Central Park.
↓
New Yorkers were shocked by the violence **which the gang committed in Central Park.**

Remember that you must move a noun phrase to the front of a relative clause unless the noun phrase is the subject and thus already at the front of the clause. In effect, this means that you must move direct objects, predicate nouns, object complements, indirect objects, or objects of prepositions.

That is the most versatile and probably the most frequently used of the relative pronouns. You can use it instead of **who, whom,** or **which.** **That** can replace any noun phrase in a relative clause, whether it's human or nonhuman, whether it functions as a subject, direct object, oblique object, predicate noun, indirect object, or object complement. Here are some example clauses with **that** as the relative pronoun:

Antonia Fraser's *Warrior Women* concerns women **who** massacred their rivals.

or

Antonia Fraser's *Warrior Women* concerns women **that** massacred their rivals.

The only comedian **whom** Robin Williams regards as a soul mate is Jonathan Winters.

or

The only comedian **that** Robin Williams regards as a soul mate is Jonathan Winters.

Oliver Sacks writes about schools **which** have harmed the deaf by teaching them only sign language.

or

Oliver Sacks writes about schools **that** have harmed the deaf by teaching them only sign language.

That is easy to use; it reduces the number of decisions you have to make when you construct a relative clause. So it has become the relative pronoun of choice. Many style manuals now recommend that writers replace **who**, **whom**, and **which** with **that** whenever possible.

Whose is different from the other relatives. Rather than replace a whole noun phrase, **whose** replaces only a possessive pronoun or a genitive noun, as in the following example:

Stewed okra is a dish.

    whose
~~The dish's~~ charms are seldom appreciated.
       ↓
Stewed okra is a dish **whose** charms are seldom appreciated.

In the previous example, **whose** replaced a genitive in the subject noun phrase of the relative clause. If you replace the possessive in an object noun phrase with **whose**, you have to move the whole noun phrase, not simply the possessive, to the front of the relative clause. Here is an example with **whose** in an object noun phrase:

Native Americans are asking for their land to be returned.

                      whose
↓ The government "appropriated" ~~their~~ territory in the nineteenth century.
       ↓

Native Americans **whose territory the government appropriated in the nineteenth century** are asking for their land to be returned.

Sometimes you have to replace the object of a preposition with a relative pronoun. In that case, you have a choice when you move the relative. You may move the whole prepositional phrase to the front of the clause, or you may move just the relative pronoun, stranding the preposition at the end of the clause. The next example shows the different choices.

The park is scheduled to become a parking lot.

which

The neighborhood kids play baseball in ~~the park~~.

↓

The park **in which the neighborhood kids play** is scheduled to become a parking lot.

or

The park **which the neighborhood kids play in** is scheduled to become a parking lot.

The second choice, with the preposition left at the end of the clause, sounds more natural. So we often construct clauses that way when we're speaking or when we're writing. But some writers and teachers prefer to front the whole prepositional phrase, especially in more formal writing.

Fronted Relatives and Functions

When you move a noun phrase to the front of a relative clause, it retains the relationship it had in the clause before it was moved: an object remains an object; a predicate noun remains a predicate noun; an object complement remains an object complement; an indirect object remains an indirect object; an object of a preposition remains an object of a preposition. Here's a sentence that has a relative clause with a direct object brought to the front. Following the sentence is a diagram of the relative clause to illustrate that the fronted noun phrase, the relative pronoun **that**, remains the direct object of the clause.

Condominium owners share the upkeep expenses.

┌─────────────────────────that
↓ Their property demands ~~upkeep expenses~~.
↓

Condominium owners share the upkeep expenses **that their property demands**.

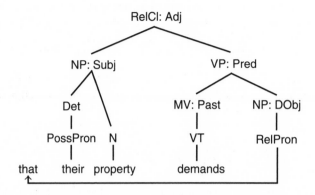

Though the relative pronoun is disjoined from the normal object position following the verb, it retains the direct object relationship. The noun phrase subject of the relative clause is **their property**; **demands that** is the predicate; **that** is the object of the transitive verb **demands**.

Before we move into the next section, here's a hint about analyzing relative clauses. Since relative clauses are combined into matrix clauses, you can reverse the process in order to parse sentences and to identify all the constituents in relative clauses. If you "pull the clause out" of the sentence you're analyzing, you should be able to reconstruct the relative clause into an independent sentence and easily identify its constituents. Here's an example:

David Franklin's *Age of Optimism* is a study of American leaders for whom anything seemed possible.

The relative clause is

for whom anything seemed possible.

You know that a relative pronoun is moved to the front of its clause and that when a relative is the noun phrase object of a prepositional phrase, the prepositional phrase can move to the front as well. So you can move the prepositional phrase back to its original position to produce

anything seemed possible for whom.

You also know that a relative pronoun replaces a noun phrase that is the same as the head of the matrix noun phrase the clause is embedded in. By this logic, **whom** in our example must have replaced the noun phrase **American leaders**. With that insight, you can rebuild the independent clause.

Anything seemed possible for American leaders.

It's generally that simple to reconstruct a relative clause as an independent clause and to be back into territory you should know well by now. The way it was is the way it is.

Deleting Object Noun Phrases

Normally, you move object noun phrases to the front of their clauses after you make the phrases into relatives. But you can also delete object noun phrases from relative clauses. Speakers and writers often delete object noun phrases because it's an efficient way to create clauses and because it saves having to decide whether to use **who**, **whom**, **that**, or **which**. The object noun phrases have been deleted from the relative clauses in the second of each of the following output sentences. Though they no longer contain relative pronouns, the dependent clauses are still relative clauses.

The administration denied all the requests.

that
The students made <del>the requests</del>.
↓

The administration denied all the requests **that the students made**.

or

The administration denied all the requests **the students made**.

I left the expressway to get a look at the tower.

which
I had seen <del>the tower</del> rising above the tree line.
↓

I left the expressway to get a look at the tower **which I had seen rising above the tree line**.

or

I left the expressway to get a look at the tower **I had seen rising above the tree line.**

The substitute teachers seemed not to like us children.

whom
We taunted ~~those substitute teachers~~ most.
↓
The substitute teachers **whom we taunted most** seemed not to like us children.

or

The substitute teachers **we taunted most** seemed not to like us children.

Embedding Relative Clauses into Dependent Clauses

So far we've embedded relative clauses only into the noun phrases of independent clauses. This section is simply a reminder that you can also embed relative clauses into other subordinate clauses. Here's a sentence with a relative clause embedded within a relative clause:

The psychologist talked to women.

The women could describe the problems.

They encountered the problems in the workplace.
↓
The psychologist talked to women **who could describe the problems they encountered in the workplace.**

They encountered in the workplace is a relative clause embedded in the noun phrase **the problems they encountered in the workplace**; the noun phrase functions as the object of the verb **describe**, which, together with **could**, is the main verb of the larger relative clause **who could describe the problems they encountered in the workplace.** This larger relative clause is embedded in the noun phrase object of the independent clause, **women who could describe the problems they encountered in the workplace.**

This sentence is a good example of the principle that large sentences are composed of little sentences, sometimes several little sentences.

Restrictive Clauses

The relative clauses in this chapter are called RESTRICTIVE or BOUND. These terms are just another way of saying that these relative clauses function as adjective clauses embedded within noun phrases. Restrictive clauses are not set off by commas. We'll discuss the differences between restrictive and nonrestrictive relative clauses in the chapter on sentence modifiers.

Summary

Clauses

Whether they are independent or dependent, clauses have the same basic constituents, a noun phrase subject and a finite verb phrase predicate. Independent clauses stand alone as sentences; dependent clauses are embedded within larger, matrix clauses as nouns, adjectives, or adverbs. The dependent clauses discussed in this chapter are restrictive relative clauses embedded within noun phrases as adjectives.

Relative Clauses

You make a clause into a relative clause by replacing one of its noun phrases with a relative pronoun and, if necessary, moving the pronoun to the front of the relative clause; if the relative replaces a genitive pronoun or occurs in a prepositional phrase, then you move the whole phrase that the relative is in. After moving the relative, you embed the relative clause within a noun phrase in a matrix clause.

The relatives are **who, whom, that, which,** and **whose.** The most common relative is **that**: to use it, you don't have to differentiate either subjects from objects, as you do between **who** and **whom,** or human from nonhuman, as you do between **which** and **who** or **whom.** Whose replaces possessive pronouns or genitive nouns.

When you're analyzing sentences, it sometimes helps to see relationships if you take the relative clauses out of their matrix clauses and change them back into complete sentences. It's important to remember that the relationships within a clause do not change, no matter where you move constituents to make a relative clause.

Grammar as a Discrete Combinatorial System

We have seen in this chapter more evidence that grammar is a discrete combinatorial system. The principle behind building grammatical units is simple: take structures you already have available and use them again and again. Use a noun phrase as a subject, a direct object, a predicate noun, or an object complement; a noun phrase is a noun phrase wherever it occurs in a clause. Use a clause as a sentence, or combine it into another clause as an adjective, noun, or adverb; a clause is a clause whether it is independent or dependent. In the next few chapters, we'll see how this combining principle works to produce clause and nonclause structures that allow us to expand sentences in a variety of ways.

Hierarchy as Underlying Design

You don't combine constituents helter-skelter. You build constituents into hierarchies because the hierarchy is the basic design of all grammatical constituents—phrases or clauses. Boxes nest within boxes.

EXERCISES

I. WRITING DEFINITIONS

Define the following words and phrases as completely as you can, giving examples whenever possible:

Dependent (subordinate) clause   Adjective clause
Independent clause   Matrix clause
Embedded   Relative pronoun
Complex sentence   Restrictive
Relative clause

II. COMBINING SENTENCES

Combine the following pairs of sentences. Make the second sentence of each pair into a relative clause, and then embed it into the first.

EXAMPLE

The first graders played "go fish" with cards.

The cards had pictures of animals on them.

↓

The first graders played "go fish" with cards **that had pictures of animals on them**.

1. The comet appears every twenty years.
   Dr. Okada discovered the comet.
2. Everyone respected the quarterback.
   The quarterback refused to give up.
3. The most valuable experiences were small ones.
   I had the experiences on my trip to Europe.
4. Children will probably become abusers of drugs or alcohol.
   Children's parents abuse alcohol.
6. Many nations are restricting emissions of noxious gases.
   The noxious gases threaten the atmosphere.

III. BREAKING OUT UNDERLYING SENTENCES

Identify the matrix clause and the relative clause in each of the following sentences. Then write out the complete sentences from which the matrix and relative clauses are derived.

EXAMPLE

Honeydew is a sweet libation that can enhance a summer brunch.

Honeydew is a sweet libation. (MC)

The sweet libation can enhance a summer brunch. (RelCl)

1. Gloria Steinem writes about the campaign in which Geraldine Ferraro ran for vice president.
2. The Sherpa guides who led us through the mountains became our steadfast friends.
3. The recent terrorist attacks should change the way you think about national resistance movements.
4. Midway was a battle that shaped naval strategy during World War II.
5. There are historical insights in the *Encyclopedia of Southern Culture* every American should be aware of.

IV. ANALYZING SENTENCES

Analyze the following sentences, identifying the structures and their functions, as far as you are able. It may help you to write out the underlying sentences from which the relative clauses are derived or to diagram the sentences.

EXAMPLE

Norman Rockwell's paintings suggest a stroll during which you experience dramatic scenes.

Explanation. The sentence is composed of the subject noun phrase **Norman Rockwell's paintings** and the verb phrase predicate **suggest a stroll during which you experience dramatic scenes**. The main verb of the matrix clause is the transitive verb **suggest**, which is in the present indicative form. **A stroll during which you experience dramatic scenes** is the noun phrase functioning as the direct object of the matrix clause. This noun phrase is composed of the head noun phrase **a stroll** and the relative clause **during which you experience dramatic scenes**. Since the relative pronoun **which** is the object of the preposition **during**, the prepositional phrase **during which** was brought to the front of the relative clause. The prepositional phrase functions as an adverb of time within the relative clause. The subject of the relative clause is **you** and the predicate is

during which ... experience dramatic scenes ___ .

Experience is a transitive verb in the present indicative form. The noun phrase **dramatic scenes** functions as the object of the verb **experience**. It is composed of the adjective **dramatic** and the head noun **scenes**. If you broke out the main clause, it would be **Norman Rockwell's paintings suggest a stroll**. If you broke out the relative clause, you would make **You experience dramatic scenes during the stroll**.

Sentences

1. My folks don't like the guy I'm dating now.
2. Lucille Ball was a glamour girl who became a clown.
3. The drug epidemic is a cancer that threatens the nation's survival.
4. Countries whose energy consumption does not decrease will suffer during the next decade.

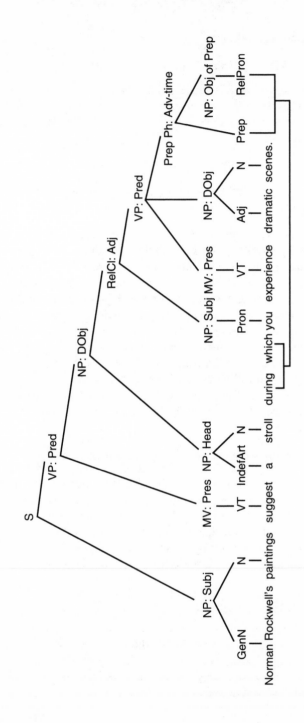

5. Dad wanted the subwoofer system, which mom considered overpriced.
6. Elephants are complex social animals that can feel compassion.
7. The American soldiers met some Haitian children who had overcome the squalor that surrounded them.
8. The cows that were stolen from Colorado ranches wound up in Utah.
9. The university dismissed the coach whose recruiting practices the NCAA questioned.
10. The joyous Cubs fan rang a bell that rivaled Big Ben.
11. The best fiction comes from writers who have a sensitive vision of the world.
12. The warden opened the gray steel door that connects death row to the gas chamber.
13. The people who had bought $42.00 tickets lounged in the Emerald Room.
14. Mercer Sullivan is an anthropologist who studies youth crime on the streets of Brooklyn.
15. The new mall established a climate in which high-class stores could thrive.
16. Woody Allen is a vulnerable artist who takes things personally.
17. Senior citizens who have suffered strokes come to the clinic for speech therapy.
18. We rode whitewater rapids that battered our raft perilously.
19. Special-education teachers succeed with students for whom there has been no hope.
20. Our Zagreb trip was complicated by a taxi driver who spoke no known language.
21. There are several ornamental grasses that will flourish in partial shade.
22. Ginger Rogers and Fred Astaire tapped and shimmied through ten movies that define Hollywood's romantic heyday.
23. John Grisham's *The Rainmaker* sold over 300,000 copies during the first week it appeared in bookstores.
24. The new tech school provides classrooms in which every student has a computer.
25. Gospel singer Fontella Bass's voice bursts with a spirit that seems to come from a different world.
26. The social pressures that encourage women to starve themselves include men's expectations and media representations of lithe models.

27. The light that gets through your dirty windows will be noticed by your guests.
28. The "killer brownie" I bought at the snack bar was sinfully rich.
29. The foods your mother prepared can keep you healthy.
30. Sue Miller's books explore the underground passages that connect family members.
31. Wisconsin boasts a dairy industry that flourishes because of lush pastures.
32. African Americans have won political influence that was denied them for centuries.
33. The prevalence of family violence has spawned a shelter network that offers women refuge.
34. Nintendo is a madness that strikes adolescent boys.
35. Laptop computers you can slip into a backpack are replacing blue books at college exams.
36. Readers who know Churchill's basic story will find this new biography dull.
37. Barbie emanates an attraction that keeps young girls hooked.
38. Apple gave us a computer anyone can use.
39. Neighborhood crime-watch groups are organizations through which police can build civilian support.
40. IBM has developed a full-sized keyboard that can collapse into a notebook computer.
41. Pectinase dissolves the white material that makes orange peel adhere.
42. The FDA monitors the food we buy.
43. Satellites read the infrared emissions that reveal the ocean's temperature.
44. Grizzly bears have eaten people who have ventured into their domains.
45. The pancreas is a gland that produces insulin.
46. Aunt Ethel's home looked like a house a kindergartner might draw.
47. Dr. Weinstein gave good news to the cancer patient she had treated with the new drug.
48. Bob Dylan's art resembles the drawings high school kids do on their notebooks.
49. Seahorses are the only fish that practice steadfast monogamy.
50. F. Scott Fitzgerald lived like the characters he wrote about.

CHAPTER 7

Reducing Relative Clauses to Phrases

Preview

This chapter is about how to reduce relative clauses to participial or prepositional phrases that you can use as adjectives within noun phrases. Here are the main points of the chapter:

- You can reduce relative clauses to phrases by deleting the subject noun phrase and BE.
- By reducing relative clauses, you produce present participial phrases, past participial phrases, or prepositional phrases.
- These phrases are restrictive and function as adjectives, just like the clauses from which they derive.
- Parsing is a matter of recognizing constituents "nested" in one another and taking them apart piece by piece.

Reducing Relative Clauses

In the last chapter, you saw how to embed relative clauses into matrix clauses to function as adjectives, as in

The students assembled on the steps of the administration
building.

The students were protesting the new dorm rules.
↓
The students **who were protesting the new dorm rules**
assembled on the steps of the administration building.

Now let's look at how you can reduce relative clauses to phrases. In the
above example, you can make the relative clause **who were protesting
the new dorm rules** into a present participial phrase **protesting the
new dorm rules** by deleting **who were**.

The students ~~who were~~ **protesting the new dorm rules**
assembled on the steps of the administration building.
↓
The students **protesting the new dorm rules** assembled
on the steps of the administration building.

In this same way, by deleting a relative pronoun and BE, you can reduce
relative clauses to produce past participial phrases and prepositional
phrases as well as present participial phrases.

Present Participial Phrases

A PRESENT PARTICIPIAL PHRASE is a phrase headed by a present participle. When you embed a participial phrase into a matrix noun phrase, it
functions as an adjective, exactly like the relative clause from which it
derives. So **the students protesting the new dorm rules** is a noun
phrase composed of a noun phrase head, **the students**, and a present
participial phrase, **protesting the new dorm rules**.

Here are some more examples of present participial phrases embedded as adjectives into matrix noun phrases:

Group therapy can help people **who are** fighting drug
addiction.
↓
Group therapy can help people **fighting drug addiction.**

I played soldier among the apple trees ~~that were~~ **growing**
in my grandpa's orchard.

↓

I played soldier among the apple trees **growing in my**
grandpa's orchard.

The hurricane ~~which was~~ **bearing down on Florida**
frightened the coastal residents.

↓

The hurricane **bearing down on Florida** frightened the
coastal residents.

Present participial phrases function in the same way as the relative
clauses from which they derive; they function as adjectives. They also
pattern in the same way within matrix clauses; they are embedded in
noun phrases to the right of a head noun.

Another thing to notice about participial phrases is that they are verb
phrases, so they retain all the internal characteristics associated with
verb phrases: they contain the same six kinds of verbs as the core sentences. The participial phrase in the diagram, **fighting drug addiction,**
is composed of the transitive verb **fighting** followed by a noun phrase
drug addiction, which functions as the object of the verb. In the sentence

I played soldier among the apple trees **growing in my**
grandpa's orchard,

growing in my grandpa's orchard is a present participial phrase that
functions as an adjective within the matrix noun phrase **the apple trees**
growing in my grandpa's orchard. Growing is an intransitive verb
followed by the prepositional phrase **in my grandpa's orchard;** the
prepositional phrase functions as an adverb of place within the verb
phrase.

One exception to the rule about deleting a relative pronoun and BE
concerns verbs that cannot be made progressive. When you change a
relative clause with such a verb into a participial phrase, you have to
make the verb into a present participle, not simply delete BE and the
noun phrase. For instance, in the following example,

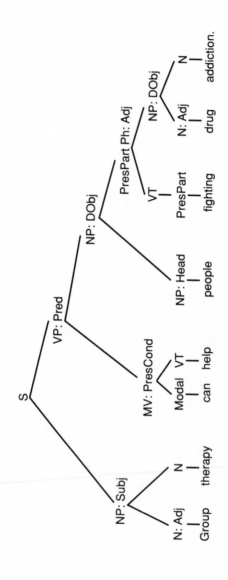

The "screwball comedies" that featured Cary Grant
virtually defined urbane humor for America in the 1930s,

the verb **feature** doesn't allow a progressive form with BE (there is no "that were featuring Cary Grant"). Nonetheless, **feature** can be made into a present participle:

The "screwball comedies" **that featured Cary Grant**
virtually defined urbane humor for America in the 1930s.
↓
The "screwball comedies" **featuring Cary Grant** virtually
defined urbane humor for America in the 1930s.

Notice that present participial phrases are nonfinite verb phrases; you delete tense when you delete the BE of the main verb.

Past Participial Phrases

Just as you can delete BE and the relative pronoun from a clause and create a present participial phrase, so you can delete BE and a relative pronoun from a clause and create a PAST PARTICIPIAL PHRASE. Here is a sentence with an embedded past participial phrase. The sentence is diagramed on the next page.

Students **who are taught phonics by their primary
teachers** can sound out unfamiliar words.
↓
Students **taught phonics by their primary teachers**
can sound out unfamiliar words.

A clause from which you derive a past participial phrase will always be passive, since that's the only construction in which BE can be followed by a past participle. The relative clause in the above example, for instance, is passive. The verb **teach** is a two-place transitive, Vg. Here is the derivation of the past participial phrase, one step at a time, as it changes from an active, independent clause to a passive to a relative clause and finally to a past participial phrase.

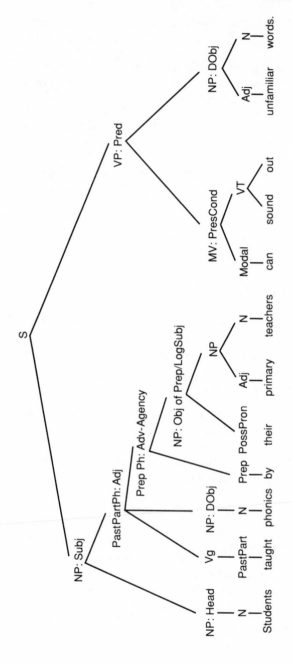

Their primary teachers teach students phonics.
↓

who
~~Students~~ are taught phonics by their primary teachers.
↓

~~who are~~ taught phonics by their primary teachers
↓

taught phonics by their primary teachers

No matter how complex a structure may seem, you can derive it easily, because even the most complex construction derives from structures and processes you've already become familiar with. The way it was is the way it is remains a basic principle of parsing.

Since the relative clause from which you derive a past participial phrase is passive, you can delete its **by** phrase just as you can delete the **by** phrase from an independent clause that is passive.

A tiny pump ~~which is~~ **implanted beneath a diabetic's skin by a doctor** can regulate insulin dosage better than injections.
↓

A tiny pump **implanted beneath a diabetic's skin** ~~by a doctor~~ can regulate insulin dosage better than injections.
↓

A tiny pump **implanted beneath a diabetic's skin** can regulate insulin dosage better than injections.

What you have left when you delete the **by** phrase is still a past participial phrase.

Prepositional Phrases

Another structure you can derive from a clause by deleting BE and the subject NP is a prepositional phrase, as in

The refrigerator ~~that is~~ **in the center of the nursery** is filled with baby formula for early-morning feeding.
↓

The refrigerator **in the center of the nursery** is filled with baby formula for early-morning feeding.

The art critic considered the paintings ~~which were~~ **from Renaissance Florence** the best in the exhibition.

↓

The art critic considered the paintings **from Renaissance Florence** the best in the exhibition.

Prepositional phrases that are embedded in noun phrases function as adjectives, just like the past and present participial phrases you derive in the same way. Prepositional phrases that occur in verb phrases function as adverbs. Constituency is the key to whether a prepositional phrase functions as an adjective or an adverb. Take a close look at the next example.

The mill **in Oak Brook, Illinois**, was a shelter **for slaves traveling on the Underground Railway**.

The prepositional phrase **for slaves traveling on the Underground Railway** functions as an adjective because it is embedded in the noun phrase **a shelter for slaves traveling on the Underground Railway**; in the same way, **in Oak Brook, Illinois**, functions as an adjective because it is embedded in the noun phrase **the mill in Oak Brook, Illinois**. But the prepositional phrase **on the Underground Railway** functions as an adverb since it occurs in a verb phrase, **traveling on the Underground Railway**. It is not embedded directly in a noun phrase; it exists within a verb phrase. The diagram on the next page makes these comments clear.

Prepositional phrases headed by **with** are difficult to derive. They seem to come from underlying phrases with **have** rather than **is with**. For instance, in the sentence

A house **with a computer and a set of encyclopedias** announces the sophistication of its occupants,

the prepositional phrase

with a computer and a set of encyclopedias

seems to derives from

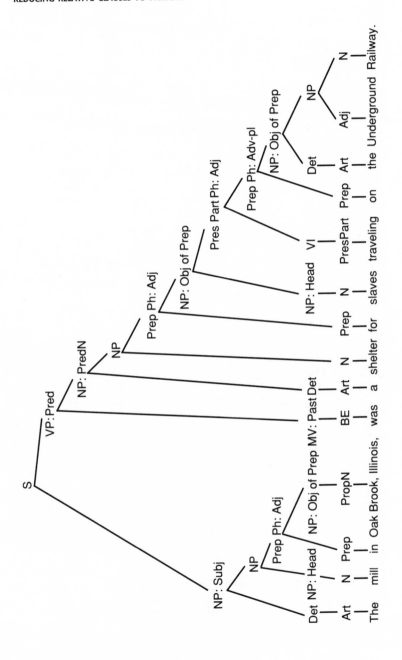

~~which has~~ a computer and a set of encyclopedias.

It is likely, though, that there is an intermediate step that turns the **has** into **is with**. We won't worry about such an intermediate step. For our purposes, it is enough to say that the phrase **with a computer and a set of encyclopedias** is derived from

~~which is~~ with a computer and a set of encyclopedias.

And we should take note that a clause that contains **is with** never occurs, except as a structure underlying derived prepositional phrases headed by **with**.

Constituency within Embedded Phrases

Some of my students find it difficult to understand the relationships within the embedded phrases. It is an important enough issue to devote a small section to in order to emphasize what has been said before.

Here are the main points. The whole phrase that is embedded within a noun phrase functions as an adjective. But the components of the embedded phrase function within the phrase just as they always do. In a present participial phrase, a transitive verb will be followed immediately by a noun phrase direct object (fighting **drug addiction**); an intransitive verb may be followed by an adverb (growing **in my grandpa's orchard**). In a past participial phrase, the verb may be followed by a prepositional phrase functioning as an adverb of agency, or the agent phrase may be deleted (implanted beneath a diabetic's skin **by a doctor**, or implanted beneath a diabetic's skin). In a prepositional phrase, the noun phrase functions as the object of the preposition (in **the center of the nursery**).

If you have trouble seeing the relationships within an embedded phrase, you may find it useful to rebuild the clause from which the phrase derives.

~~who were~~ **fighting drug addiction**

~~that were~~ **growing in my grandpa's orchard**

~~which is~~ **implanted beneath a diabetic's skin by a doctor**

~~which is~~ **in the center of the nursery**

The relationships within the predicate or prepositional phrase of the re-built clause will be the relationships within the embedded phrase. The embedded phrase itself, the whole phrase, functions as an adjective within the matrix noun phrase into which it is embedded. The constituents of the embedded phrase, though, are just that: constituents of the embedded phrase. The issue is one of constituency. The whole embedded phrase is a constituent of its matrix noun phrase; the components of the embedded phrase are constituents of the embedded phrase—whether that embedded phrase is a present participial, past participial, or prepositional phrase.

Single-Word Participles, Adverbs, and Adjectives

To be consistent, we should derive single-word participles, adverbs, and adjectives in the same way we derive multi-word phrases. When you embed a single word, you generally have to move it to the front of its head noun, as with these participles:

> The Empire State Building achieved fame **that was enduring** in *King Kong.*
>
> ↓
>
> The Empire State Building achieved fame **enduring** in *King Kong.*
>
> ↓
>
> The Empire State Building achieved **enduring** fame in *King Kong.*

> The captain from our intelligence unit interrogated the guerrillas ~~who were~~ **captured**.
>
> ↓
>
> The captain from our intelligence unit interrogated the guerrillas **captured**.
>
> ↓
>
> The captain from our intelligence unit interrogated the **captured** guerrillas.

Or these adjectives:

The relievers have given the Reds pitching ~~which is~~ **consistent**.
↓
The relievers have given the Reds pitching **consistent**.
↓
The relievers have given the Reds **consistent** pitching.

In this same way, a one-word adverb that functions as an adjective in a noun phrase derives from an embedded clause. These one-word adverbs functioning as adjectives usually occur before a noun, though sometimes they can follow a noun.

Harry longed for the blonde who lived in the apartment ~~which was~~ **upstairs**.
↓
Harry longed for the blonde who lived in the apartment **upstairs**.

or

Harry longed for the blonde who lived in the **upstairs** apartment.

When you diagram one-word participles, adjectives, or adverbs, you normally make the word a constituent with the head noun as a noun phrase before you make a constituent with the determiner, as in these diagrams:

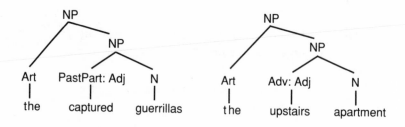

Here is a diagram of the sentence about the Reds' pitching staff:

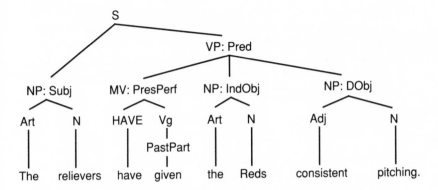

You should be aware that deriving single-word adjectives, participles, and adverbs from clauses will sometimes produce underlying clauses that sound strange. As an example, to derive the word **alley** in **alley cats**, you'd have to suppose there was a clause **the cats were alley** (or perhaps **from the alley**).

Deriving individual participles, adjectives, and adverbs from underlying clauses may help you with your grammatical analysis. If it doesn't, don't feel compelled to derive every single word used as an adjective in a noun phrase. The main point to understand is that these single words function like adjectives within noun phrases. As long as you're careful about their constituency, your analyses should be okay.

Restrictive Phrases

Like the relative clauses from which they derive, the phrases discussed in this chapter are restrictive; they are bound within noun phrases and function as adjectives. Because they are restrictive, the phrases are not set off by commas.

Parsing, Onion Peeling, and "Thermogrammatics": Some Irreverent Thoughts

Building sentences and taking sentences apart lead to several metaphors that might help you to understand grammatical structure and parsing. We've mentioned some in earlier chapters.

The first chapter notes that the relationships among the structures in long sentences are like nested boxes, boxes that fit one within another.

In later chapters, we said the same thing in a different way, referring to the fact that grammar is a discrete combinatorial system. Because phrases and clauses fit within one another, you can make long complex sentences from just a few kinds of phrases and clauses. Look at the following sentence about meals that begin with spicy foods and end with exquisite desserts.

> Dinners that begin with "fireworks" should end with fantasies
> like hazelnut eclairs.

A sentence such as this, with several embedded structures, may look daunting to parse. But if you remember that even the longest, most complicated sentence is composed of smaller constituents nested within it, you can take the sentence apart piece by familiar piece.

This insight on nesting leads to the second point. Parsing is basically a matter of identifying those constituent pieces. In the 1992 presidential campaign, Bill Clinton's staff put a sign above his desk that read, "It's the economy, Stupid." They wanted the candidate to keep focused on what they saw as the central issue of the campaign. During that campaign year, some of my students made copies of a sign that read

It's Constituency, Stupid!

They said they put the signs over their desks to remind themselves that constituency is always the central issue in grammatical analysis. Let's parse the example sentence to illustrate the importance of constituency and nesting. Here it is again:

> Dinners that begin with "fireworks" should end with fantasies
> like hazelnut eclairs.

The predicate in the sentence contains the following constituents that "fold into" one another. First, the noun **hazelnut** (functioning as an adjective) is embedded into the NP **hazelnut eclairs**.

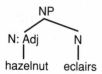

Then the NP becomes the object of the preposition **like** in the prepositional phrase **like hazelnut eclairs.**

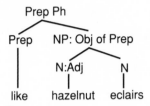

In turn, the prepositional phrase is embedded into the noun phrase **fantasies like hazelnut eclairs,** where it functions as an adjective.

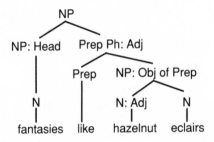

This noun phrase is the object of yet another prepositional phrase, **with fantasies like hazelnut eclairs.**

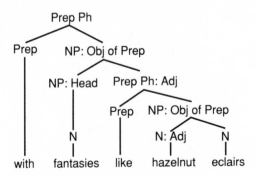

And this prepositional phrase functions as an adverb of manner within the verb phrase predicate **should end with fantasies like hazelnut eclairs.**

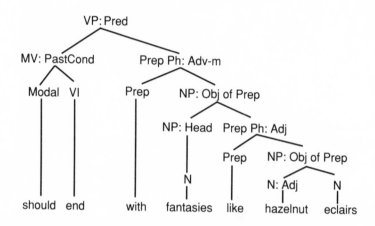

The noun phrase subject is built the same way, with constituents folding into one another to make larger constituents. First, the noun **"fireworks"** becomes the object of the preposition **with**; the prepositional phrase **with "fireworks"** functions as an adverb of manner with the verb **begin**; the verb phrase **begin with "fireworks"** functions as the predicate of the relative clause **that begin with "fireworks"**; and the relative clause functions as an adjective within the noun phrase **dinners that begin with "fireworks."** The diagram of the complete sentence is on the next page.

Here's another metaphor for parsing. In class, I've sometimes compared parsing sentences to peeling onions, taking off one layer at a time. When you peel off one onion layer, the one beneath it looks similar; you peel layer from layer until you reach the innermost layer. A student stopped me one day to remark that parsing is more like "existential onion peeling, beginning with the innermost layer and working your way out." She was right. It's probably best to think of parsing as identifying one constituent at a time and "working your way out" from the center of the onion.

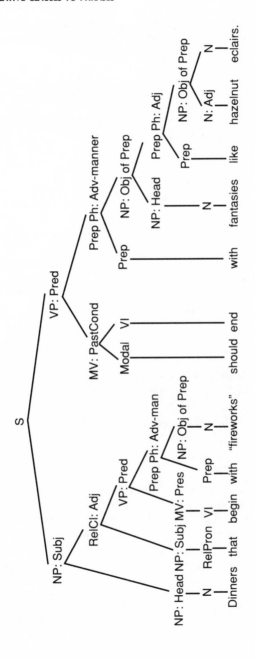

You can also look at a sentence in terms of the clauses that underlie the embedded constituents and the processes that generate them. At the core of the example sentence is a main clause.

Dinners should end with fantasies.

Three clauses underlie the structures embedded within the main clause; the first becomes a relative clause embedded into the subject noun phrase of the main clause:

that
~~Dinners~~ begin with fireworks
↓
that begin with fireworks.

The second becomes a prepositional phrase embedded into the noun phrase **the fantasies**.

~~The fantasies are~~ like eclairs.
↓
like eclairs.

And the third sentence becomes an adjective embedded into the noun phrase **eclairs**.

~~The eclairs are~~ hazelnut.
↓
hazelnut

Either way you look at the sentence, you can see that the constituents that enfold within one another and the processes that create the embedded structures are familiar. You've seen them all before in earlier chapters.

One final metaphor. Grammar is the ultimate recycler; it wastes neither parts nor processes. It uses both over and over again. Mathematicians may refer to this "ecological" characteristic as the discrete combinatorial power of grammar. My students have called this view of grammatical construction "Morenberg's first law of thermogrammatics": grammatical constituents are neither created nor destroyed, just changed in form. Well, if it works for you . . . .

Problems Identifying Constituents

Even when you understand the principle of how clauses are combined
into larger structures and how constituents fit within other constituents,
you sometimes face difficult decisions when you try to identify certain
sentence components and their relationships. Sometimes a sentence may
be ambiguous for one reason or another. That is, it may be understood
in more than one way. Here is an ambiguous sentence:

> Anne Tyler wrote the book in our living room.

The sentence may mean either that Anne Tyler wrote the book while
she was in our living room or simply that our living room contains a
book that Anne Tyler wrote, wherever she might have written it.

Ambiguity can be caused by many factors—sound or meaning or
grammar. The ambiguity of the example sentence is grammatical ambiguity: it's caused by a constituency problem. Specifically, the sentence is ambiguous because the prepositional phrase **in our living room**
may function as an adverb of place, forming a constituent with the verb
phrase **wrote the book in our living room**, as in the following diagram.

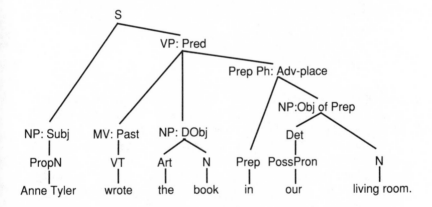

Or it may function as an adjective phrase, forming a constituent with
the object noun phrase **the book in our living room**, as in the next diagram.

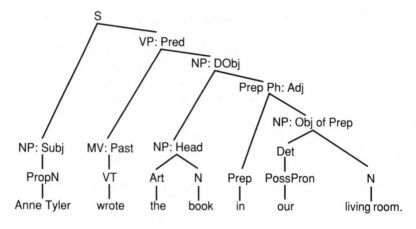

When you come upon a sentence like this with two possible constituent analyses, you may not be able to decide which analysis is correct unless you have more information than a single sentence can give you. In speech or writing, you can usually tell which is the correct interpretation because the context provides more information. But when you get such a sentence as an individual item in a grammar book, probably the best thing to do is to indicate that you understand both possible analyses.

Summary

Each of the structures discussed in this chapter—present participial phrases, past participial phrases, prepositional phrases, adverbs, and adjectives—can be derived from relative clauses by deleting subject noun phrases and BE. When you delete a form of BE, you delete finiteness as well. The structures you derive in this way are used to expand noun phrases, and, though they belong to different grammatical classes, all function as adjectives, just like the relative clauses from which they derive. These structures can be embedded at several levels, either in clauses or in other phrases. With just a small number of structures, you can construct many different complex phrases and clauses. When you parse sentences, you should look for constituents and how they nest within one another so that you can take them apart piece by piece.

EXERCISES

I. WRITING DEFINITIONS

Define the following words and phrases as completely as you can, giving examples whenever possible:

> Present participial phrase
> Past participial phrase
> Restrictive phrase

II. BREAKING OUT UNDERLYING SENTENCES

Identify the main clauses and embedded phrases in each of the following sentences. Then write out the complete sentences from which the main clauses and embedded phrases are derived. Don't derive single-word adjectives or nouns that precede head nouns, like **British** in the example.

EXAMPLE

> The British sloop sailed across waters haunted by pirate ships.
> ↓
> The sloop sailed across waters. (MC)
> The waters were haunted by pirate ships. (past participal phrase)

1. The possums in the neighborhood foraged among the rubbish.
2. Our motorboat passed tiny shacks built on palm-wood stilts.
3. Two Arab women carrying buckets of water from the well walked by our Land Rover.
4. A British botanist named William Burchell invented the African safari.
5. The rainbows arching over Iguacu Falls link Brazil and Argentina in a colorful bond.

III. COMBINING SENTENCES

Combine the following pairs of sentences to make the structures indicated in parentheses:

EXAMPLE

The antipasto features tender squid.

The antipasto is displayed in the glass case. (past participal phrase)
↓
The antipasto displayed in the glass case features tender squid.

1. Overcast skies ruined our weekend.
   The overcast skies were punctuated by thunderstorms. (past participal phrase)
2. The debate vexes federal lawmakers.
   The debate is about taxes. (prepositional phrase)
3. The hotel guests listened to musicians.
   The musicians were playing Tahitian songs. (present participal phrase)
4. The bank robbers shot at the police helicopter.
   The police helicopter was hovering above their car. (present participal phrase)
5. The region is a tourist mecca.
   The region is below Mexico City. (prepositional phrase)

IV. ANALYZING SENTENCES

Analyze the following sentences. Draw diagrams if that helps you to identify constituents and relationships. You may also want to write out the underlying clauses, but don't derive single-word adjectives and nouns that precede head nouns. You may find it helpful to work from "the inside out," identifying constituents and then deciding whether those constituents fit within or next to other constituents.

EXAMPLE

The mother fox caring for the pups threatened the human intruders.

> *Underlying Clauses*
> The mother fox threatened the human intruders.
> The mother fox was caring for the pups.

Explanation. **The mother fox caring for the pups** is the noun phrase subject of the sentence; **threatened the human intruders** is the verb phrase predicate. The main verb is the transitive verb **threatened**; its status is past indicative. The object of **threaten** is **the human intrud-**

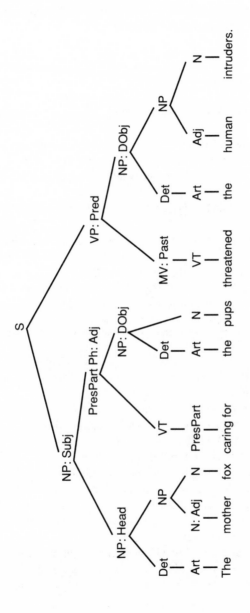

ers. The noun phrase subject of the clause is composed of the head noun phrase **the mother fox** and the present participial phrase **caring for the pups**, which functions as an adjective.

Sentences

1. The reporter describing the murder scene didn't reveal the gory details.
2. Most of the doctors trained in Ohio practice in other states.
3. George Harrison posed as a monk in prayer.
4. Our national frustration with welfare is exploited by some politicians.
5. The books sold at this sleazy newsstand are not available in the city library.
6. Wall Street traders investing in foreign markets have earned 12% interest this year.
7. The restaurant served shrimp boiled in a special creole sauce.
8. The Red Cross sent relief to all the countries stricken with malarial dysentery. [**With malarial dysentery** functions as an instrumental adverb; **malarial dysentery** functions as the logical subject of the passive that underlies the past participial phrase **stricken with malarial dysentery**. Passives like this have instruments rather than agents.]
9. Rural communities across America lack physicians.
10. The police scattered the young men loitering outside the convenience store.
11. Bighorn Canyon National Park contains multi-layered canyons blanketed by juniper woodlands and rolling prairies.
12. The New York Philharmonic aims at lucid performances filled with orchestral detail polished to a high sheen.
13. There are no quick fixes for broken children.
14. Shaq looks like a monster. But he is a gentle man with a great smile.
15. The judge denied the objection made by the defense attorney.
16. The casino's credit-checking system discourages players who want to gamble excessively.
17. NASA draws upon knowledge accumulated over decades.
18. Children are unnerved by parents suffering job distress.
19. The first city destroyed by an atomic bomb was Hiroshima.

20. The land around this church was the first property blacks owned in our town after the Civil War.
21. There are several Vietnamese dishes on the restaurant's menu.
22. Some trees growing at an angle can straighten themselves up.
23. Companies advertising in *Vogue* aim toward women in their thirties.
24. The three teenage girls admitted to the hospital yesterday had attempted suicide.
25. Major dance companies throughout the world still perform Balanchine's ballets.
26. Penguins in Antarctica can't avoid the throngs of human tourists.
27. New Hampshire is the state with the first presidential primary.
28. The peak covered by new snow attracted most of the skiers.
29. The Druid ritual begins with a sudden shout that surprises the audience.
30. The Miami Dolphins face a difficult defensive task.
31. The physicians in the rehab program have compulsive behavior patterns.
32. Kids selling crack on the streets have become common sights in our big cities.
33. Throngs crowding the Anchorage streets cheered the dogsled teams starting the Iditarod race.
34. The apiary at Miami University is surrounded by a wall that protects the bees from onlookers. [**From onlookers** functions as a goal adverb; the goal (intent) of the wall is to keep onlookers away.]
35. Pop singers like Linda Ronstadt often cross over and record country tunes. [**Often** is an adverb of frequency that introduces the predicate and is a part of it.]
36. My friends in politics have complex personalities.
37. Your Dodge dealer can provide details about the rebate.
38. The two Egyptian statues carved in granite completed the Louvre's Middle Kingdom exhibit.
39. The vet sedated the zoo's tiger with a tranquilizer made for house cats.
40. Hideo Nomo was the first major league player from Japan since the 60s.
41. Leslea Newman's *Fat Chance* is a good book for any young woman struggling with bulimia or anorexia.

42. Parents who overprotect their children may be abusing them with love.
43. The first hookless fasteners produced in 1893 snagged and tore clothes. But zippers have improved and become commonplace on clothes, camping gear, and luggage.
44. Jerry Garcia would play a phrase, repeat it, and toy with it like a cat toying with a mouse.
45. Humphrey Bogart's character in *Casablanca* is tough but sentimental.
46. Winterset, Iowa, has become a mythical place in the hearts of middle-aged Americans entranced by the romantic power of *The Bridges of Madison County*.
47. Elvis's leather outfit is one of the gems displayed at the Rock and Roll Hall of Fame and Museum in Cleveland.
48. The AARP is the most powerful lobbying group in Washington.
49. Television has made Olympic gymnasts like Mary Lou Retton and Nadia Comaneci into household names.
50. Two Argentine paleontologists excavated the remains of a carnivorous dinosaur like Tyrannosaurus Rex.

CHAPTER 8

Making Noun Clauses, Gerunds, and Infinitives

Preview

Subordinate clauses can function as nouns, adverbs, or adjectives. You've seen relative clauses embedded in noun phrases as adjectives, and you've seen how relative clauses can be reduced to phrases. This chapter takes up subordinate clauses that function as nouns and that can be reduced to gerund and infinitive phrases. Here are the main points of the chapter:

- There are two types of noun clauses: that-clauses and Wh-clauses.

- The **that** of that-clauses is a subordinate conjunction; it has no function within the clause. It simply introduces it.

- When that-clauses function as subjects, they can sometimes be extraposed to the ends of sentences.

- Except for **whether**, the wh-words that introduce noun clauses also function within their clauses in noun or adverb slots.

- Some noun clauses can be reduced to infinitive phrases; like the clauses they replace, these infinitive phrases function as nouns because they fill noun phrase slots.

- Infinitive phrases that function as nouns may be introduced by **to** or **for . . . to**, though they sometimes occur without a subordinator.
- Like noun clauses, infinitive phrases can be extraposed.
- Some infinitive phrases function as adverbs of reason.
- Gerunds are **-ing** verb forms that function as nouns.
- Gerund phrases may make constituents with genitives; these are called gerunds with genitive phrases.
- Because they are verb forms that fill noun slots, both gerunds and infinitives are known as verbal nouns.

That-Clauses

The first noun clauses we'll look at are called that-clauses because they are usually introduced by the word **that**. That-clauses can occur in almost any slot in a sentence that nouns can occur in—as subjects, direct objects, object complements, or predicate nouns. Here is a noun clause functioning as a direct object of the matrix verb **claim**:

Chinese cooks claim **that snake meat keeps you warm in winter**.

To demonstrate that the subordinate clause **that snake meat keeps you warm in winter** functions as a direct object, you can turn the matrix sentence into a passive, making the clause into a grammatical subject, as any object noun phrase would become in a passive sentence.

That snake meat keeps you warm in winter is claimed by
    Chinese cooks.

Since the subordinate clause fills a noun phrase slot and functions as a direct object, it is a noun clause. You can think of the sentence **Chinese cooks claim that snake meat keeps you warm in winter** as composed of two underlying clauses, with the second becoming a noun clause and replacing **this** in the matrix.

Chinese cooks claim **this**.

Snake meat keeps you warm in winter.
                    ↓
Chinese cooks claim **that snake meat keeps you warm in winter**.

When **that** which introduces a noun clause it is an introductory word. **That** is called a SUBORDINATE CONJUNCTION or a SUBORDINATOR. It is not a pronoun: it does not replace a noun phrase within the noun clause. Its function is to mark the subordinate clause, to indicate that it is a noun clause. Some grammarians argue that the subordinator attaches to the noun clause, though it does not become a constituent of the clause; some argue that it is simply a component of the noun phrase and never attaches to the clause. The intricacies of these arguments are best left to grammatical theorists. We'll accept the first view for the sake of simplicity and consistency. So, when we analyze a sentence which includes a that-clause, we will show the subordinator attached to the noun clause but not as a component of the clause. To show that the subordinator is not a component of the core clause (though it is attached to it), the diagram pictures a noun clause within a noun clause. The outer clause contains the subordinator and remains one level above the core clause. This device of a clause within a clause is an attempt to indicate that the subordinator is attached to the clause but that it does not become a constituent of it. The diagram of the example sentence, with the direct object noun phrase highlighted in a rectangle, is on the next page. Note that we haven't attached the subordinator to the core noun clause in the diagram, only to the outer noun clause.

Here are two more sentences to illustrate that-clauses in different noun phrase positions; the first noun clause functions as a subject, the next as a predicate noun.

This worries the president's economic advisors.

High interest rates are slowing home sales.
↓
That high interest rates are slowing home sales worries the president's economic advisors.

The problem is **this**.

Children watch far too much TV.
↓
The problem is **that children watch far too much TV**.

The subordinator **that** does not have to appear when a noun clause functions as a direct object or as a predicate noun. You may say either

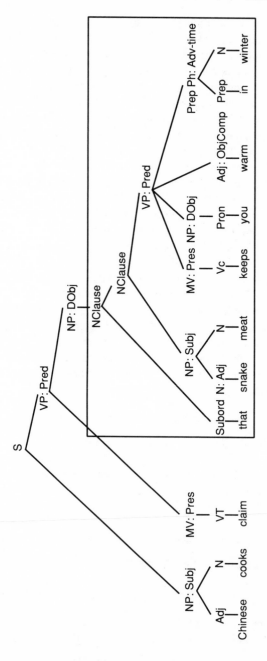

The Federal Aviation Administration conceded **that** the UFO sighting had occurred.

or

The Federal Aviation Administration conceded the UFO sighting had occurred.

But **that** has to appear when the noun clause functions as the subject of a sentence. You may not say

*Industrial plants will cut thousands of jobs this year worries Labor Department officials.

You must introduce a subject noun clause with **that**. You have to say

That industrial plants will cut thousands of jobs this year worries Labor Department officials.

Distinguishing Noun Clauses from Relative Clauses

Since that-clauses look like relative clauses, you'll have to be careful not to confuse the two. The major difference between relative clauses and noun clauses is that relative clauses are embedded into noun phrases following noun phrase heads and function as adjectives. Noun clauses fill whole noun phrase slots; they replace noun phrases and function like nouns. Here is the sentence with the noun clause about snake meat again, followed by a sentence with a similar relative clause.

Chinese cooks claim **that snake meat keeps you warm in winter.** (NC)

Chinese cooks prepare snake-meat dishes **that keep you warm in winter.** (RC)

The noun clause fills a noun phrase slot; it functions as the direct object of the verb **claim**, as we proved when we made the sentence passive. The clause follows the transitive verb **claim** and is a constituent of the verb phrase, as any direct object noun phrase would be. The subordinator **that** introduces the noun clause but has no function within it.

In the second example, the clause **that keep you warm in winter** sits next to the noun phrase **snake-meat dishes**, which functions as the head of the noun phrase **snake-meat dishes that keep you warm in winter**. The relative clause is a constituent of a noun phrase. In addition, the **that** functions as the subject within the relative clause; it does not simply introduce the relative clause. As with most questions about grammatical analysis, the answer as to whether a clause is a noun clause or a relative clause lies in constituency. Remember the sign that some students posted over their computers?

> **It's Constituency, Stupid!**

It's a useful reminder for anyone who loses sight of the central issue in parsing.

Moving That-Clauses

Sometimes when a that-clause functions as a subject, you can move it to the end of the sentence and fill the subject position with an expletive **it**, as in the following example.

> **That the Iraqi army invaded Kuwait** surprised American diplomats.
>
> ↓
>
> **It** surprised American diplomats **that the Iraqi army invaded Kuwait**.

This movement from the subject position is called EXTRAPOSITION. When you extrapose a clause and fill its subject position with an expletive **it**, the clause functions as the logical subject and the expletive as the grammatical subject. Some grammarians focus only on the surface form of sentences and claim that an extraposed clause functions as a complement to the noun phrase object; they call it a COMPLEMENT TO A NOUN PHRASE or a NOUN PHRASE COMPLEMENT. In the same way, they would claim that, in the next example, the extraposed noun clause functions as a complement to the predicate adjective **remarkable;** they call it a COM-

PLEMENT TO AN ADJECTIVE. You should be aware that you can look at extraposed clauses in both ways—in terms of their surface relationships (complement to a noun or adjective) or in terms of their underlying relationship (logical subject). The diagram on the next page lists both relationships.

That Barbie has sold well for decades is remarkable.

↓

It is remarkable **that Barbie has sold well for decades.**

Some sentences with expletives in the grammatical subject position and noun clauses at the end don't seem to be derived from underlying sentences in which the noun clauses begin as subjects and are later extraposed. Nonetheless, the expletives in such sentences, as in the following example, are called grammatical subjects and the noun clauses are called complements, or logical subjects.

It is seldom **that nations apologize.**

We probably extrapose clauses because sentences with long predicates and short subjects sound better to us than do sentences with long subjects and short predicates.

Wh-Clauses

Another class of noun clauses is called WH-CLAUSES. Wh-clauses, like that-clauses, are named for the words that introduce them, the subordinators **who, when, where, how, how often, why,** and **whether.** Wh-clauses can function as subjects, objects, predicate nouns, complements, and objects of prepositions. Here is an example of a Wh-clause functioning as the subject of a sentence.

What software manufacturers pray for is a hot-selling product
like Quicken.

Wh-subordinators are different from the subordinator **that;** Wh-subordinators not only introduce noun clauses, but they also function as content words within the subordinate clauses. In the example sentence, for instance, the subordinator **what** both introduces the noun clause **what**

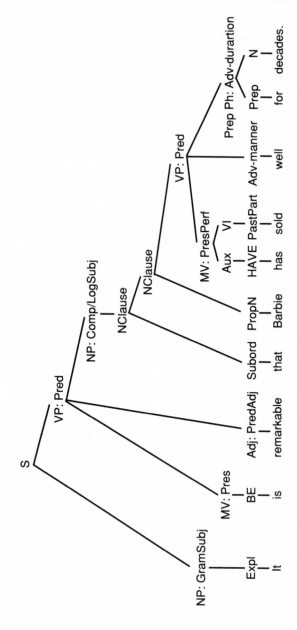

software manufacturers pray for and functions within the noun clause as the object of the two-word transitive verb **pray for**. It is both a subordinator and a pronoun. In the derivation of the last example, this can be shown by replacing the indefinite pronoun **something** with **what** and then moving **what** to the front of the clause.

```
  ┌──────────────────────────── what
  ↓
```

Software manufacturers pray for **something**.

This is a hot-selling product like Quicken.
            ↓

What software manufacturers pray for is a hot-selling product like Quicken.

Producing Wh-noun clauses is similar to producing relative clauses or Wh-questions. In each, you replace a noun phrase or adverb phrase with a pronoun or pro-adverb and move the pro-form to the front of the clause; the pro-form you move retains its original function within its own clause: if it started out as a direct object, it remains a direct object; if it started out as an adverb of time, it remains an adverb of time. With Wh-noun clauses, though, the pro-forms are subordinators as well. In the example sentence, **what** is a pronoun that functions both as the object of the two-word transitive verb **pray for** and as a subordinator that introduces the noun clause. The diagram of the sentence, with the noun clause highlighted by a rectangle, is on the next page.

Wh-words in noun clauses are the same words as interrogative pronouns and pro-adverbs. **Who, whom**, and **what** replace nouns. **Who** and **whom** replace human nouns; **what** replaces nouns other than humans. **When, where, how often**, and **why** replace adverbs of time, place, frequency, and reason, respectively. In the derivations we illustrate, the Wh-pronouns substitute for indefinite pronouns in underlying clauses, while the Wh-pro-adverbs substitute for such indefinite adverbs as **sometime, somewhere, somehow**, or **for some reason**. But Wh-pronouns could as easily substitute for nouns or adverbs with more content.

It might seem odd that noun clauses can be introduced by pro-adverbs; it is a fact nonetheless. These subordinate clauses are noun clauses not because of what introduces them but because of how they function and where they are embedded in matrix clauses. In the following example, the subordinate clause **how rock music fills a spiritual void in**

190   DOING GRAMMAR

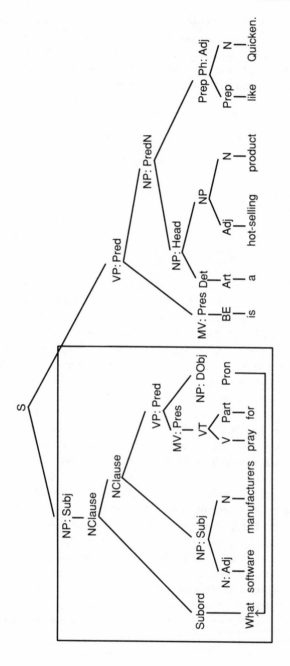

our society replaces **this** in the matrix; it fills a noun phrase slot and functions as the object of the transitive verb **explain**.

Bloom's book explains **this**.

```
                                    ─── how
  ↓ Rock music fills a spiritual void somehow in our society.
                          ↓
```

Bloom's book explains **how rock music fills a spiritual void in our society**.

The diagram on the next page illustrates the point that the clause **how rock music fills a spiritual void in our society** functions as an object within the matrix and is therefore a noun clause.

Like that-clauses, Wh-noun clauses can function in almost any noun phrase position in a matrix. Here are Wh-noun clauses functioning in different relationships. The first functions as the object of a preposition; the second functions as a direct object following a Vg verb.

The Depression-era photographs remind us of **this**.

```
          ─── who
  ↓ We are some people.
               ↓
```

The Depression-era photographs remind us of **who we are**.

The school superintendent told the governor **this**.

```
                                                    ─── how
  ↓ Her tax proposals would affect educational spending somehow.
                          ↓
```

The school superintendent told the governor **how her tax proposals would affect educational spending**.

The main point is that you can turn a clause into a noun clause by "wh-ing" (double u aiching) a noun or adverb and then embedding the clause into a noun phrase slot in a matrix sentence. Clauses with wh-words are called INDIRECT QUESTIONS because they seem to be related to Wh-question sentences. The wh-word is moved to the front of the clause, just like the wh-word of a Wh-question sentence. This is true of all the wh-words we've looked at so far.

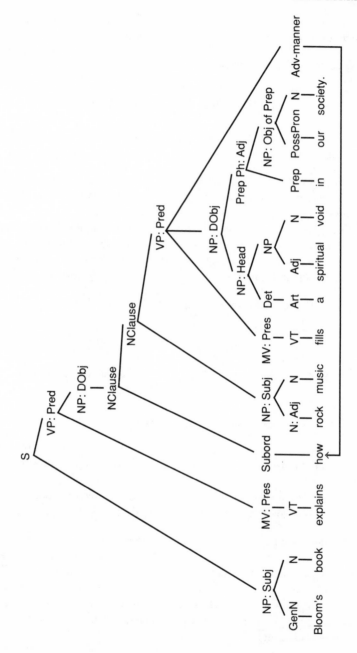

But one Wh-subordinator is different—**whether**. **Whether** has neither a noun nor adverb function within its own clause; it is not a pronoun or pro-adverb: it is only a subordinator. **Whether** seems to make indirect question sentences into something more like yes/no questions than Wh-questions. Take a look at the next example, for instance, where the noun clause functions as the object of **asking**.

> Police officials are asking **whether the war against drug
> traffickers will succeed.**

The sentence can be paraphrased as a matrix clause followed by a yes/no question.

> Police officials are asking, **"Will the war against drug
> traffickers succeed?"**

Not only can whether-clauses be paraphrased by yes/no questions, but they can also function as predicate nouns in sentences that indicate the clauses are Wh-questions.

> The question is **whether the president is a tough negotiator.**

In addition, clauses with **whether** can be paraphrased with **whether or not**, giving the same option as a yes/no question would.

> Police officials are asking **whether or not the war against
> drug traffickers will succeed.**

All of these characteristics seem to emphasize the relationship of whether-clauses to yes/no questions.

One other fact about clauses with **whether**. Contemporary writers and editors often use **if** as a subordinator in place of **whether**, though some teachers and editors still consider **whether** more correct as a subordinator to introduce noun clauses. Thus, you can always say

> Historians can't decide **whether** J. Edgar Hoover was a brilliant
> administrator or simply a skilled manipulator of public
> opinion.

You can sometimes say

> Historians can't decide **if** J. Edgar Hoover was a brilliant

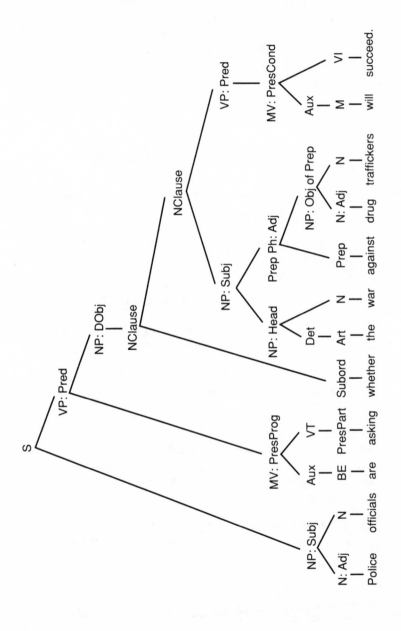

administrator or simply a skilled manipulator of public
opinion.

The diagram on page 194 illustrates the major structural and functional
points about clauses with **whether**: that they are noun clauses and that
whether is neither a pronoun nor a pro-adverb but simply a subordinator.

Infinitives that Function As Nouns

Some noun clauses can be reduced to INFINITIVE PHRASES. Remember
from chapter 2 that an infinitive is the base form of a verb, the tense-
less form. In the following example, the underlying clause **they should
avoid fatty foods** can be made into a noun clause, or it can be reduced
to an infinitive phrase **to avoid fatty foods**.

> Dieters know **this**.

> They should avoid fatty foods.
> ↓
> Dieters know **that they should avoid fatty foods**.

> or

> Dieters know **to avoid fatty foods**.

In the example, the infinitive phrase, like the noun clause, functions as
the object of the matrix verb **know**.

Since an infinitive is a verb, the structures within the infinitive phrase
remain in the same relationships with the verb as when the phrase was
a predicate in the underlying clause. The way it was is still the way it
is! So **fatty foods** is a noun phrase that functions as the object of the
transitive verb **avoid** within the infinitive phrase. The verb and noun
phrase together remain a verb phrase constituent. The diagram of the
sentence illustrates both points: (1) that the infinitive phrase functions
in a noun phrase slot as the object of the matrix verb, and (2) that the
infinitive phrase remains a verb phrase constituent, with all its internal
relationships intact. The diagram indicates that the verb **avoid** is the
head of the infinitive phrase. Phrases have heads; clauses have subjects.

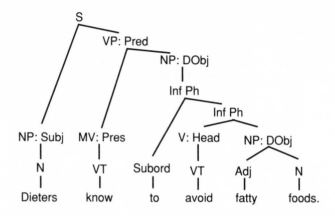

There are two situations that may cause you problems. The first is that you cannot always make a clause into both an infinitive phrase and a noun clause, but only into one or the other. You can combine the next two sentences, for instance, into a single sentence with an infinitive phrase.

The prince's main job is **this**.

The prince attends ceremonial dinners.
↓
The prince's main job is **to attend ceremonial dinners**.

But you cannot combine them into a single sentence with a noun clause. There is no

*The prince's main job is **that he attends ceremonial dinners**.

The second is that you'll sometimes have to decide whether an infinitive functions as the head of an infinitive phrase that functions as an object or whether it is the head of the main verb constituent. In

Judge Ito asked **to see the evidence**,

the **to** forms a constituent with **see the evidence**, which functions as the object of the transitive verb **asked**. But in

Judge Ito **wanted to see** the evidence,

wanted to see is a main verb; **to** forms a constituent with **wanted**.
Wanted to is a semi-modal; **see** is the head of the main verb; and **the
evidence** functions as the direct object of **see**. You might want to look
back at the discussion of modals and semi-modals in chapter 3.

Words That Introduce Infinitives

The word **to** often introduces infinitives. Some grammarians say that **to**
replaces the tense of the verb. Whether or not **to** actually replaces tense,
to does function in relation to an infinitive phrase much like **that** functions in relation to a noun clause—as a subordinator. And just as **that**
does not always have to occur with a noun clause, **to** does not always
have to occur with an infinitive phrase. Here are two sentences as il-
lustration. **To** introduces the infinitive phrase in the first sentence but
does not in the second.

> The Peace Corps allows Americans **to teach survival skills**.

> The Peace Corps lets Americans **teach survival skills**.

Since the verbs **allow** and **let** are Vc verbs, the infinitive phrases, **to
teach survival skills** and **teach survival skills**, both function as object
complements.

Some infinitive phrases are introduced by the subordinator **for . . . to**.
For and **to** are disjoined, but they work together as a single subordinator, as in

> IRS identifies laundered drug money.

> **This** is tough.
>
> ↓
>
> **For** IRS **to** identify laundered drug money is tough.

The noun phrase that sits between the **for** and **to** is called the subject
of the infinitive. In the example, **IRS** functions as the subject of the infinitive phrase **for IRS to identify laundered drug money**. But notice
that such a subject also functions as the object of the preposition **for**.

This fact becomes more clear when you put a pronoun in the slot following **for**. A pronoun will always be in the object form, as in

> For **her** to win this tournament would demand more strength and endurance than Graf can muster today.

Her is the object form of the personal pronoun. The verb phrase constituent of an infinitive phrase introduced by **for . . . to** is called a PARTIAL PREDICATE, to differentiate it from a predicate, which must show tense.

Though they have a subject, infinitive phrases introduced by **for . . . to** remain phrases because they lack finiteness (tense and agreement). Remember that, except for an imperative, a clause must contain both a noun phrase subject and a finite verb phrase predicate, a verb phrase with tense. Without a finite verb phrase, a construction is a phrase. The IRS sentence is diagramed on the next page.

Like noun clauses, infinitive phrases can sometimes be extraposed. In the following example, the infinitive phrase **to look like a *Vogue* model** functions as the subject of the sentence:

> **To look like a *Vogue* model** is the goal of many teenage girls.

You can move the infinitive phrase to the end of the sentence if you insert an expletive **it** in the subject position.

> **It** is the goal of many teenage girls **to look like a *Vogue* model**.

The expletive **it** is the grammatical subject; the infinitive phrase is the logical subject as well as the complement to the noun phrase **the goal of many teenage girls**.

Infinitive phrases introduced by **for . . . to** can be extraposed also. Here is a sentence with an extraposed **for . . . to** infinitive phrase:

> **For terrorists to poison a city's water supply** would be easy.
>   ↓
> **It** would be easy **for terrorists to poison a city's water supply**.

In this case, the extraposed infinitive phrase functions both as the complement to the predicate adjective **easy** and as the logical subject, while the expletive **it** functions as the grammatical subject of the sentence.

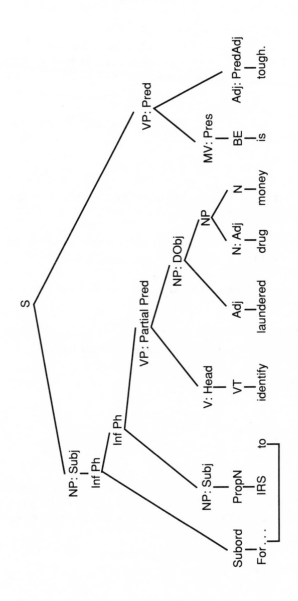

Infinitives That Function As Adverbs

Some infinitives function as adverbs, not as nouns. ADVERBIAL INFINI-TIVES are often introduced by the subordinator **in order to**. In the following sentence, the infinitive phrase **in order to keep its economy in gear** functions as an adverb of reason; it tells why Japan must overcome serious obstacles.

> Japan must overcome serious obstacles **in order to keep its economy in gear**.

The sentence is diagramed on the next page.

The three-word subordinator **in order to** can often be reduced to the single word **to**, as in the following:

> Physicists study the structure of atoms ~~in order~~ **to find out how the world works**.
> ↓
> Physicists study the structure of atoms **to find out how the world works**.

The subordinator **in order to** is the key to identifying adverbial infinitives. An infinitive phrase introduced by **in order to** functions as an adverb. No doubt about that. When an infinitive is introduced by **to**, you can identify it as an adverbial infinitive if you can change the **to** into **in order to**.

Gerunds

Like infinitives, GERUNDS are nonfinite verbs; gerunds are **-ing** verb forms that function as nouns. **Becoming a Hollywood playboy** is a gerund phrase that fills the direct object slot in the next example.

> Nick Nolte has resisted **this**.
>
> ~~Nick Nolte~~ becomes a Hollywood playboy.
> ↓
> Nick Nolte has resisted **becoming a Hollywood playboy**.

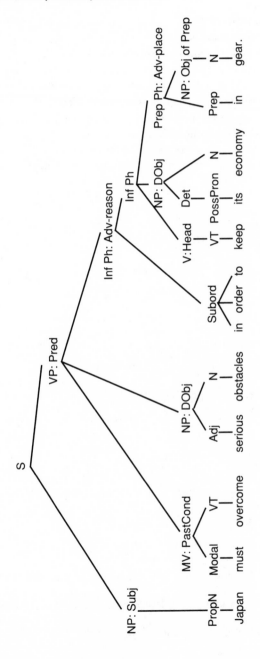

Gerunds are derived from clauses. In this case, the gerund phrase **be-coming a Hollywood playboy** originates from the verb phrase of the clause **Nick Nolte becomes a Hollywood playboy**. Though it functions as a noun, the gerund phrase retains its internal structure as a verb phrase. In the original clause, **become** is a linking verb followed by a predicate noun, **a Hollywood playboy**. In the gerund phrase, the gerund **becoming** is a linking verb followed by a predicate noun, **a Hollywood playboy**. One last point to note about the structure of gerunds. The **-ing** of a gerund phrase is a subordinator, like the **to** of an infinitive phrase. Here is the sentence diagramed to illustrate the relationships:

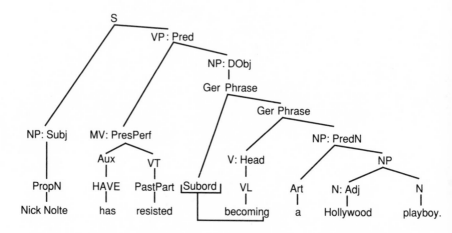

Gerunds can occur in several different noun positions. The next example shows a gerund phrase functioning as the subject of a sentence.

This is difficult for rural towns.

~~Rural towns~~ recruit doctors.

↓

Recruiting doctors is difficult for rural towns.

And here is a gerund phrase functioning as the object of a preposition:

Merrill Lynch sells partnerships for **this**.

~~The partnerships~~ invest in real estate.

Merrill Lynch sells partnerships for **investing in real estate.**

As you've probably anticipated, you have to learn to differentiate gerund from present participle. It shouldn't be much of a problem. Gerunds, like present participles, are **-ing** verb forms. But that is their only similarity. Present participial phrases always derive from underlying structures that contain **be** plus **-ing**. Gerunds never do. Present participial phrases never fill noun phrase slots: they are always adjectives (or, as we'll see in the next chapter, adverbs). Gerund phrases always fill noun phrase slots; a gerund is a verbal noun and only a verbal noun. The **-ing** of present participles is an inherent feature of verbs; a present participle is one principal part of a verb. The **-ing** of a gerund is actually a subordinator, like the **to** of infinitives.

Most gerund phrases begin with the **-ing** verb, but there is a gerund form that contains its own subject as a possessive pronoun or genitive noun; such a gerund phrase is called a GERUND WITH GENITIVE. Here is an example:

Willie Nelson sings.

This still enthralls audiences.

Willie Nelson's singing still enthralls audiences.

In the example sentence, the subordinator is the **'s**, along with the **-ing**, just as the subordinator in a **for . . . to** infinitive phrase is the disjoined subordinator **for . . . to.** The Willie Nelson sentence is diagramed on the next page.

The diagram illustrates a few basic points. **Willie Nelson's singing** is a gerund-with-genitive phrase (a gerund phrase which carries its own subject, **Willie Nelson's,** and in which the gerund, **singing,** functions as a partial predicate). The gerund-with-genitive phrase functions as the subject of the sentence. The **'s . . . -ing** is a subordinator.

Gerund-with-genitive phrases. like other gerund phrases, can function in various noun phrase slots. Here is a gerund-with-genitive phrase that functions as a direct object:

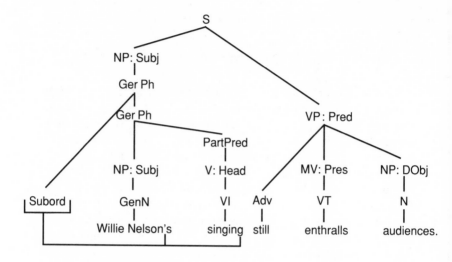

The ballerina improved **this** as a martial arts student.

The ballerina dances.

↓

The ballerina improved **her dancing** as a martial arts student.

The main point in this section on gerunds is that a gerund is an **-ing** verb phrase that functions as a noun.

Putting Structures and Processes Together

Through the years, I've found that some students look for only those structures and processes in sentences that a particular chapter is about. If the chapter is on noun clauses and related structures, they look for noun clauses, infinitives, and gerunds. A sentence in the exercises that contains a relative clause instead of a noun substitute can throw them for a loop. Yet only in a grammar book chapter do you find sets of sentences put together with just a few related structures and processes. When we write and speak, we are likely to combine many structures into single sentences.

From the point of view of a grammar course or a grammar book, grammar is cumulative. What you learn in the first week (or the first chapter) will still be important in the fifteenth week (or the tenth chapter). Understanding the second chapter depends on your understanding the first. Understanding the tenth chapter depends on your understanding the first through the ninth. To be successful at grammatical analysis, then, you have to remember that you might find almost any combination of structures and processes within an individual sentence. The fact that constituents can be put together in novel, creative ways is part of the design of language.

Here, for instance, is a sentence that includes a long gerund phrase functioning as the object of the preposition—**by gathering friends together to share the dishes that make southern food unique**:

Kentuckians celebrate the Derby by **gathering friends together to share the dishes that make southern food unique**.

Within the gerund phrase is an adverbial infinitive phrase, **to share the dishes that make southern food unique**. And within that is a restrictive relative clause, **that make southern food unique**. The main verb of the independent clause, **celebrate**, is a transitive verb in the present tense. The main verb of the relative clause, **make**, is a Vc.

Summary

Underlying clauses can be formed into clauses and phrases that function as nouns: noun clauses, infinitive phrases, and gerund phrases. There are two kinds of noun clauses—that-clauses and Wh-clauses. Noun clauses can fill almost any noun phrase slot. **That** and the wh-words that introduce noun clauses are subordinators; the wh-words also function as nouns or adverbs within their own clauses.

Both infinitive and gerund phrases are verb phrases filling noun slots. They can occur simply as phrases or with their own subjects.

EXERCISES

I. WRITING DEFINITIONS

Define the following words and phrases as completely as you can, giving examples whenever possible:

Noun clause   Indirect question
Infinitive phrase   Noun phrase complement
Gerund phrase   Extraposition
That-clause   Wh-clause
Gerund with genitive   Subordinate conjunction
Adverbial infinitive   Subordinator
Partial predicate   Complement to an adjective

II. BREAKING OUT UNDERLYING SENTENCES

Identify the main clauses and embedded phrases in each of the following sentences. Then write out the complete sentences from which the main clauses and embedded phrases are derived.

EXAMPLE

Corolla owners love what Toyota does for them.
↓
Corolla owners love this.

Toyota does something for them.

1. Eliminating liquor and tobacco billboards may reduce substance abuse.
2. Scientists do not fully understand how superconductors work.
3. People join groups like Alcoholics Anonymous to control all sorts of addictions.
4. Japanese students in American business schools learn to understand Western business practices and Western culture.
5. It is increasingly obvious that city dwellers consider themselves environmentalists.

III. COMBINING SENTENCES

Combine the following pairs of sentences. Make the second of each pair into a noun clause, infinitive phrase, or gerund phrase, according to the instructions in parentheses.

EXAMPLE

The main question is this.

Congress wants to enact some amount of tax reform. (Wh-noun clause)

↓

The main question is how much tax reform Congress wants to enact.

1. Psychiatrists don't know this.
   Some people become compulsive for some reason.
2. This can be difficult for arthritics.
   Arthritics turn a doorknob.
3. A mother bird will attempt this.
   A mother bird distracts predators from her nest. (infinitive phrase)
4. This occurred to the vice president.
   Some TV reporters are carnivorous. (extraposed that-clause)
5. Researchers recorded whale songs.
   Researchers wanted to analyze their patterns. (adverbial infinitive phrase)

IV. ANALYZING SENTENCES

Analyze the following sentences. Feel free to use diagrams if those help you to see and understand functions. You may find it helpful to break the exercise sentences down into their component sentences and to work from "the inside out," identifying constituents and then deciding whether those constituents fit within or next to other constituents. Notice that these exercise sentences may have constructions discussed in other chapters as well as gerunds, infinitives, and noun clauses.

EXAMPLE

Eating in Japanese restaurants taught me that raw fish won't hurt you.

The example sentence derives from three underlying sentences.

I eat in Japanese restaurants.

This taught me **this**.

Raw fish won't kill you.

Explanation. The example is a complicated sentence that contains both a gerund phrase and a noun clause. The gerund phrase, **eating in Japanese restaurants**, functions as the subject of the sentence. The head

of the gerund phrase is the intransitive verb **eat** followed by a prepositional phrase, **in Japanese restaurants**, that functions as an adverb of
place. The main verb of the sentence, **taught**, is a two-place transitive
Vg. The personal pronoun **me** functions as an indirect object; the noun
clause **that raw fish won't kill you** functions as the direct object.

Sentences

1. Robert McNamara's book asserts that American troops should not
   have fought in Vietnam.
2. James Cagney is remembered for playing gangsters on the screen.
   But he considered himself a singer and dancer.
3. That the Raiders returned to Oakland angered LA football fans.
4. It angered LA football fans that the Raiders returned to Oakland.
5. The journalism class asked the visiting reporter why she prefers the
   police beat.
6. America cannot postpone confronting environmental problems.
7. Psychologists who study aphasia want to understand how memory
   works.
8. The defense attorney's probing displeased the judge.
9. Doctors know that certain hormones can intensify depression.
10. The basic rule in the White House is that debate should be internal.
11. The Nicaraguan refugee went to Los Angeles to join her sister.
12. Some book reviewers criticize Pat Conroy for retelling the story of
    his dysfunctional family in each of his novels.
13. It doesn't take long for Crystal Gayle's audience to understand that
    she is Loretta Lynn's sister.
14. Psychiatrists have not shown why Freudian therapy works.
15. The British revere Winston Churchill for rallying their country
    against Nazi aggression.
16. Internet surfers use electronic bulletin boards to swap software.
17. The Israeli press chided the Syrians for what they called unfriendly
    activity.
18. Walking down Main Street can be dangerous after dark.
19. Computer companies haven't shown teachers how they can use tech-
    nology in the classroom.
20. It takes skill and luck for a gambler to win at blackjack.
21. Thomas Edison became famous for inventing the light bulb.
22. Inner-city teens often envision themselves dying in a gang war.

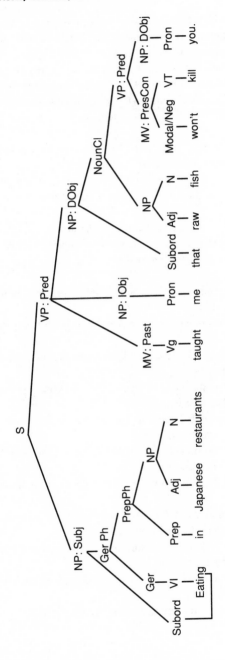

23. Calling a Texan a liar will usually provoke a fight.
24. Twenty percent of Americans don't believe that murderers should be executed by the state.
25. Father Chabot wonders whether the city cares about kids.
26. Holocaust survivors want to prevent genocide by preserving the memory of the atrocities visited upon them.
27. It may surprise parents that infant seats don't protect children in serious crashes.
28. The barren diner in Edward Hopper's *Nighthawks* suggests that urban America is lonely and sad.
29. It takes a solid pitching staff for a team to win a pennant.
30. A survey by a cooking magazine found that Americans eat leaner food now.
31. President Truman decided to use the atomic bomb.
32. It is Russian policy to control oil production around the Black Sea.
33. The unemployment rate resists falling below 7 percent of the labor force.
34. The experiment will determine whether the new radium therapy can cure leukemia.
35. The tourist bureau's map makes finding your way around Chicago a breeze.
36. Neuroscientists have found differences in how men and women use their brains.
37. Modeling is an industry that abuses its young and masks the carnage in layers of hairspray.
38. Entomologists believe that termite flatulence causes 20 percent of the world's methane.
39. That the continent's ice shelves are cracking indicates that Antarctica is warming.
40. Thomas Jefferson claimed to abhor slavery, but he owned slaves all his life.
41. Lionel Dahmer's *A Father's Story* explores how the innocent boy he remembers became a vicious killer.
42. Julia Roberts admits it's hard for her to listen to former hubby Lyle Lovett's music.
43. Painting the Sistine Chapel's ceiling was Michelangelo's greatest achievement.
44. Jane Bryant Quinn makes money make sense.

45. The B-29 veered sharply after dropping its deadly load on Hiroshima.
46. Oceanographers know that reefs play a crucial role in an ocean's ecosystem.
47. It is clear that the South has become a Republican dominion.
48. Playing one parent against the other is a fundamental skill of adolescents.
49. Bones found in a quarry near Shanghai encourage some biologists to believe that primates originated in Asia.
50. It is difficult to be honest with your parents.

CHAPTER 9

Adding Modifiers to Sentences

This chapter introduces nonrestrictive modifiers. Nonrestrictive modifiers look like the equivalent restrictive structures (a nonrestrictive participial phrase looks like a restrictive participial phrase; a nonrestrictive relative clause looks like a restrictive relative clause, etc.). Nonrestrictive modifiers differ in one important way from their restrictive counterparts: nonrestrictive modifiers are not bound within phrases. They are added to clauses. Because they have a different relationship with matrix clauses, nonrestrictive modifiers also differ in meaning from restrictive modifiers.

Preview

- Nonrestrictive modifiers have the same structure as equivalent restrictive modifiers. But they are added to matrix clauses, not embedded within phrases. This is the central difference between restrictive and nonrestrictive modifiers.

- Because they are added to clauses, nonrestrictive modifiers are set off from core constituents by commas, dashes, colons, or parentheses.

- Nonrestrictives are sometimes called free modifiers because they can often move to different positions in a sentence. They can be placed at the beginning or end of a sentence, or even be used to separate the subject from the predicate.

- Absolute phrases, unlike the other nonrestrictive modifiers, have no restrictive counterparts.

- Nonrestrictive modifiers don't mean the same thing as restrictive modifiers. Restrictive modifiers imply that there is a larger or different group than that mentioned in the main clause. Nonrestrictive modifiers, on the other hand, state that the group mentioned in the modifier is exactly the same as the one mentioned in the main clause. Nonrestrictive modifiers are additional comments.

- Nonrestrictive modifiers don't function in the same way as restrictive modifiers. Because they are bound within noun phrases, restrictive modifiers function as adjectives. Because they are added to sentences, nonrestrictive modifiers function as sentence adverbs.

Nonrestrictive Modifiers

In previous chapters, you've seen how sentences are expanded by clauses or phrases embedded as adjectives or nouns. The relative clauses, noun clauses, infinitive phrases, gerund phrases, participial phrases, and other structures described in the earlier chapters are bound into phrases within matrix clauses. The relative clauses, infinitive phrases, participial phrases, and other structures described in this chapter are not bound within phrases but added to clauses. Because they are not bound within phrases, nonrestrictive modifiers are set off from the core sentence constituents by punctuation marks that indicate their parenthetical nature: commas, dashes, colons, or parentheses.

Traditionally, these separate structures are called NONRESTRICTIVE MODIFIERS. Though some grammarians refer to them as FREE MODIFIERS, or SENTENCE MODIFIERS, these three names are interchangeable. Nonrestrictive modifiers are free in the sense that they can often be moved to different locations in a sentence: they can be placed at the end or beginning of a main clause or sometimes even within the main clause, separating the subject from the predicate. Here is a nonrestrictive prepo-

sitional phrase first placed at the beginning of a sentence, then between
the subject and the predicate, and finally at the end of the sentence:

> **Except for fools and lunatics**, everyone knows nuclear war would
> be catastrophic.

> Everyone, **except for fools and lunatics**, knows nuclear war would
> be catastrophic.

> Everyone knows nuclear war would be catastrophic—**except for
> fools and lunatics**.

Whether you are able to move a modifier to the beginning or end of a
matrix clause or to use it to interrupt the subject and predicate generally depends on the meaning relationship between the modifier and its
matrix clause. This is an important point. Since they are not bound within
phrases, nonrestrictive modifiers are generally considered sentence modifiers, additions to matrix clauses. As sentence modifiers, they do not
function as adjectives but as sentence adverbs.

The structures that can occur as nonrestrictive modifiers are not new
to you. Most of the structures that occur as restrictive modifiers can also
occur as nonrestrictive modifiers: relative clauses, participial phrases,
infinitive phrases, prepositional phrases, adjectives, and adverbs. There
is only one new structure discussed in this chapter, absolute phrases.
We'll look first at nonrestrictive relative clauses.

Nonrestrictive Relative Clauses

NONRESTRICTIVE RELATIVE CLAUSES are constructed exactly the same as
their restrictive cousins. Relative pronouns replace noun phrases and—
if they are not subject noun phrases—move to the front of the relative
clause, as in

> No entertainer brought more joy to filmgoers than Fred Astaire.

>   **who**
> ~~Fred Astaire~~ turned energy, dignity, and wit into pure dance.
>   ↓

> No entertainer brought more joy to filmgoers than Fred Astaire,
> **who turned energy, dignity, and wit into pure dance.**

Princess Diana often upsets the royal family with her antics.

```
            ┌─────────────────────────── whom
            │ The press enjoys writing about P̶r̶i̶n̶c̶e̶s̶s̶ ̶D̶i̶a̶n̶a̶.
            ↓                              ↓
```

Princess Diana, **whom the press enjoys writing about**, often upsets the royal family with her antics.

Though they are constructed in the same way, restrictive and nonrestrictive relative clauses do not function in the same way; nor do they mean the same thing. Restrictive relative clauses imply that there is a larger or different group from the one named in the main clause. For instance, the next example, with a restrictive relative clause, says that there is a group of biologists who studies racial genetics. But it implies that there is also a group of biologists who do not study racial genetics, as the second sentence indicates.

Biologists **who study racial genetics** have been criticized by groups on both ends of the political spectrum. But those who study less controversial areas of life are generally untouched by such criticism.

If we make the relative clause nonrestrictive, we'll change the meaning of the sentence radically.

Biologists, **who study racial genetics**, have been criticized by groups on both ends of the political spectrum.

The new sentence no longer implies that there is a group of biologists who do not study racial genetics as well as one that does. It makes two equivalent statements, one in the main clause and one in the relative clause: that biologists have been criticized by groups on both ends of the political spectrum and that biologists (all of them) study racial genetics. Here's another pair of sentences to indicate how restrictive relative clauses imply larger groups while nonrestrictive ones do not.

The town's cops keep a careful eye on the high school boys who hang out at the pool hall.

The town's cops keep a careful eye on the high school boys, who hang out at the pool hall.

In the first example, the cops watch carefully only the boys who hang out at the pool hall; we must presume there is a group of boys who do not hang out at the pool hall. In the second example, the cops keep a careful eye on the high school boys, all of whom, we are told, hang out at the pool hall.

Nonrestrictive modifiers imply nothing about different groups. They typically make comments that are in addition to those in the main clause and equivalent to those in the main clause. That's why nonrestrictive modifiers are thought of as being added to rather than bound within matrix clauses. It's almost as if nonrestrictive modifiers were compound structures. For instance, if you wanted to make two equivalent statements about the Beatles, both that the band has become a cultural icon and that they made British rock popular in the United States, you could construct two separate sentences joined by the conjunction **and**:

> The Beatles have become a cultural icon. **And** they made British rock popular in the United States.

Or you could say the same thing by making one of the statements into a nonrestrictive relative clause, like so:

> The Beatles, **who made British rock popular in the United States**, have become a cultural icon.

With the nonrestrictive clause, it's as if you said "the Beatles have become a cultural icon, and, by the way, the group made British rock popular." Because of that "and-by-the-way" relationship, you can delete the nonrestrictive modifier without changing the meaning of the main clause.

Nonrestrictive modifiers relate differently to matrix clauses and attach to matrix clauses in a different way than do restrictive modifiers. The diagram on the next page illustrates how a nonrestrictive relative clause attaches to a matrix:

The diagram indicates that the nonrestrictive relative clause is not bound within the matrix clause; the relative clause is shown as essentially equivalent to the matrix. It is moved between the subject and predicate of the matrix, interrupting the main clause.

As we've seen, nonrestrictive modifiers are most movable. Not relative clauses. They must immediately follow a noun phrase.

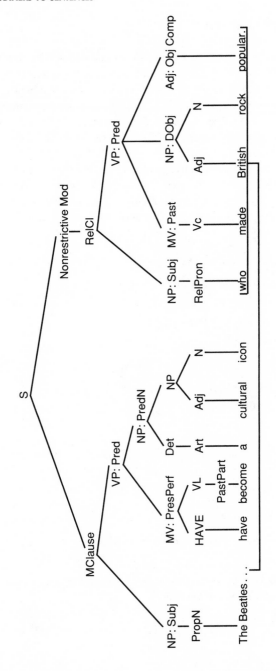

Participial Phrases

NONRESTRICTIVE PRESENT PARTICIPAL PHRASES look like restrictive participial phrases: they occur in both past and present participle forms. And they are derived exactly like restrictive participial phrases. You derive nonrestrictive participial phrases from clauses by deleting the subject and BE; you derive past participial phrases by deleting the grammatical subject and BE from passive clauses; sometimes you delete the agent phrase as well.

But, like any nonrestrictive modifier, they are not bound within a noun phrase. They have a different relationship with the matrix than bound modifiers. And they are movable. Here are examples of nonrestrictive participial phrases—both present and past—in various sentence positions:

Steinbeck produced *The Grapes of Wrath* in five months.

~~Steinbeck was~~ writing in longhand.

↓

Steinbeck produced *The Grapes of Wrath* in five months, **writing in longhand**.

or

Steinbeck, **writing in longhand**, produced *The Grapes of Wrath* in five months.

or

Writing in longhand, Steinbeck produced *The Grapes of Wrath* in five months.

Three Senators reversed their vote on the controversial tax bill.

~~Three Senators were~~ prodded by public opinion.

↓

Prodded by public opinion, three senators reversed their vote on the controversial tax bill.

or

Three senators, **prodded by public opinion**, reversed their vote on the controversial tax bill.

or

Three senators reversed their vote on the controversial tax bill, **prodded by public opinion**.

Since nonrestrictive participial phrases aren't embedded in noun phrases, they don't function as adjectives. They function as adverbs. Notice that the present participial phrase of the example on page 218, **writing in longhand**, is not only an additional commentary, but its action also takes place at the same time as the action in the main clause. That is, the writing in longhand and the production of *The Grapes of Wrath* occurred at the same time. In this case, the participial phrase functions as an adverb of attendant circumstance. This is a fancy way of saying that the present participial phrase is an additional commentary whose action takes place at the same time as the action in the main clause. Nonrestrictive present participial phrases often function as adverbs of attendant circumstance.

Nonrestrictive past participial phrases often show cause or reason, as in the second example, where the senators reversed their vote because they were **prodded by public opinion**. The past participial phrase functions as an adverb of reason. We often place past participial phrases before the main clause, since we generally state causes before effects. The example sentence is diagrammed on the next page. So, nonrestrictive participial phrases share the same structure as their restrictive kin. But they function differently because they are attached to matrix clauses differently.

Appositive Nouns and Adjectives

Appositive Noun Phrases

Perhaps the most familiar nonrestrictive modifiers are APPOSITIVE NOUN PHRASES. These are the structures we typically call appositives. Appositive noun phrases occur next to other nouns and explain them, as in the following, where **the candidate's wife** tells us who Juliana is:

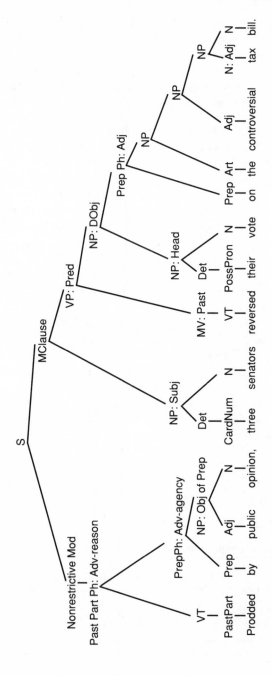

Next, the reporters questioned Juliana.

~~Juliana~~ is the candidate's wife.

↓

Next, the reporters questioned Juliana, **the candidate's wife.**

Appositive noun phrases derive from predicate nouns following a verb BE, as in the example, where the subject noun phrase **Juliana** and **is** are deleted in order to leave the predicate noun phrase **the candidate's wife.** This noun phrase is then attached to the main clause as a nonrestrictive modifier. Here is the sentence diagramed.

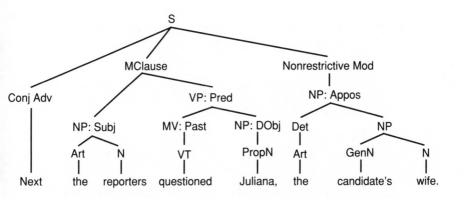

Appositive noun phrases can be complex because noun phrases can be long and complicated—including within them other phrases or even clauses. In the example below, the noun phrase **a dazzling but destructive woman** contains a compound adjective:

Daisy is Fitzgerald's ideal "southern belle."

~~Daisy is~~ a dazzling but destructive woman.

↓

Daisy, **a dazzling but destructive woman**, is Fitzgerald's ideal "southern belle."

or

A dazzling but destructive woman, Daisy is Fitzgerald's ideal "southern belle."

Notice that the appositive noun phrase, **a dazzling but destructive woman**, can precede **Daisy**, the noun it is in apposition to. The next appositive noun phrase, **the males in the bee colony**, has a prepositional phrase—**in the bee colony**—functioning adjectivally within it.

> Drones exist solely to mate with a queen.
>
> ~~Drones are~~ the males.
>
> ~~The males are~~ in the bee colony.
> $$\downarrow$$
> Drones, **the males in the bee colony**, exist solely to mate with a queen.

In the next example, the noun phrase **an old man whose stringy hair was tied back in a single braid** contains a restrictive relative clause, **whose stringy hair was tied back in a single braid**.

> The tourists retreated from the panhandler.
>
> ~~The panhandler was~~ an old man.
>
> **whose**
> ~~The old man's~~ stringy hair was tied back in a single braid.
> $$\downarrow$$
> The tourists retreated from the panhandler, **an old man whose stringy hair was tied back in a single braid**.

Appositive Adjective Phrases

Though less often mentioned in grammar books, APPOSITIVE ADJECTIVES occur with some frequency, particularly in narrative writing. Like appositive nouns, they derive from sentences with the verb BE, and they serve to identify or define noun phrases they sit next to in the matrix. Appositive adjectives originate as predicate adjectives. Here are some examples:

> It is a large school building.
>
> ~~It is~~ square and high.
> $$\downarrow$$
> It is a large school building, **square and high**.

Many adolescents see overeating as the perfect rebellion.

~~Overeating~~ is safe but obnoxious.

$$\downarrow$$

Many adolescents see overeating as the perfect rebellion—**safe but obnoxious**.

~~The Simpsons' life is~~ chaotic.

~~The Simpsons' life is~~ absurd.

~~The Simpsons' life is~~ entirely banal.

$$\downarrow$$

The Simpsons' life—**chaotic, absurd, and entirely banal**—has become the model for too many American families.

or

Chaotic, absurd, and entirely banal, the Simpsons' life has become the model for too many. American families.

Appositive adjectives attach to matrix clauses in exactly the same way as appositive nouns.

Absolute Phrases

ABSOLUTE PHRASES, sometimes called NOMINATIVE ABSOLUTES, are different from the other nonrestrictive modifiers; they contain both a noun phrase subject and a partial predicate, a predicate lacking finiteness. They look enough like clauses that students sometimes confuse the two. But if you understand how to derive them from clauses, you should be able to identify absolute phrases without difficulty.

To construct an absolute, you generally delete BE from a clause, whether it is the verb BE or the auxiliary BE. In the next example, the verb BE is deleted from the clause **a razor blade was in her grip** in order to produce the absolute **a razor blade in her grip**:

The detective looked at the young lady lying in the pool of blood.

A razor blade ~~was~~ in her grip.

$$\downarrow$$

The detective looked at the young lady lying in the pool of blood,
a razor blade in her grip.

The diagram of the sentence on the next page indicates the structure of
the absolute and its relationship to the main clause.

In the previous example, we deleted the verb BE to produce the absolute.
In the next example, we'll delete the auxiliary BE that precedes a present participle.

The turkey hen brooded her downy poults during the storm.

Her outstretched wings ~~were~~ providing shelter for the baby birds.
↓
The turkey hen brooded her downy poults during the storm—**her
outstretched wings providing shelter for the baby birds**.

Or you can delete the auxiliary BE that precedes a past participle in a
passive clause.

Buildings crumbled along San Francisco's Market Street.

Their foundations ~~were~~ damaged by the quake.
↓
Buildings crumbled along San Francisco's Market Street, **their
foundations damaged by the quake**.

Abolute phrases are used in interesting ways. Absolute phrases are
the only structures in English that allow you to narrow in on a scene as
if you were using a zoom lens on a camera. You can draw a general
scene in a main clause, like **the detective looked at the young lady lying in the pool of blood**. Then you can zoom in on the scene with an
absolute, focusing specifically on the **razor blade in her grip**. You can
zoom in on the outstretched wings of the turkey hen or note the damaged foundations of the buildings on Market Street after the quake.

Absolutes are sometimes mistaken for clauses because they contain
a noun phrase subject and a partial predicate, what is left after you delete
BE from a finite verb phrase. But after you delete BE, the verb phrase is
not finite. So an absolute cannot be a clause, though it has a subject and
a partial predicate. A clause must have both a noun phrase that functions as a subject and a verb phrase that functions as a predicate, a fi-

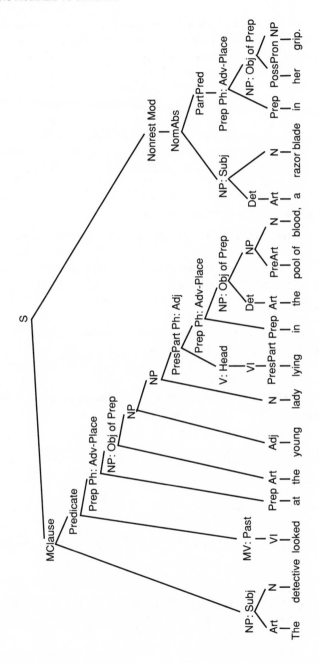

nite verb phrase. **A razor blade in her grip**, for instance, is an absolute phrase because it is composed of a noun phrase subject, **a razor blade**, and a prepositional phrase that functions as a partial predicate, **in her grip**. To make the absolute phrase into a clause, you'd have to replace **was** in order to create a complete predicate, **was in her grip**.

Since the action in an absolute generally occurs at the same time as the action in the main clause, absolutes are attendant circumstances. And they move with some freedom before or after the main clause, or between the subject and the predicate. Here are two example sentences, with absolute phrases in various positions; the second has a conjoined pair of absolutes:

The fullback charged into the end zone

His legs ~~were~~ pumping like the pistons of a fine-tuned engine.
↓
The fullback charged into the end zone, **his legs pumping like the pistons of a fine-tuned engine**.

or

His legs pumping like the pistons of a fine-tuned engine, the fullback charged into the end zone.

or

The fullback—**his legs pumping like the pistons of a fine-tuned engine**—charged into the end zone.

The Range Rover sat near the water hole.

Its lights ~~were~~ off.

And its engine ~~was~~ silent.
↓
The Range Rover sat near the water hole, **its lights off and its engine silent**.

or

Its lights off and its engine silent, the Range Rover sat near the water hole.

or

The Range Rover—**its lights off and its engine silent**—sat near the water hole.

Sometimes absolute phrases are introduced by the preposition **with**, as in

A twinkle ~~was~~ in his eye.

The old man said good-bye to his grandson.

↓

With a twinkle in his eye, the old man said good-bye to his grandson.

The United States and Canada share the busiest border in the world.

One hundred million people cross every year.

↓

The United States and Canada share the busiest border in the world—**with one hundred million people crossing every year**.

Our English teacher read "Stopping by Woods" as Robert Frost might have.

The spoken lines took on a life of their own.

↓

Our English teacher read "Stopping by Woods" as Robert Frost might have, **with the spoken lines taking on a life of their own**.

With is considered an introductory word, like a subordinate conjunction. It is not a part of the absolute itself. So absolute phrases that are introduced by **with**, like **with a twinkle in his eye** or **with one hundred million people crossing every year**, are not prepositional phrases. They remain absolute phrases.

Adverb Clauses

Though ADVERB CLAUSES are not in the strictest sense nonrestrictive modifiers, they do share two characteristics with nonrestrictive modifiers. They have similar freedom of movement around and within a main clause, and—when they precede or interrupt a main clause—they must be separated from it with a comma or a dash. They differ from nonrestrictive modifiers because they derive within the predicate of a main clause, not as an additional comment separate from the main clause. They are, after all, adverbs. Adverb clauses are subordinate clauses that function in the full range of adverb roles, including manner, place, time, reason, and condition. Here are a few examples of adverb clauses:

Robert Waller became a celebrity **after he published *The Bridges of Madison County*.** (adverb of time)

or

After he published *The Bridges of Madison County*, Robert Waller became a celebrity.

or

Robert Waller, **after he published *The Bridges of Madison County*,** became a celebrity.

Many night-blooming plants would die out **if bats did not disperse their seeds.** (adverb of condition)

or

If bats did not disperse their seeds, many night-blooming plants would die out.

or

Many night-blooming plants—**if bats did not disperse their seeds**—would die out.

Americans will be able to weekend in Hong Kong or Australia **because aerospace planes will be so fast.** (adverb of reason)

or

Because aerospace planes will be so fast. Americans will be able to weekend in Hong Kong or Australia.

Midas was attracted to gold **just as moths are attracted to bright
lights.** (adverb of manner)

or

Just as moths are attracted to bright lights, Midas was attracted
to gold.

Civilian life was destroyed **where the German armies swept
through Russia.** (adverb of place)

or

Where the German armies swept through Russia, civilian life
was destroyed.

The words that introduce adverb clauses, like **where, just as, because, if,** and **after** in the examples above, are often the same as the
prepositions that precede noun phrases to make prepositional phrases.
But they are not called prepositions when they introduce adverb clauses:
like the words that introduce noun clauses, the words that introduce adverb clauses are called subordinate conjunctions or subordinators. These
subordinators have no function within the adverb clauses they introduce;
they do not replace any constituents within the clauses.

The diagram on the next page of the second version of the Robert
Waller sentence to illustrate the structure of adverb clauses and their relationship to main clauses. Since the adverb clause originates within the
predicate, I've shown it beginning there, under **VP: Pred,** and moving
to the front of the sentence, attached to **S.** This is an attempt to show
that adverb clauses are not separate, additional structures, like nonrestrictive modifiers.

What the subordinators in adverb clauses do is establish specific adverb relationships like time, place, manner, and condition that link the
content of adverb clauses to the content of main clauses. Notice how
the relationships between the subordinate and main clause change when
you switch from one subordinator to another.

   If it rained on the beach, we retreated under the palm trees.
   (condition)

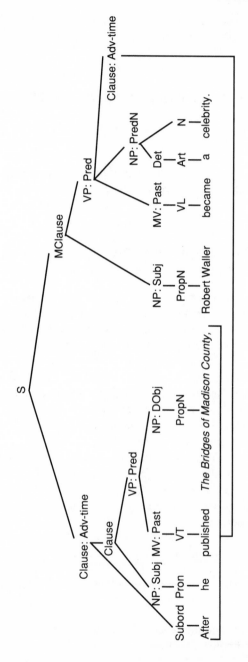

Unless it rained on the beach, we retreated under the palm trees. (negative condition)

Before it rained on the beach, we retreated under the palm trees. (time)

Because it rained on the beach, we retreated under the palm trees. (reason/cause)

As soon as it rained on the beach, we retreated under the palm trees. (instancy)

Whenever it rained on the beach, we retreated under the palm trees. (frequency)

While it rained on the beach, we retreated under the palm trees. (duration)

Putting Sentence Modifiers Together

Writers often put more than one nonrestrictive modifier into a sentence. Using sentence modifiers is one way a writer has of changing the pace, the rhythm, and the movement of her sentences. Here are just a few examples of sentences with at least two free modifiers each. The first example has a present participial phrase and a nominative absolute. It begins with the present participial phrase to reflect the movement of the gymnast's twisting flip: **hurling herself into a full twisting flip**. The sentence moves through the main clause, which compares her rotation to an artillery shell; then it concludes with an absolute phrase that focuses on the relation of the gymnast's head to the ground: **her head pointed improbably at the floor**.

> **Hurling herself into a full twisting flip**, the gymnast rotated like an artillery shell—**her head pointed improbably at the floor**.

The next sentence uses a nonrestrictive relative clause to interrupt the main clause. It concludes with a summarizing noun phrase appositive.

> Thomas Hart Benson, **whom Harry Truman called the best painter in America**, was a swaggering Hemingway-like character, **a "roughneck artist."**

Here's a sentence that opens with a prepositional phrase; following the main clause are a pair of present participial phrases compounded into a single phrase:

> **In the old West**, marshals were the shock troops who enforced federal laws, **hunting fugitives or collecting taxes**.

In the next sentence, a pair of absolute phrases follow the main clause. The second absolute comments on the first.

> The hunter stepped into the clearing—**his rifle in his left hand, barrel up**.

The final example has three appositive noun phrases following the main clause—one on how the house looks, one on how it feels, one on how it smells. By focusing on the individual parts of the house, the three absolutes produce a sense that the writer has covered completely the subject of how the architect's design creates the home's enveloping warmth.

> Good design creates the enveloping warmth of architect Tanaka's house—**the sensuous curves of the ceiling, the texture of coarse concrete walls, the fragrance of heated tatami floors**.

A Final Word on Taking Sentences Apart

One goal of a course in grammar must be to prepare students to analyze sentences they will run across in everyday life—in their own writing and that of their classmates; in novels, poems, and psychology texts; in magazines like *Reader's Digest*, *Newsweek*, and *The Smithsonian*. Here, for instance, is the opening sentence from a *National Geographic* article on Tibetan nomads. The sentence is long and complex, with restrictive and nonrestrictive structures. It's also an interesting sentence, like many you'll run across in professional writing or in successful student writing. You should by now be able to analyze it successfully. Try your hand at taking it apart and naming the parts before you read the analysis below. Try to reconstruct the underlying clauses that are combined into the larger sentence also. And don't forget that no matter how long or complex a sentence becomes, you simply peel off one familiar layer at a time to analyze it.

Sitting beside a dung fire in his black yak-hair tent,
aromatic smoke whirling around his head, Trinley, a 63-
year-old Tibetan nomad, rhythmically pumped the fire
with his goatskin bellows.

The base of this sentence is the main clause **Trinley . . . rhythmically pumped the fire with his goatskin bellows**, upon which several nonrestrictive structures are hung. The subject of the matrix is the proper noun **Trinley**; the predicate is **rhythmically pumped the fire with his goatskin bellows**. The predicate begins with **rhythmically**, an adverb of manner; the main verb is **pumped**, the past tense form of the transitive verb, which is followed by a direct object, **the fire**. The matrix is completed by a prepositional phrase, **with his goatskin bellows**, which functions as an instrumental adverb (it names the instrument used to pump the fire). Preceding the matrix are two nonrestrictive structures— a present participial phrase, **sitting beside a dung fire in his black yak-hair tent**, and a nominative absolute, **aromatic smoke whirling around his head**. Interrupting the subject and predicate of the main clause is the noun phrase appositive, **a 63-year old Tibetan nomad**. Underlying the main clause and the modifiers are the following sentences:

Trinley sat beside a dung fire in his black yak-hair coat.

Aromatic smoke was whirling around his head.

Trinley rhythmically pumped the fire with his goatskin bellows.

Trinley is a 63-year-old Tibetan nomad.

You should be able to combine the small sentences into the larger sentence, label all the constituents, and identify all the relationships. In the last chapter, we'll suggest reasons why writers construct sentences the way they do; for now, we'll restrict ourselves to analyzing the structures and their relationships.

Summary and Implications

Many different structures can be nonrestrictive modifiers—including relative clauses, participial phrases, prepositional phrases, noun or adjective phrases, and nominative absolutes. Nonrestrictive modifiers are not bound within a matrix phrase; they are attached to and nearly equivalent with the main clause. Because they are not embedded within a phrase, they are generally set off from other constituents by commas, parentheses, colons, or dashes; nonrestrictive modifiers are parenthetical comments. Another consequence of not being embedded within phrases is that nonrestrictive modifiers have more freedom of movement within a sentence than restrictive modifiers. They often begin a sentence, end it, or interrupt the sentence by separating the subject from the predicate. Unlike restrictive modifiers, nonrestrictive modifiers do not imply a larger group but function as additional commentary, often as adverbs of attendant circumstance. Adverb clauses, though they are not strictly nonrestrictive, have the same freedom of movement as nonrestrictive modifiers.

Another important point in this chapter is that, with the grammar you have learned, you can analyze and discuss even complex sentences by student or professional writers. If you remember that every sentence, no matter how complex, can be broken down into underlying sentences, you can peel away the layers of complex structures until you reach the core and then systematically rebuild all the structures and relationships. Getting to the core of sentences and understanding the system that produces them is what doing grammar is about.

EXERCISES

I. WRITING DEFINITIONS

Define the following words and phrases as completely as you can, giving examples whenever possible:

Nonrestrictive modifiers/
   sentence modifiers
Nonrestrictive relative clauses
Nonrestrictive present
   participial phrases
Nonrestrictive pastparticipal phrases

Appositive noun phrases
Appositive adjectives
Absolute phrases/nominative
   absolutes
Adverb clauses

II. BREAKING OUT UNDERLYING SENTENCES

Identify the main clause, the embedded constituents, and the nonrestrictive constituents in each of the following sentences. Then write out the underlying sentences from which the final constituents are derived.

EXAMPLE

> Camels will eat every seedling that sprouts, guaranteeing that their
> grazing land will remain barren.
>
> ↓
>
> Camels will eat every seedling.
>
> Every seedling that sprouts.
>
> Their eating guarantees this.
>
> Their grazing land will remain barren.

1. Route 27, which meanders through Florida's citrus and cattle country, takes you into the state's agricultural heartland.
2. Cliff Stoll's book on computer espionage, *The Cuckoo's Egg*, grabs
   you—its short sentences and terse paragraphs creating an exciting
   pace.
3. Where the plague appeared in the fourteenth century, death was sudden and terrifying.
4. The decor of her apartment, planned by a Japanese decorator, evokes
   Yoko's oriental heritage.
5. After you cross the Golden Gate Bridge, driving north from San
   Francisco, Highway 101 loses its city slickness, becoming a country
   road that winds through rolling hills.

III. COMBINING SENTENCES

Combine the following core sentences to make main clauses and the
nonrestrictive structures indicated in parentheses.

EXAMPLE

> Photography became a tool of journalism soon after its invention.
>
> Photography traveled with the U.S. Army during the Mexican War
> in 1846. (present participial phrase)
>
> ↓
>
> Photography became a tool of journalism soon after its invention,
> traveling with the U.S. Army during the Mexican War in 1846.

1. William Faulkner read a great deal in his youth. (adverb clause)
   William Faulkner disliked school.

2. Scientists have found the fossil of the oldest know vertebrate.
   The oldest known vertebrate is a jawless fish. (appositive noun phrase)
3. The wind streamed past the schooner.
   The wind was whipping its mainsail. (present participial phrase)
4. Young John Kennedy lived a happy youth.
   His leisure time was spent in play and study. (nominative absolute)
5. Edsel Ford rode to town with his parents.
   Edsel was wedged between them on the front seat of the Model T. (past participial phrase)

IV. ANALYZING SENTENCES

Analyze the following sentences, identifying the structures and functions. If you wish, you may use diagrams to show relationships. Remember to differentiate between restrictive and nonrestrictive modifiers.

EXAMPLE

> Julie bakes her mother's rhubarb pie, using safflower oil in the crust instead of Crisco.

Explanation. This sentence is composed of a main clause, **Julie bakes her mother's rhubarb pie,** and a nonrestrictive present participial phrase, **using safflower oil in the crust instead of Crisco.** The subject of the main clause is the proper noun **Julie;** the predicate is the verb phrase **bakes her mother's rhubarb pie,** which has a transitive verb **bakes** and a noun phrase direct object, **her mother's rhubarb pie.** The head of the participial phrase, **using,** is a transitive verb, followed by a noun phrase direct object, **safflower oil.** The participial phrase is completed by two prepositional phrases functioning adverbially; **in the crust** is an adverb of place, and **instead of Crisco** is an adverb of contrast.

Sentences

1. The courthouse design, maligned by local residents, earned praise from architects.
2. Many LA buildings have been abandoned and torched, leaving streets barren and empty.

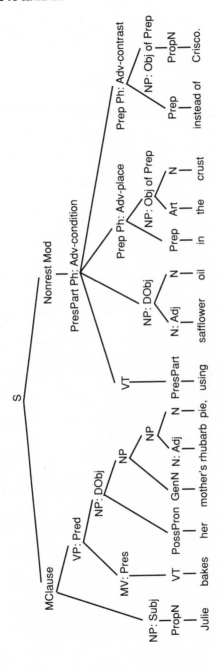

3. Buried in a remote Guatemalan rainforest, the ancient city of Tikal contains thousands of Mayan structures.

4. As I walk to my car, I can see the snowcapped mountains that brought me to Wyoming.

5. The *J.B. Ford*—the freighter I worked on as a teenager—steams no more.

6. Hoping to catch a last glimpse of their families, the children lingered for a moment before boarding the camp bus.

7. Bruce Springsteen, who exemplifies intelligent rock and roll, has become a political symbol.

8. Pelted by wind and rain, we struggled with the tent flaps in order to keep dry.

9. The camera-toting tourists swarmed from the monorail, joining Epcot's early morning rush.

10. When I think of my grandfather now, I see him on a tractor, tilling ground in wind that cuts a bitter day.

11. The lions rose, yawning and stretching, as they began their search for the day's first meal.

12. Several dozen boats sit on the dry bed of the Aral Sea—their anchors buried in the sand.

13. The Range Rover sat near the salt lick, lights off and engine silent, concealing three hunters and their equipment.

14. I stood for hours at Cincinnati's riverfront dock, awaiting the arrival of a Mississippi steamboat—a paddlewheeler named the *Memphis Queen.*

15. The mother bear curled up beside a tree, while the cub grazed on grass, an important part of a young bear's diet.

16. The mayor of Djénné pointed to the town's masterpiece of Muslim architecture, the great mosque in the city square.

17. I hit the gas pedal instead of the brake, the policeman on the corner staring as I ran the red light.

18. Canyon Ranch—a former dude ranch converted into a fitness spa— is not just a fat farm for the rich.

19. Looking as if their world had collapsed, Mom and Dad sat silently on the front porch after the doctor had hurried inside.

20. Since eating well is highly esteemed in New Orleans, restaurant lore is a colorful dimension of social chatter.

21. Stately and erect, the United Artists Tower looms prominent along the skyline overlooking Nashville's Music Row.

22. As Caribbean cooking becomes popular, plantains—exotic bananas eaten as a starch—may replace potatoes at the American table.

23. To defend the government of South Vietnam, American forces tore the country apart.

24. One of the strangest comic book villains is Catwoman—whose heart belongs to crime and to Batman.

25. Barefoot and disheveled, my son stood shamefaced before me, as I had once stood before my father.

26. Keeshawna's birthday cake was like those baked by my southern grandmother— moist, rich, and sticky.

27. Unlike my mother—who had to drop out of school at 16—I was heading for college.

28. When FDR's funeral train passed through towns, thousands turned out to say good-bye—heads bowed, openly weeping.

29. The diver was swimming alone, ascending in a slow spiral, when he noticed the shark.

30. At breakfast, powdered sugar from a beignet—a yeasty cousin to the doughnut— dusted my newspaper.

31. Our English teacher read "Stopping by Woods" as Robert Frost might have read it, with the spoken lines taking on a life of their own.

32. The Harlem Renaissance comes alive in Van Der Zee's photo exhibit because the photographer lived in Harlem during the 1920s, taking pictures.

33. The night sky displays wondrous objects: giant galaxies that look like pinwheels, gauzy nebulae that drift through the Milky Way.

34. Some of the most memorable geographic places never existed: like Tolkien's Middle Earth and Swift's Lilliput.

35. Tangy and cool—gazpacho hits the spot when the weather turns hot and muggy.

36. Bears are solitary animals—loners accustomed to ranging over large areas.

37. Although he was anxious to see his family, Seymour waited patiently for the next plane.

38. When Chubby Checker introduced the Twist in 1960, no-touch dancing replaced ballroom dancing.

39. Overcrowding—because it threatens the stability of the population—is a prison's greatest problem.

40. Cincinnati public radio's series of African American concerts was called "Karamu," the Swahili word for celebration.

41. Jonas Salk, who perfected his vaccine in 1955, released parents and children from the great dread of summertime, paralytic polio.

42. *Citizen Kane*, despite critical acclaim, did not make a profit during its first release.

43. South Dakota's Black Hills are considered sacred by the Lakota Sioux, who believe humans and spirits meet in harmony among these ancient rocks.

44. It's hard to believe that Sam Cooke, who had a heavenly voice, came to a hellish end—shot by a clerk in a sleazy motel.

45. The chef of the new brew pub understands her mission—to turn out high-quality munch-chow.

46. Rachel Carson's *Silent Spring*, published in 1962, triggered an environmental revolution that protected animals and humans from poisonous pesticides.

47. To the Pilgrims, the American continent was sacred soil, a new promised land.

48. Yellowstone authorities allow buffalo herds to range freely so that researchers can observe their natural migratory patterns.

49. Mickey Mantle ran the bases like a charging bull, his head down, his legs pumping furiously.

50. The federal government owns hundreds of tourist attractions—including the Grand Canyon, the White House, and Steamtown, a railroad theme park in Scranton, Pennsylvania.

CHAPTER 10

What Can You Do Now That You Can Do Grammar?

The Rhetoric of Sentences

Preview

What #@!$% good is knowing how to do grammar? That's the question you're probably asking at this point. It's the right question to ask. And it deserves a thoughtful answer. In the previous chapter, I mentioned that one goal of a grammar book should be to give students enough information and practice to enable them to parse sentences in the real world—in books and magazines and in their own writing. Learning how to analyze real sentences is an important goal. But, while parsing for the sake of parsing alone might be of some interest to students who just like to analyze structures and relationships, that isn't enough reason for most of us to expend all the time and effort necessary to become proficient at the task. So what can this newfound knowledge of nouns, verbs, subjects, predicates, gerunds, infinitives, nonrestrictive modifiers, passives, extraposition, clauses, and constituency give you beyond the analytic skills to peel away layers of sentences like some manic Zen cook peeling away layers of onions from the inside out?

I hope to show in this chapter that the hard work you've put into the grammar lessons can help you become not only a better sentence analyzer but a more knowledgeable writer and a more perceptive student of literature as well. The conscious knowledge of grammar you've gained by working through the first nine chapters should help you to reflect on what you read and write and to understand yourself as both a language maker and a language user. This conscious knowledge of grammar gives you the language to talk about and to question the stylistic components of literature and of your own writing. I hope you learn to see grammar as a language that enables you to think about and to talk about language. If *analyzing* and *identifying* were key words in earlier chapters, *reflecting* is the key word in this chapter. Much of the reflection centers on the the various ways that grammar gives you to compose sentences. What the chapter asks you to do is reflect on those options and consider why you write sentences the way you do and how you react to the sentences other writers compose. After all, if every sentence can be composed in many different ways, the way you choose to write a sentence must change its effect. Part of effective writing is to match grammatical structure with meaning.

Here are the main points in the chapter:

- Grammar is concerned with the acceptability of sentences while rhetoric is concerned with their effectiveness.

- A writer's style is determined by the sentences she makes from among the options allowed by grammar. Effective writers construct sentences that reflect upon and enhance the meaning of their writing.

- You can make sentences more clear, cut the gibberish from them, by following a few basic principles.

- As students grow older, they embed more clauses into matrix clauses and produce, in stages, longer, more complex, grammatical structures. Their little sentences grow into big sentences. More effective writers use more nonrestrictive modifiers, and they generally employ a large repertoire of structures, restrictive and nonrestrictive

- Just a few rules underlie our punctuation practice; these are concerned with internal and end punctuation. But the options you have in using punctuation marks can affect the feel and movement of sentences.

Punctuation not only helps the reader wend her way through sentences, it also affects the rhetoric of sentences.

Reflecting on Literature: Style and Meaning

When we reflect on language in the way I propose in this chapter, we move away from purely grammatical concerns into rhetorical concerns. Francis Christensen claimed that grammar tells you the structures and relationships that are possible in a language, while rhetoric tells you what structures and relationships are effective in a given context. Rhetoric is concerned with quality. Grammar is concerned with acceptability.

To introduce my linguistics students to the idea that the syntactic component of language is creative and can produce an unlimited number of sentences from a small core of structures, I give them two sentences to combine into one sentence in as many different versions as they can construct. I've sometimes used the two sentences **It surprised me** and **Jane arrived late** as the input. You're allowed to add "small words" and change word forms (say, from an adjective to a noun, "late" to "lateness"), but you must keep the basic nouns, verbs, and adjectives in some form. Normally, students will come to the next class with 50 to 70 sentences. A few years ago, a math major determined he would set the all-time record; he did. He conducted a factor analysis on his output and produced 467 different sentences. He claimed he could have gone on, but grew weary of the task. Here are some possibilities:

That Jane arrived late surprised me.

It surprised me that Jane arrived late.

I was surprised when Jane arrived late.

Jane's late arrival surprised me.

It was Jane's late arrival that surprised me.

It was surprising to me that Jane arrived late.

I was surprised by Jane's late arrival.

The lateness of Jane's arrival was surprising to me.

For Jane to arrive late surprised me.

Jane arrived late, surprising me.

Jane arrived late, and I was surprised.

The surprising thing to me was the lateness of Jane's arrival.

Jane arrived late; I was surprised.

Because Jane arrived late, I was surprised.

What a surprise it was to me when Jane arrived late.

You get the idea. The point here is that the grammar of English allows each of these versions; all 15 are acceptable English sentences, along with at least 452 others. Grammar does not care that, in certain contexts, one or the other of these sentences is more effective. Rhetoric does. Grammar is concerned with acceptability; rhetoric is concerned with quality. A writer has a number of options when she writes a sentence; her final choices are called her STYLE. Style is a concern of rhetoric. One characteristic of an effective writer is that her stylistic choices fit her content: the way you say things affects what you say. Let me show you what I mean.

In the last chapter, I presented a sentence about a Tibetan nomad. I used the sentence there to make the point that you should be able to parse even long, complex sentences that contain several nonrestrictive modifiers. Here's the sentence again:

> Sitting beside a dung fire in his black yak-hair tent, aromatic smoke whirling around his head, Trinley, a 63-year-old Tibetan nomad, rhythmically pumped the fire with his goatskin bellows.

The author could have written

> Trinley was a 63-year-old Tibetan nomad. He sat beside a dung fire in his black yak-hair tent. Aromatic smoke was whirling around his head. He rhythmically pumped the fire with his goatskin bellows.

You have to ask yourself why she chose to begin the sentence with a present participial phrase, pair it with a nominative absolute, and interrupt the main clause with an appositive noun phrase. My three-sentence revision is just as acceptable from a grammatical standpoint. But my three sentences don't capture the strangeness of the scene with anywhere near the effectiveness of the original sentence. By juxtaposing a present participial phrase with an absolute phrase (when you might expect parallel phrases), and by interrupting the strange scene described in the main clause with a matter-of-fact detail, the writer shows just how odd the scene was to her. She wants to capture that oddness for the reader, who's probably sitting on a comfortable sofa in a climate-controlled house in an American suburb. The scene is foreign to the writer and to the reader. The structure of the sentence emphasizes that point.

Here's a brief example from an Ernest Hemingway novel. In the first chapter of *The Sun also Rises*, Hemingway introduces Robert Cohen, a character who acts as a foil to the protagonist, Jake Barnes. Jake, the narrator as well as protagonist, is decisive and—most of all—realistic. Robert is indecisive and unrealistic. Cohen is used by other people, especially women. So Jake often talks about him in passive constructions in order to emphasize the fact that Cohen seldom acts on his own but is acted upon. Here are several sentences about Cohen from the first chapter of the novel. The first and last examples are gerund phrases derived from passive clauses.

> . . . [Cohen] learned [boxing] painfully and thoroughly to counter-act the feeling of inferiority and shyness he had felt on **being treated as a Jew at Princeton.** (3)
>
> He . . . **was married by the first girl who was nice to him**.
>
> **[Cohen's] divorce was arranged. . . .**
>
> **[Cohen] had been regarded purely as an angel. . . .**
>
> **He had been taken in hand by a lady who hoped to rise with the magazine.**
>
> . . . Cohen never had a chance of **not being taken in hand**.

Hemingway could easily have made each of these constructions active. Cohen could have married the first girl, or arranged his own divorce, or acted as an angel, for instance. You have to believe that Hemingway chose the passive versions to emphasize grammatically the point he was trying to make about Cohen's dependence on others for guidance. After all, Hemingway didn't introduce any other character in the same way.

Here's another example. Tom Romano is known by English teachers for a book about teaching writing in high school, *Clearing the Way*. Romano has written, but not yet published, an adolescent novel titled *Blindside*. The first chapter introduces the main character, Nick, and his girlfriend, Julie. When the novel opens, Nick is in Julie's bedroom. Her parents come home unexpectedly, and Nick has to scramble for his clothes and escape through the front door just as her parents open the door from the garage into the kitchen. He runs through the neighborhood to get as far away as quickly as possible. The following paragraph describes Nick's run:

> Nick took long strides, pumping his arms, running with more purpose than he ever had on a football field. He shot through the subdivision that quiet October morning, keeping aslant the windows of Julie's house. He rocketed through backyards, vaulting low fences, ducking clothes lines, rousing dogs to clamorous barking, staying away from the street should Mr. Kelly decide to leave the house as unexpectedly as he'd arrived.

Romano could have written that paragraph in this way:

> Nick took long strides and pumped his arms. He ran with more purpose than he ever had on the football field. He shot through the subdivision that quiet October morning as he kept aslant the windows of Julie's house. He rocketed through backyards, vaulted low fences, and ducked clothes lines. Though it roused dogs to clamorous barking, he stayed away from the street should Mr. Kelly decide to leave the house as unexpectedly as he'd arrived.

In fact, at the end of the chapter, Romano writes a paragraph that looks like my revision of the original running paragraph. When Nick reaches relative safety on the other side of town, Romano describes the scene in this way:

> Nick took a deep breath where he stood at the edge of uptown Medville. He looked up High Street. Cars waited at the light, ready to head his way. At the moment the light turned green and Nick instinctively stuck out his thumb, he felt something wrong. He patted his back pocket. Empty. Nick felt a sharp giving sensation in his bowels. His wallet was gone. And instantly he knew where it was—somewhere on the living room floor at Julie's.

Can you characterize the sentences in Romano's two paragraphs and explain why he wrote the sentences he did? Can you explain how the sentences in Romano's two paragraphs affect you as a reader and how they contribute to the meaning and movement of the first chapter in *Blindside*? Let's try to reflect on those questions, using our knowledge of grammar.

To begin with, the first paragraph from the novel contains only three sentences; but it has seven nonrestrictive present participial phrases. The present participles, because they are verbs and because present participles represent ongoingness, capture Nick's movement, making it appear both swift and instantaneous, as if it's occurring in front of our eyes. In the first two sentences, the participial phrases follow the main clauses, moving away from them. In the last sentence, the participles precede the main clause. The placement of the participles in relation to the main clause seems to show that Nick, moving from the Kelly's house as rapidly as possible, can't run from the image of Mr. Kelly, who can impose himself unexpectedly into Nick's life. Had Romano written this paragraph as I did, without present participial phrases, he might have produced acceptable sentences, but he would have created a conflict between the meaning of the paragraph and the structure of the sentences. The sentence structures wouldn't have supported the necessary movement of Nick's run. And they wouldn't have been nearly as effective as they are the way Romano crafted them, with the syntax commenting on and supporting the meaning.

If the first example paragraph from *Blindside* is about swiftness and movement, the second is about stasis, lack of movement. Nick stops. He assesses his situation. So the sentences have no present participles, no verbs as free modifiers. There are nine sentences and five free modifiers. These include an adverb clause **where he stood at the edge of uptown Medville**, a prepositional phrase with compound relative clauses embedded in the noun phrase object of the preposition, **at the moment the light turned green and Nick instinctively stuck out his thumb**, and an appositive adjective, **empty**, which is punctuated as a fragment to emphasize Nick's shock of recognition. There is a second appositive adjective phrase, **ready to head his way**, and another prepositional phrase, **somewhere on the living room floor at Julie's**. These free modifiers don't move, swiftly or otherwise. They make generalizations about the scene: Nick's pocket is empty, and cars are ready to head Nick's way. The free modifiers in this paragraph orient us to Nick's situation, to where he is in relation to traffic, and to where he is in town. A different set of circumstances demands a different set of sentence structures.

What we've done in this section is to use our conscious knowledge of grammatical structures and relationships to analyze literary style in selections from two novels and from a *National Geographic* article. Knowing how to do grammar has allowed us to understand how literary style is determined by the structures a writer chooses from among her options. And it has allowed us to reflect on how sentence structure can contribute to meaning.

Getting Rid of Gibberish

In recent years, a national movement has developed to make legal, business, and academic prose more clear and understandable. Proponents of this Plain English Movement believe that clear prose in these areas would make all our lives easier and less complicated. After all, clearly written insurance policies and mortgages would demand fewer lawyers to untangle their prose; clear writing would allow the general public to better understand the contracts they sign and give people greater access to knowledge. You can write clear prose by following a few simple principles: put your actions in verbs, not nouns; make the subjects of your sentences the agents of the actions; and put old information that links your sentence to previous ones in the subject position, new or less familiar information in predicates. The last principle about old and new information relates to concepts of coherence and cohesion, which go beyond our brief discussion of sentence options. And the first two principles need to be qualified with "everything else being equal," or "normally." They're useful principles, nonetheless.

In the previous section, we saw how Hemingway used passive sentences to emphasize the fact that Robert Cohen seldom acts on his own but is often acted upon by others. The Hemingway examples show that passives can be used effectively. But, as the first two principles of clear prose indicate, passives and certain other constructions, particularly abstract noun phrases, often make prose unclear; business, academic, and government documents are often not written carefully by thoughtful writers aware of their options. Here are two sentences from a CIA memo composed in 1957 and declassified in 1986. The memo, written by Robert Armory, Jr., a deputy director of the agency, to the Director of Central Intelligence, concerns the U.S. position on disarmament.

It is understood that the three papers presently available are being consolidated by the Disarmament Staff and that this revised consolidated paper is to be agreed to by Defense, JCS, and AEC. It is suggested that CIA's comments be withheld pending receipt of the Stassen draft.

The first sentence contains three passive clauses. Two of them are noun clauses extraposed from the grammatical subject position of the third clause, itself a passive clause with a deleted agent. Let's look at that sentence again, slowly. **That the three papers presently available are being consolidated by the Disarmament Staff** is a noun clause; conjoined to it is another noun clause, **and that this revised consolidated paper is to be agreed to by Defense, JCS, and AEC.** The pair of conjoined noun clauses are extraposed from the grammatical subject position of the independent clause and replaced by the expletive **it: it is understood** .... If this isn't confusing enough, the sentence is made obscure because the agent of the independent clause is deleted. So the reader is left to guess who understands both that the papers are being consolidated and that the consolidated paper will be agreed to. We are also not told in the next sentence who suggests **that CIA's comments be withheld,** because another agent is deleted from a passive construction. (I knew Hemingway, Mr. Armory. And you're no Ernest Hemingway!) It would be easy to joke about agents being deleted from CIA documents in order to cause confusion. But such obscure, confusing writing is typical of many government agencies, not only the CIA.

How could Mr. Armory have cleared up his prose? If he had been aware of the difficulty he was causing the reader, he might have written

I understand that the Disarmament Staff is consolidating the three available papers and that Defense, JCS, and AEC will agree to the consolidated paper. I suggest that CIA not comment on the paper until we receive the Stassen draft.

In short, Mr. Armory could have begun his sentences with human subjects that revealed exactly who was understanding and who was suggesting. He also could have made all the clauses active and compounded the two embedded noun clauses as direct objects of the active verb **understand**. To make the context of the commenting more clear (when the CIA might comment), Armory might have turned the prepositional phrase **pending receipt of the Stassen draft** (which contains an abstract noun phrase functioning as the oblique object) into an adverb clause, **until we receive the Stassen draft**. Here again, a human subject and an active verb make the original vague statement into a clear, specific one.

If you were the personnel director of a large organization and had to fire several hundred employees in order to cut personnel expenditures, you might want to hide yourself within opaque prose, deleting agents of passive sentences so you don't take responsibility for the downsizing. But more often, obscurity and lack of clarity can be costly. A dozen or so years ago, a Pennsylvania county established an environmental authority to oversee such actions as sewage disposal by boroughs within the county. The Authority, as it is called in the following excerpt, contracted to provide support for the environmental activities of the various boroughs. Recently one borough sued the Authority to pay for a new sludge-treatment plant, claiming that the county Authority had contracted not only to help the boroughs plan and design facilities but to build them as well. Such was not the intent of the arrangement according to those on the original Authority who helped compose the agreement. Here is the sentence that the case rested on:

> In order to provide the Borough with the facilities and equipment necessary to dewater its sludge in order to meet PA DER criteria for disposal of same in the lined landfill, the Authority will provide the necessary capital for the design and construction of the dewatering equipment.

The original drafters of the contract, it seems, got lost in the abstractness of their prose and the confusion of one adverbial infinitive embedded in another (**In order to provide . . . in order to meet . . .**). A confusion of infinitive phrases and abstract noun phrases. Not enough agents as subjects and too few active verbs. The Authority did want to provide capital for designing facilities that the borough could later construct (that was the sense the writers had of **in order to provide**). The Authority, though, didn't want to pay for the construction. The original members of the Authority could probably have saved the resulting lawsuit if they had written the following:

> The Authority will provide the capital to design both the facilities and equipment that the Borough will need to dewater sludge so that the Borough can dispose of its sludge in the lined landfill according to PA DER criteria.

Often just being aware of your options as a writer and paying attention to subjects, objects, and active verbs can solve problems of clarity.

Constructing Effective Sentences

In the mid 1960s, Kellogg Hunt showed how the written sentence structure of students changes between fourth and twelfth grade. Hunt measured these changes, calculating the length of various grammatical constituents. In terms of grammatical skills, he summed up this growth with the statement "little sentences grow into big ones." What he meant was that as students develop more skills in writing, they embed more clauses into matrix clauses and produce, in stages, longer, more complex, grammatical structures. When they begin to write, they use single clauses or they conjoin clauses. Later they use relative clauses, embedding rather than simply conjoining. Next, they reduce many of those relatives into restrictive phrases. Finally, the better writers, in about ninth or tenth grade, begin using more and more nonrestrictive modifiers, and they generally employ a large repertoire of structures, restrictive and nonrestrictive. The sentences of the more effective student writers begin looking like the sentences of skilled adult writers. The less effective writers don't naturally develop all of these later skills; typically they employ a smaller repertoire of structures and use fewer nonrestrictive structures.

This is not to say that all you have to do to improve your writing is to use more nonrestrictive modifiers or to use a greater variety of syntactic structures. While it is true that you have to learn to judiciously employ a range of syntactic structures in order to improve your writing, what Hunt's research really points to is that the better writers are more aware of the options open to them and understand the necessity to match their syntax more closely with their content. They use a greater variety of grammatical structures and processes—nonrestrictive modifiers, noun clauses, gerunds, passives—whatever they need to make their syntax reflect upon and enhance their content. They generally have more solid content as well.

Becoming a better writer is not simply a case of throwing more nonrestrictive modifiers into your own sentences willy-nilly; nor is it simply a case of gaining more awareness of your syntactic options. But improving your style, especially when you revise, is one step towards becoming a more effective writer. And some writing teachers believe that consciously using your stylistic options can enhance your content, making the improvement of style doubly effective. This was Francis Christensen's argument for making style the center of the writing curriculum. Whether you believe that stylistic concerns should be the core of the writing curriculum or an adjunct to other issues in the process of writing, it's hard to deny that effective student writers have mastered stylistic techniques.

Here is the writing of Marly Ellis, who submitted a portfolio of her writing to Miami University's portfolio assessment program in 1994. This is a program for high school students entering Miami to "test out of" first-year composition classes. Most of the students submitting portfolios have done well as writers in high school. The writing in Marly's portfolio shows why her teachers considered her a good writer—in no small part because she can write interesting sentences that make use of grammatical options to reflect upon their content. She is a good writer because she does what a writer must do. Her narrative called "Balance" is the story of an anorexic teenage girl named Mourning. The three example paragraphs that follow are from "Balance"; Mourning is in her bedroom, balancing herself between sanity and madness.

> Looming ghost-like in the center of the room, she tells herself, "Mourning, you're gonna get your life together. But for now just fill yourself up, take in the air and hold it, or you'll just vanish in the sky like a sick helium balloon." So she counts her breath and lines up on the rug in her room, filling up with air so she won't whisper into nothing, wondering when it was that she lost sight of so much of herself. She hangs there, poised in air, taking in the breaths and feeling herself grow stronger. She needs the balance.

> And maybe she would just stay there, suspended like a daydream personified, but her mother comes mincing up the stairs. Mourning can hear her creeping footsteps down the hallway, nervous and tight. A soft knock on the door confirms her guess. "Come in, Mother," Mourning whispers in her head, softly, breathlessly, "Come in." She doesn't speak out loud because she doesn't want to waste the air.

> Her mother bumps in anyway, face messy with nervous smiles and an overflowing breakfast tray in one pale hand. She hesitates imperceptibly when she sees her daughter wavering in the middle of her room as if there were a tightrope, body clenched and linear in the stillness.

We don't have to calculate the words per clause to see whether Marly has reached a "mature" level of sentence structure. She has. Anyone who reads her sentences knows she is a writer. She proves it in many ways. One way is how she uses nonrestrictive modifiers. Rewrite her second paragraph without the nonrestrictive modifiers if you want to see how much such modifiers add to her writing:

> And maybe she would just stay there, but her mother comes mincing up the stairs. Mourning can hear her creeping footsteps down the hallway. A soft knock on the door confirms her guess. "Come in, Mother," Mourning whispers in her head, "Come in." She doesn't speak out loud because she doesn't want to waste the air.

Or break down Marly's sentences into their underlying structures and then rebuild the paragraph with other options in order to see how the same content might have been said differently.

1. a. And maybe she would just stay there.
   b. She was suspended like a dream.
   c. The dream was personified.
   d. But her mother comes mincing up the stairs.
2. a. Mourning can hear her footsteps down the hallway.
   b. Her footsteps are creeping.
   c. Her footsteps are nervous.
   d. And her footsteps are tight.
3. a. A knock confirms her guess.
   b. The knock is soft.
   c. The knock is on the door.
4. a. Mourning whispers "Come in, Mother" in her head.
   b. Mourning whispers softly.
   c. And Mourning whispers breathlessly.
5. a. Mourning whispers "Come in" in her head.
6. a. She doesn't speak out loud for this reason.
   b. She doesn't want to waste the air.

If we can combine **It surprised me** and **Jane arrived late** in 467 different ways, how many ways could we combine those seventeen sentences? More than we could count. Here is just one possible variation built from the sentences underlying Marly's paragraph:

> And maybe she would just stay there and be suspended like a dream personified. But her mother comes mincing up the stairs. Mourning can hear her creeping, nervous, and tight footsteps down the hallway. Her guess is confirmed by a soft knock on the door. In her head, Mourning whispers softly

and breathlessly, "Come in, Mother." Mourning whispers "Come in" in her head. In order not to waste the air, she doesn't speak out loud.

This version doesn't have the effect of Marly's original. It doesn't capture in syntax Mourning's attempt to balance reality and unreality. But if you understand that grammar gives you many options for revision, you might be able to work toward a more effective version in the way that Marly must have. If you see that you have to ask the same questions about your own sentences that you would ask about Hemingway's or Romano's, then you understand how reflecting about sentence structure can help you become a more effective writer. Will nonrestrictive modifiers help you produce the effects you need? Will a passive or active sentence make a better characterization? Do your sentences need to show movement or stasis? If you want to show a tenuous balance between reality and unreality, can you do it like Marly did, by having Mourning's mother perceive her on a tightrope, balanced in a nominative absolute?

> She hesitates imperceptibly when she sees her daughter wavering in the middle of her room as if there were a tightrope, **body clenched and linear in the stillness**.

Did Marly put in the nonrestrictive modifiers or structure her sentences the way she did because she had a grammar course to show her how to do so? Probably not. I don't think Hemingway did either. Some people come to their knowledge of sentence structure and other attributes of writing through reading, through intuition, without a conscious knowledge of the terminology. But for those of us who want to learn how to write better, doing grammar can provide the kind of conscious awareness of our own language that will help us reflect on how to improve our sentences and to know that we can change them. A conscious knowledge of language might alert us to add a nonrestrictive modifier, or suggest that we might combine two sentences into one, or allow us to realize that we can make a passive into an active sentence. Doing grammar can help us see into our own writing, just as it can help us see into the writing of others.

Using Punctuation to Improve Sentence Effectiveness

When I was an undergraduate, one of my English teachers, Dr. Larkin, liked to refer her students to a handbook when we made an error in punctuation. In the margin of our paper might be written directions like "CS. 27c." With that cryptic note, Dr. Larkin was telling us that the handbook had a section 27c that would clear up a CS (comma splice) error. Dr. Larkin assumed we could understand the instructions in the section. I never could, because they were couched in grammatical terminology that made no sense to me. Not only did the rules make no sense, but there seemed to be hundreds of them, unrelated to one another or to any pattern I could discern. Who could make sense of them all? Who wanted to? I didn't.

But you now have a working knowledge of grammar and have mastered most of its terminology, so presumably you could understand the hundreds of punctuation rules. But maybe you don't have to, since there are very few principles that underlie all the rules, and the principles make sense once you understand the logic behind them. Most punctuation can be addressed in three principles. The first concerns end punctuation marks; the second and third concern internal punctuation marks. Fourth and fifth principles might be added to take care of exceptions.

The end punctuation marks refer to those marks that you put at the end of independent clauses—periods, semicolons, question marks, and exclamation points. The internal punctuation marks refer to those marks that you use to set off either compound phrases and clauses within sentences or nonrestrictive phrases and clauses within sentences—commas, dashes, colons, and parentheses. There are just a few end punctuation marks and a few internal punctuation marks, and the principles for using them are pretty straightforward.

1. End sentences (independent clauses together with their nonrestrictive modifiers, if any) with end punctuation marks. You may also separate independent clauses by a comma and a coordinate conjunction.

EXAMPLES

Though we have been deluged with reports and studies, backed by abundant anecdotes, documenting the academic deficiencies of our young people, most states have not yet implemented serious school reforms. We continue to muddle along with old-fashioned schools and old-fashioned curriculums.

With each step on the moon, the Apollo 11 astronauts launched a perfect umbrella-shaped spray of dust particles. But the most

amazing part of their moonwalk was the moon itself—an alien
panorama of ashen rocks and forbidding craters.

or

With each step on the moon, the Apollo 11 astronauts launched a
perfect umbrella-shaped spray of dust particles, but the most
amazing part of their moonwalk was the moon itself—an alien
panorama of ashen rocks and forbidding craters.

2. Separate the phrases in a series of three or more compound phrases
with commas. The last phrase in the series should be separated by a
comma and a coordinate conjunction. This is true for subordinate
clauses, too.

EXAMPLES

Mom asked my new friend Rosa what her father did, where her
family was from, **and** why they had moved to Springfield.

The Reds' new pitcher worked 7 innings, struck out 8 batters,
and gave up 3 hits.

The Boy Scouts who trashed the old cemetery were **neither**
brave, clean, **nor** reverent.

3. Separate nonrestrictive modifiers from main clauses and from other
nonrestrictive modifiers by commas, dashes, parentheses, or colons.
Separate conjunctive adverbs from main clauses with commas, and
separate names in direct address with internal punctuation.

EXAMPLES

Flies and aphids suck the juices from plants—preferring soft leaves,
like those of basil, rather than the tough leaves of rosemary,
thyme, or oregano.

When the Step Pyramid was built in 2630 B.C., it was the world's
finest tomb; indeed, it was the world's largest building.

Probably the most quoted movie line is "Play it again, Sam." It
even became the title of a Woody Allen film. But that's not what
Humphrey Bogart's character Rick Blain actually said to the piano
player in *Casablanca*. All he said was, " Play it!"

Those are the three standard principles. The fourth and fifth might read

4. Use a comma when the reader might otherwise misread your sentence. This often relates to initial modifiers, when you might confuse the subject of the sentence with the object of the modifier's verb.

EXAMPLE

As her parents watched, the toddler walked across the room.

Not

As her parents watched the toddler walked across the room.

Another possibility for misreading occurs when a modifier follows a negative main clause. The first example sentence implies that the Raiders lost for different reasons than the referee's call. The second says that the Raiders didn't lose, and the reason they didn't lose was the referee's bad call.

EXAMPLE

The Raiders didn't lose because the referee made a bad call.

Does not mean

The Raiders didn't lose, because the referee made a bad call.

5. Ignore the first four principles for rhetorical reasons (for effect). But know that to ignore one of those principles puts you in jeopardy. Unless you've convinced your readers that you have both grammatical and rhetorical control of your text, many people (teachers included) will think you made a mistake.

Those five principles basically outline "correct" punctuation. But, since the principles provide you with options, you can use punctuation not only to make your writing correct but to make it more effective as well. To explore the rhetorical aspect of punctuation, I've taken some examples from the writing Shiri Frank submitted to Miami's portfolio assessment program in 1991. Shiri was a bright young woman, eighteen years old and just about to enter Miami University, when she died in an auto accident. In the following, Shiri was trying to communicate an experience she had while walking alone in the woods:

> With my arms up, I coasted sideways through the path, doing goofy
> imitations of a Jane Fonda workout.

Shiri began the sentence with a nominative absolute separated from the
main clause by a comma; she ended the sentence with a present participial phrase separated from the main clause in the same way. Commas
are the normal internal punctuation mark; they don't call attention to
themselves. If she had wanted to emphasize, say, the action in the participial phrase, Shiri might have used a dash or even a colon.

> With my arms up, I coasted sideways through the path—doing
> goofy imitations of a Jane Fonda workout.

> or

> With my arms up, I coasted sideways through the path: doing
> goofy imitations of a Jane Fonda workout.

The dash might have been a good choice; it makes the reader pause for
a moment longer, adding emphasis. The colon would have been too formal for the breezy content of the sentence. The comma makes the participial phrase essentially equal to the absolute, probably the effect Shiri
was after. She knew when to use the longer pause; she uses dashes in
several places throughout the portfolio. In her introduction, for instance,
Shiri sets off in dashes a comment about the paper she wrote on Eliot's
"The Hollow Men."

> The last contribution to my assessment—an analysis of "The
> Hollow Men"—serves as a necessary and a universal
> message.

Commas would have sufficed, as in

> The last contribution to my assessment, an analysis of "The
> Hollow Men," serves as a necessary and a universal
> message.

But commas wouldn't have foregrounded the appositive noun phrase in
the way the dashes do.

Shiri knew how to control punctuation marks, both internal and end
marks. In one place in her woods piece, Shiri described a change of temperature caused by the thick foliage.

> Once inside the woods, I felt the cooler temperature; the light
> from the sun had been filtered by the canopy of new and
> old trees standing together.

Shiri used a semicolon to separate the two independent clauses. Look what would have happened had she used a period instead.

> Once inside the woods, I felt the cooler temperature. The light
> from the sun had been filtered by the canopy of new and
> old trees standing together.

The period would have nearly isolated the ideas in the two clauses from one another. The semicolon indicates they are both independent clauses but closely related to one another, close enough to be placed within the same sentence. Shiri seemed to have understood how to vary end punctuation. She certainly used periods to separate sentences most of the time, as you would expect. But when the occasion called for a different option, she didn't hesitate. In another place in the woods, she sat behind a waterfall and put her hand in the water.

> I stuck my hand through the water, and the power of the fall
> pushed it downward.

What if she had separated these two sentences differently? Shiri could have written

> I stuck my hand through the water. And the power of the fall
> pushed it downward.

> or

> I stuck my hand through the water. The power of the fall
> pushed it downward.

Either of these options would have been perfectly acceptable. But they would have made the separation between the ideas greater and more abrupt. The conjunction and the comma make a gentle segue. A more abrupt transition might have disrupted the misty vision Shiri attempted to portray here.

There are two main points in this discussion of punctuation. The first is that, once you understand how to analyze sentences, a confusion of punctuation rules can be reduced to a few understandable principles.

The second point is that when you understand how to punctuate, you can use punctuation rhetorically, in order to enhance the effect of your writing, just as you use grammatical structures for effect. Shiri was a good writer, which means that she knew more about writing than simply how to do it correctly. She obviously knew more than grammar and punctuation rules as well. But her ability to use punctuation for rhetorical effect enhanced her writing. It showed how much control she had over the written word, and it added a sophisticated dimension to her writing. Dr. Larkin may have gotten us to punctuate correctly through her handbook instructions. I don't remember, though, that she ever showed us how punctuation could have a positive effect on our writing.

Summary and Implications

This chapter started out with a question: What #@!$% good is knowing how to do grammar? I hope the chapter has been a satisfactory, if incomplete, answer. The basis of the answer is that good writers and good readers are aware of the options grammar gives us to construct sentences, to clarify them, to punctuate them, and to choose the most effective among them. Studying grammar makes that knowledge conscious. It gives us a language with which to think about language.

You don't learn grammar simply to parse sentences or to draw diagrams. You learn grammar so that you can understand how language works. If you are interested in the structure of language, as a linguist is, you build on that knowledge of how your language works and look at how other languages work, in order to discern basic principles of language or to investigate how the mind processes language, or to view language in a social context. If you're not a linguist, you likely want to learn grammar so that you will have the means to reflect on your writing and on the writing of others.

EXERCISES

I.   Take a paragraph or two from a writer you like a lot and analyze its sentence structure. Then break those sentences down into their underlying components and write them in a way different from the original. What have you discerned about the author's style with this exercise? Write a one- or two-page paper in which you relate the author's sentence structure to her content, in effect analyzing her style. You can analyze the writing in a novel, a short story, a poem, or a magazine or newspaper article.

II. Take a paper that you are writing for this or any other class. Revise it using your knowledge of grammatical options. You may want to add free modifiers, to revise sentences, or to punctuate it anew. Keep notes on the changes you make, and write a page or two reflection on how your changes made the paper more effective. Or on why you went back to the original versions.

III. In an article entitled " Grammars of Style: New Options in Composition," Winston Weathers explores what he calls Grammar B. In short, Weathers asks you to perceive your text in other than standard ways. For instance, he suggests using fragments or arranging comparisons on the page in columns rather than in paragraphs that follow one after another. Read Weathers' article and write a paper using the principles of Grammar B. Add a brief reflection on the Grammar B processes you used and how they affect your content. (An abridged version of "Grammars of Style" appears in Richard L. Graves, ed. *Rhetoric and Composition: A Sourcebook for Teachers*. Upper Montclair, NJ: Boynton/Cook, 1984, pp. 133–147; the original article appeared in *Freshman English News* 4(Winter 1976): 1–4, 12–18.)

IV. Take a paragraph or two from a textbook or academic article you think is written in academic gibberish, or take a paragraph from a confusing government or legal document, break its sentences down into their underlying structures, and revise the text to make it more clear. Write a page or two reflection on why your revised text is more clear than the original. Or couch your reflection as a letter to the author explaining why the original text is unclear and how she might make it both more clear and more interesting.

Appendix:
Selected
Answers

This unit identifies the constituents and functions of ten sentences from the analyzing sentences and identifying verb types exercises in chapters 1 through 9. Except for chapter 1, the answers are given in simplified diagram form rather than branching diagrams, in order to conserve space. The teacher's manual contains analyses of the other sentences in those exercises.

Chapter 1. Identifying Verb Types

3. **Vg–** "Disney World offers visitors family entertainment" "Visitors" = NP:IObj; "family entertainment" = NP:DObj.
6. **Vc–** Computer spreadsheets make business analysis (to be) easy. "Business analysis" = NP:DObj; "easy" = AdjPh:ObjComp.
8. **BE–** "A national treasure" = NP:PN. It has the same referent as "Yellowstone."
10. **VT–** "The fraternity" = NP:DObj.
13. **VL–** "Limitless" = AdjPh:PredAdj.
21. **Vc–** You can't quite say that "Coren calls border collies (to be) the smartest dogs." Nonetheless, "the smartest dogs" = NP:ObjComp.

In a sense, Coren does "designate border collies (to be) the smartest dogs." And "smartest dogs" does rename "border collies."

23. **VI**– "Around the fire station" = PrepPh:Adv-place.

33. **VT**– "Her perennials" = NP:DOb; "with care" = PrepPh:Adv-manner. The sentence doesn't make a very good passive because of the universal rule in language that NPs that refer to the same person or thing cannot cross one another in a sentence rearrangement (this is called the crossover principle). The possessive pronoun "her" refers to "my neighbor."

44. **Vg**– or **Vc**– This sentence is ambiguous. If "found" is Vg, then "Oprah" = NP:IObj; "an interesting guest" = NP:DObj. If "found" is Vc, then "Oprah" = NP:DObj; "an interesting guest" = NP:ObjComp. He found an interesting guest for her; or he found her (to be) an interesting guest.

48. **VL**– "Inexplicable" = AdjPh:PredAdj

Chapter 2. Analyzing Sentences

2. A dancer's body — is — her living voice.
NP:Subj — BE — NP:PredN
———— VP:Pred ————

6. Dr. Jeckyl — became — a different person — after — his experiment.
NP:Subj — VL — NP:PredN — Prep — NP:Obj/Prep
———— PrepPh:Adv-time ————
———— VP:Pred ————

11. The International Olympic Committee — returned — Jim Thorpe's medals — to — his family — in — 1983.
NP:Subj — Vg — NP:DObj — Prep — NP:Obj/Prep — Prep — NP:Obj/Prep
———— PrepPh:Adv-reception ———— PrepPh:Adv-time
———————————— VP:Pred ————————————

Note: Though you can't say **returned his family Jim Thorpe's medals**, **return** is a Vg verb. **His family** is a perceptive receptor of the medals, not a place.

16. The Senate — came up with — a compromise bill — despite — White House opposition.
NP:Subj — VT — NP:DObj — Prep — NP:Obj/Prep
———— PrepPh:Adv-condition ————
———— VP:Pred ————

18. The 1948 Chrysler Town and Country convertible — makes — an unforgettable impression — at — antique car shows.
NP:Subj — VT — NP:DObj — Prep — NP:Obj/Prep
———— PrepPh:Adv-place ————
———————————— VP:Pred ————————————

21. Jell-O sales — plummeted — during — the '70s.
NP:Subj — VI — Prep — NP:Obj/Prep
———— PrepPh:Adv-time ————
———— VP:Pred ————

31. South Africans elected Mandela   their first president.
    NP:Subj   Vc   NP:DObj ——NP:ObjComp——
                          ————VP:Pred————

37. Distance   comes   from   a balanced golf swing
    NP:Subj   VI   Prep   NP:Obj/Prep
                        ——PrepPh:Adv-place——
                ————VP:Pred————

Note: It would be all right to consider the prep phrase the source of the distance—Adv-source, rather than Adv-place.

40. Lead-based paint remains a danger   in   older housing projects.
    NP:Subj   VL   NP:PredN Prep ——NP:Obj/Prep——
                                             ——PrepPh:Adv-place——
                     ————————VP:Pred————————

48. Fifteen million Americans suffer from carpal tunnel syndrome.
    NP:Subj   VI   Prep   NP:Obj/Prep
                                             PrepPh:Adv-source——

Note: You might argue that **suffer from** is a two-word transitive verb. But the passive is so bad—**Carpal tunnel syndrome is suffered from by millions of Americans**—that it would be difficult to sustain that argument.

Chapter 3. Expanding Verb Phrases

1. The state legislature might   offer parents school vouchers next year.
   NP:Subj   Modal   Vg   NP:IObj NP:DObj   NP:Adv-time
                         Aux
                         MV:PastCond
                         ————————VP:Pred————————

8. Winston Churchill was a complicated giant on the world stage.
   — NP:Subj — BE — NP:PredN — Prep NP:Obj/Prep
                MV:Past — PrepPh:Adv-place —
                ——— VP:Pred ———

12. Stingrays could have been cruising near the beach.
    NP:Subj Modal HAVE BE VI Prep NP:Obj/Prep
                  PastPart PresPart — PrepPh:Adv-place —
                  — Aux —
                  — MV:PastPerfProgCond —
                  ——— VP:Pred ———

16. The silo might have blown up.
    NP:Subj Modal HAVE VI
                  PastPart
            — Aux —
            — MV:PastPerfCond —
            ——— VP:Pred ———

27. The Japanese have rebuilt their cities several times this century.
    — NP:Subj — HAVE VT NP:DObj NP:Adv-frequency NP:Adv-time
                PastPart
       — Aux —
       — MV:PresPerf —
       ——— VP:Pred ———

30. The Reds fans were screaming for a hit in the ninth inning.
    NP:Subj BE VT NP:DObj Prep NP:Obj/Prep
            PresPart — PrepPh:Adv-time —
       — Aux —
       — MV:PastProg —
       ——— VP:Pred ———

Note: Sentence 30 is difficult. I analyzed **scream for** as a two-word transitive. You could probably justify **scream** as intransitive. In that case, **for a hit** would be a prep phrase functioning as an adverb of reason or perhaps condition.

33. Communism   seems to   be   dying   around   the world.
    NP:Subj   Modal   BE   VI   Prep   NP:Obj/Prep
                   ——Aux——   PresPart   ——PrepPh:Adv-place——
                   ——MV:PresProgCond——
                   ————————————————VP:Pred————————————————

35. The Weather Bureau   had   been   playing   Chicken Little   with   the coastal residents.
    NP:Subj   HAVE   BE   VT   NP:DObj   Prep   ——NP:Obj/Prep——
                                   PastPart PresPart   —PrepPh:Adv-accompaniment—
                          ——Aux——
                          ——MV:PastPerfProg——
                          ————————————————VP:Pred————————————————

45. Newman's blue eyes   can   make   older women   mushy.
    ——NP:Subj——   Modal   Vc   NP:DObj   AdjPh:ObjComp
                          Aux
                          MV:PresCond
                          ————————————VP:Pred————————————

50. A banjo player   was   sitting   in front of   Woolworth's.
    ——NP:Subject——   BE   VI   ——Prep——   NP:Obj/Prep
                      Aux   PresPart   ——PrepPh:Adv-place——
                      —MV:PastProg—
                      ————————————VP:Pred————————————

Chapter 4. Exploring Noun Phrases

2. The   torte   recipe   required   a cup of   almonds.
   D/Art   Adj   N   VT   PreArt   N
   Det   ——NP——   MV:Past   Det
   ——NP:Subj——   ——NP:DObj——
                                           ————VP:Pred————

11. Anti-smoking activists are dancing   on   the   Marlboro Man's grave.
    Adj   N   BE   VI   Prep D/Art   GenN   N
                             Aux PresPart   Det   —GenN— NP
    —NP:Subj—   —MV:PresProg—   NP:Obj/Prep
                                                                  PrepPh:Adv-place
                                                                  VP:Pred

Note: **Danced on** can be a two-word VT. **The Marlboro Man's grave was danced on by anti-smoking activists** is an acceptable passive.

14. Napoleon crowned himself   emperor of   France   in   1804.
    ProperN   Vc   ReflexPron N   Prep ProperN   Prep N
    NP:Subj   MV:Past NP:DObj   NP:Obj/Prep   NP:Obj/Prep
                                                   —PrepPh:Gen—   —PrepPh:Adv-time—
                                               —NP:ObjComp—
                                               VP:Pred

16. Longwood Gardens unfolds in   4 miles   of   paths.
    ProperN   VI   Prep PreArt   N
    NP:Subj   MV:Pres   Det   NP:Obj/Prep
                                     —NP:Obj/Prep—
                                     —PrepPh:Adv-extent—
                                     VP:Pred

19. Anti-adoption advocates have   been attacking the   concept of   adoption.
    Adj   N   HAVE   BE   VT   D/Art N   Prep N
                                           PastPart   PresPart Det   NP:Obj/Prep
    —NP:Subj—   —Aux—   —PrepPh:Gen—
                          —MV:PresPerfProg—   NP
                                                                            NP:DObj
                                                     VP:Pred

21. The   modern study   of   grammar   began   with   Noam Chomsky's   Syntactic Structures   in   1957.
    D/Art   Adj   N   Prep   N   VI   Prep   GenN   PropN   Prep   N
    Det   NP:Obj/Prep MV:Past   ——NP:Obj/Prep——   NP:Obj/Prep
                             ——PrepPh:Gen——   ——PrepPh:Adv-source——   PrepPh:Adv-time
                             ——NP——   ——VP:Pred——
    ——NP:Subj——

30. Ireland kept   European culture   alive   during the Dark Ages.
    PropN   Vc   Adj   N   Adj:ObjComp   Prep   PropN
    NP:Subj MV:Past   NP:DObj   NP:Obj/Prep
                                                               ——PrepPh:Adv-duration——
                                              ——VP:Pred——

40. Charleston puts   on   a   pretty face   for   its   visitors.
    ProperN   V   Part   I/Art   Adj   N   Prep   PossPr   N
    NP:Subj   ——VT——   Det   NP:DObj   Det   ——NP:Obj/Prep——
                ——MV:Pres——   ——NP——
                                                                ——PrepPh:Adv-goal——
                                              ——VP:Pred——

Note: You might consider **for its visitors** an adverb of reason.

42. Calvin Klein's world   is   a   world   of   subdued chic.
    GenN   N   BE   I/Art   N   Prep   Adj   N
    ——NP:Subj——   MV:Pres Det   NP: Obj/Prep
                                                            ——PrepPh:Gen——
                                            ——NP——
                                            ——NP:PredN——
                                            ——VP:Pred——

Note: You could argue that **a world of** is a pre-article. I've assumed that **world** is the head of the phrase and **of subdued chic** is a genitive, because **world** is the head of the noun phrase subject. This way, the predN and the subject are more clearly parallel.

47. Goya   ranks   behind   Picasso   as   Spain's   greatest   artist.
     PropN   VI   Prep   PropN   Prep   GenN   Adj   N
     NP:Subj   MV:Pres   NP:Obj/Prep ——————————————————————————————— NP ———
                         ——PrepPh:Adv-place——   NP:Obj/Prep ——————————
                                                              ——PrepPh.:Adv-manner——————
                         ——————————————————————— VP:Pred ——————————————————————————

Chapter 5. Rearranging and Compounding

1. The   sporty   Jaguar   is   called   the   XJR.
    D/Art   Adj   PropN   BE   Vc   D/Art   PropN
    Det   —— NP ——   PastPart   Det   NP:ObjComp
    ——————— NP:GramSubj ———————   MV:PresPass
                                        ——————————— VP:Pred ——————————

Note. The article *the* with **sporty Jaguar** or **XJR** is labeled as article because it is separate from the proper nouns. That is, you can talk about **this Jag, an XJR**, etc. When the article is insepable from a proper noun (the Atlantic Ocean), it is part of the proper noun. You cannot normally talk about **this Atlantic Ocean** or **an Atlantic Ocean**.

                                     ——————————— MV:PresInt ———————————┐

3. Why   do   school   buildings   sit   empty   most of   the   day?
    Adv-reason DO   N:Adj   N   VI   Adv-manner   PreArt   D/Art   N
                Aux   —— NP:Subj ——   Det   Det   ——————
                                                                              ——————— NP ———————
                                                                   ——— NP:Adv-frequency ————————

Note: The VP predicate begins with **do ... sit** and continues **empty most of the day**. The pro-adverb replaces an adverb like **for some reason**.

11.

What	values	are	taught	by	our	schools?
Det	N	BE	VT	Prep	PossPron	N
		Aux	PastPart		Det	
NP:GramSubj		MV:PresPassInt				

NP:Obj of Prep/LogSubj
PrepPh:Adv-agency
VP:Pred

Note: The Pro-det **what** replaces an article or demonstrative like **these**.

18.

Bake	the	mixture	in	the	oven	for	20	minutes.
VT	D/Art	N	Prep	D/Art	N	Prep	CardN	N
MV:Imp	Det			Det			Det	

NP:DObj
NP:Obj/Prep
PrepPh:Adv-place
NP:Obj/Prep
PrepPh:Adv-duration
VP:Pred

21.

Seafood	is	featured	on	the	menu	of	the	new	Mexican	restaurant.
N	BE	Adj:PredAdj	Prep	D/Art	N	Prep	D/Art	Adj	Adj	N
NP:Subj	MV:Pres			Det			Det			

NP
NP:Obj/Prep
PrepPh:Gen
NP
NP:Obj/Prep
PrepPh:Adv-place
VP:Pred

Note: You could analyze **is featured** as a passive, with **BE** as an Aux and **featured** as a past participle. I've elected to call **BE** a verb and **featured** a pred adj. If you conclude that the sentence is passive, you have to assume an agent like **by the management/someone**.

27.
There	was	no	warning	before	the	quake.
Expl	BE	PreArt	N	Prep	D/Art	N
NP:GramSubj	MV:Pres	Det			Det	
		NP:PredN/LogSubj				NP:Obj/Prep
						PrepPh:Adv-time
					VP:Pred	

36.
Rap	rhythms	and	gospel	messages	make	Christian	hip-hop	a	strange	musical	blend.
N:Adj	N	Conj	Adj	N	Vc	Adj	N	I/Art	Adj	Adj	N
NP			NP		MV:Pres	NP:DObj		Det		NP	
NP:Subj									NP		
									NP:ObjComp		
					VP:Pred						

40.
Why	can't	we	afford	good	nursing	care	in	America?
Adv-reason	M/neg	PersPron	VT	Adj	Adj	N	Prep	PropN
	Aux	NP:Subj				NP		NP:Obj/Prep
	MV:Pres Cond Int					NP:Obj/Prep		PrepPh:Adv-place
								VP:Pred

Note: The VP begins with **can't . . . afford** and continues **good nursing care in America [why].** The interrogative pro-adverb **why** replaces an adverb like **for some reason.**

44.
White	teenage	girls	define	beauty	in	terms of	physical	perfection.
Adj	Adj	N	VT	N	Prep	PreArt	Adj	N
	NP		MV:Pres	NP:DObj				NP
NP:Subj								NP:Obj/Prep
								PrepPh:Adv-manner
						VP:Pred		

In contrast, black teenage girls define it in terms of the right attitude.

In contrast,	black	teenage	girls	define	it	in	terms of	the	right	attitude.
ConjAdv	Adj	Adj	N	VT	PersPron	Prep	PreArt	D/Art	Adj	N
				MV:Pres	NP:DObj		Det	Det		

NP:Subj (black teenage girls)
NP (teenage girls)
NP:Obj/Prep
PrepPh:Adv-manner
VP:Pred

50. Most single-parent families don't define it happen by choice.

Most	single-parent	families	don't		happen	by	choice.
PreArt	Adj	N	DO/Neg		VI	Prep	N
Det					MV:Pres		

NP:Subj
NP
NP:Obj/Prep
PrepPh:Adv-manner
VP:Pred

Chapter 6. Constructing Relative Clauses

1.

My	folks	don't	like	the	guy	I	'm	dating	now.
PossPr	N	DO/Neg	VT	D/Art	N	PersPr	BE	VI	Adv-time
Det		Aux		Det		NP:Subj			
		MV:Pres			NP:Head		MV:PresProg		

NP:Subj
NP:DObj
VP:Pred
RelCl:Adj
VP:Pred
NP:DObj
VP:Pred

Note: The obj NP of the relative clause has been deleted. The underlying form of the relative clause would be **I'm dating whom**. Without the deletion, the relative clause would be **whom I'm dating now**.

~~a guy~~ now.

4. Countries whose energy consumption does not decrease will suffer during the next decade.
   N   RelDet N:Adj N   DO   Neg VI   M   VI   Prep D/Art OrdN N
   NP:Head Det   Aux   Aux   Det
                       ——NP——   Aux   MV:PresCond   ——NP——
                    ——NP:Subj——   MV:Pres   ——NP;Obj/Prep——
                                               VP:Pred   ——PrepPh:Adv-duration——
              ————RelCl:Adj————   ——VP:Pred——
         ————————NP:Subj————————

7. The American soldiers met some Haitian children who had overcome the squalor that surrounded them.
   D/Art Adj   N   VT PreArt Adj   N   RelPr HAVE VT   D/Art N   RelPr VT   PersPron
   Det   ——NP——   ——PastDet——NP——   NP:Subj ——MV:PastPer—— VT   Det   N   NP:DObj
   ————NP:Sub————   ——MV:Past——   ————————————————————NP:Subj MV:Past VP:Pred
                                 ——NP:Head——   ——RelCl:Adj——
                                                                                    ——NP:DObj——
                                              ——NP:Head——
                                                                    ——VP:Pred——
                                         ——NP:DObj——   ——RelCl:Adj——
                                    ——VP:Pred——
                              ——VP:Pred——

15. The new mall established a   climate in   which high-class stores could thrive . . .
    D/Art Adj N   VT   I/Art N   Prep RelPr Adj   N   M   VI
    Det   ——NP—— MV:Past   Det   ——NP:Obj/Prep—— N   M   VI
    ——NP:Subj——   ——NP:Head——   ——PrepPh:Adv-place——   MV:PastCond
                                                                         ——RelCl:Adj——
                                                             ——NP:Subj——
                                                          ——NP:DObj——
                                                       ——VP:Pred——
                              ——NP:DObj——
                           ——VP:Pred——

Note: The predicate of the relative clause is disjoined, and the prep phrase has been moved to the front of the clause: **could thrive in which** is the predicate.

20. Our — Zagreb — trip — was — complicated — by — a — taxi — driver — who — spoke — no — known — language.

Our	Zagreb	trip	was	complicated	by	a	taxi	driver	who	spoke	no	known	language.
PossPr	N:Adj	N	BE	VT	Prep	I/Art	N:Adj	N	RelPr	VT	PreArt	Adj	N
Det			Aux	PastPart		Det			NP:Subj	MV:Past	Det		

— NP — | — NP — | — NP — | — NP —
— NP:GramSubj — | MV:PastPass | — NP:Head — | NP:DObj
| | | | NP:Obj/Prep/LogSubj
| | | | PrepPh:Adv-agency
| | | | VP:Pred
| | | | RelCl:Adj
| | | | VP:Pred

Note: The independent clause is passive. The relative clause is embedded into the logical subject. The underlying active form of the independent clause would be **A taxi driver who spoke no known language complicated our Zagreb trip.**

29. The — foods — your — mother — prepared — can — keep — you — healthy.

The	foods	your	mother	prepared	can	keep	you	healthy.
D/Art	N	PossPr	N	VT	M	Vc	PersPr	Adj:ObjComp
Det		Det		MV:Past	Aux	MV:PresCond	NP:DObj	

— NP:Head — | — NP:Subj —
| RelCl:Adj | VP:Pred | MV:PresCond | VP:Pred
| NP:Subj | VP:Pred

Note: The Object NP **the foods** has been deleted from the relative clause. The clause underlying the relative clause is **your mother prepared the foods.**

32. African Americans — have — won — political — influence — that — was — denied — them — for — centuries.

African Americans	have	won	political	influence	that	was	denied	them	for	centuries.
PropN	HAVE	VT	Adj	N	RelPr	BE	Vg	PersPr	Prep	N
NP:Subj	Aux	PastPart			NP:GramSubj	Aux	PastPart	NP:IObj		
	MV:PresPerf		— NP:Head —			MV:PastPass				NP:Obj/Prep

— PrepPh:Adv-duration
VP:Pred
RelCl:Adj
— NP:DObj —
VP:Pred

Note: The RelCl is in passive form. The agent phrase **by society** has been deleted. The independent passive clause underlying the relative clause is **political influence was denied them (by society) for centuries.** The active form is **society denied them political influence for centuries.**

40. IBM has developed a full-sized keyboard that can collapse into a notebook computer.

IBM	PropN — NP:Subj
has	HAVE — MV:PresPerf
developed	VT — MV:PresPerf
a	I/Art — Det
full-sized	Adj
keyboard	N — NP:Head — NP
that	RelPr — NP:Subj
can	M — Aux — MV:PresCond
collapse	VI
into	Prep
a	I/Art — Det
notebook	N:Adj
computer	N — NP

Phrase labels: NP:Obj/Prep — PrepPh:Adv-place — VP:Pred — RelCl:Adj — NP:DObj — VP:Pred

44. Grizzly bears have eaten people who have ventured into their domains.

Grizzly bears	N — NP:Subj
have	HAVE — Aux — MV:PresPerf
eaten	VT — MV:PresPerf
people	N — NP:Head
who	RelPr — NP:Subj
have	HAVE — Aux — MV:PresPerf
ventured	VI — MV:PresPerf
into	Prep
their	PossPr
domains	N — NP:Obj/Prep — PrepPh:Adv-place

Phrase labels: VP:Pred — RelCl:Adj — NP:DObj — VP:Pred

50. F. Scott Fitzgerald lived like the characters he wrote about.

F. Scott Fitzgerald	PropN — NP:Subj
lived	VI — MV:Past
like	Prep
the	D/Art — Det
characters	N — NP:Head
he	PersPr — NP:Subj
wrote	VT — MV:Past — VP:Pred
about.	

Phrase labels: NP:Obj/Prep — PrepPh:Adv-manner — VP:Pred — RelCl:Adj — NP:Obj/Prep — VP:Pred

Note: The Object NP **the characters** has been deleted from the relative clause: The underlying clause is **he wrote about the characters.**

Chapter 7. Reducing Relative Clauses to Phrases

3. George Harrison posed as a monk in prayer.
   George Harrison — PropN — NP:Subj
   posed — VI — MV:Past
   as — Prep
   a — I/Art — Det
   monk — N — NP:Head
   in — Prep
   prayer — N
   PrepPh:Adj
   NP:Obj/Prep
   PrepPh:Adv-manner
   VP:Pred

6. Wall Street traders investing in foreign markets have earned 12% interest this year.
   Wall Street — N:Adj — NP:Head
   traders — N
   investing — VI
   in — Prep
   foreign — Adj
   markets — N — NP
   have — HAVE — MV:PresPerf
   earned — VT
   12% — CardN
   interest — N — NP:DObj
   this — Demon — Det
   year — N — NP:Adv-time
   PrepPh:Adv-place
   PresPartPh:Adj
   NP:Subj
   VP:Pred

11. Bighorn Canyon National Park contains multi-layered canyons blanketed by juniper woodlands and rolling prairies.
   Bighorn Canyon National Park — PropN — NP:Subj
   contains — VT — MV:Pres
   multi-layered — Adj
   canyons — N — NP:Head
   blanketed — VT
   by — Prep
   juniper — N:Adj
   woodlands — N — NP
   and — Conj
   rolling — PresPart:Adj
   prairies — N
   NP:Obj/Prep
   PrepPh:Adv-agency
   PastPartPh:Adj
   NP:DObj
   VP:Pred

19. The first city destroyed by an atomic bomb was Hiroshima.
   The — D/Art — Det
   first — OrdN
   city — N — NP:Head
   destroyed — VT
   by — Prep
   an — I/Art — Det
   atomic — Adj
   bomb — N — NP
   was — BE — MV:Past
   Hiroshima — PropN — NP:PredN
   NP:Obj/Prep
   PrepPh:Adv-agency
   PastPartPh:Adj
   NP:Subj
   VP:Pred

25. Major   dance   companies   throughout   the   world   still   perform   Ballanchine's   ballets.
    Adj   N:Adj   N   Prep   D/Art   N   Adv-frequ   VT   GenN   N
    ——— N:Adj ——   —— NP:Obj/Prep ——   MV:Pres   —— NP:DObj ——
    ———— NP:Head ————   ——— PrepPh:Adj ———   —————— VP:Pred ——————
    ————————— NP:Subj —————————

28. The   peak   covered   by   new   snow   attracted   most of   the   skiers.
    D/Art   N   VT   Prep   Adj   N   VT   PreArt   D/Art   N
    Det   NP:Obj/Prep   MV:Past   Det
    — NP:Head —   — PrepPh:Adv-instrument —   — NP —
                                                   —— PastPartPh:Adj ——   —— NP:DObj ——
    ———————————————— NP:Subj ————————————————   ———— VP:Pred ————

Note: **By new snow** isn't an agent because **new snow** can't motivate itself; it isn't animate. Nonetheless, **new snow covered the peak** underlies the past participial phrase. Some passive sentences have instruments not agents as logical subjects.

33. Throngs   crowding   the   Anchorage   streets   cheered   the   dogsled   teams   starting   the   Iditarod   race
    N   VT   D/Art   PropN:Adj   N   VT   D/Art   N:Adj   N   VT   D/Art   PropN:Adj   N
    NP:Head   Det   NP   MV:Past Det   Det   NP
                                                  — NP:DObj —   — NP:Head —   — NP —
                           —— PresPartPh:Adj ——   —— PresPartPh:Adj ——
    —————— NP:Subj ——————   ————— NP:DObj —————
                                                                                                      ———————— VP:Pred ————————

35. Pop   singers   like   Linda Ronstadt   often   cross over   and   record   country   tunes.
    Adj   N   Prep   PropN   Adv-frequency   VI   Conj   VT   N:Adj   N
    N:Adj   NP:Obj/Prep   MV:Pres   MV:Pres   NP:DObj
    — NP:Head —   —— PrepPh:Adj ——   —— VP:Pred ——   — VP:Pred —
                                                                                           ———————— VP:Pred ————————
    ———————— NP:Subj ————————

Note: **Often** is an adverb of frequency that introduces the first predicate (of the compound predicates) and is attached to it, though not exactly a component of the verb phrase.

44. Jerry Garcia would play a phrase, repeat it, and toy with it like a cat toying with a mouse.

Jerry Garcia	would	play	a	phrase,	repeat	it,	and	toy with	it	like	a	cat	toying with	a	mouse.
ProperN	M	VT	I/Art	N	VT	PersPron	Conj	VT	PersPr	Prep	I/Art	N	VT	I/Art	N
			Det								Det			Det	

NP:Subj
NP
NP:DObj
NP:DObj
NP:Head
NP:DObj
PresPartPh
NP:Obj/Prep
PrepPh:Adv-manner
PrepPh:Prep
VP
VP
VP:Pred
MV:PastCond

Note: The phrases **would play ... repeat ..., and toy with ...** together make a main verb that is past conditional. The heads of the main verb constuent are compounded. The main verb could read **would play ... [would] repeat ..., [would] toy with.** Actually, more than the heads are compounded. So are the object noun phrases that follow them.

50. Two Argentine paleontologists excavated the remains of a carnivorous dinosaur like Tyrannosaurus Rex.

Two	Argentine	paleontologists	excavated	the	remains	of	a	carnivorous	dinosaur	like	Tyrannosaurus Rex.
CardN	N:Adj	N	VT	D/Art	N	Prep	I/Art	Adj	N	Prep	PropN
Det			MV:Past	Det			Det				

NP:Subj
NP:Adj
NP:Head
NP:Head
NP:Obj/Prep
PrepPh:Adj
PrepPh:Gen
NP:DObj
VP:Pred

Chapter 8. Making Noun Clauses, Gerunds, and Infinitives

2.
James Cagney	is	remembered	for	playing^Sub	gangsters	on	the	screen.
PropN	BE	VT	Prep	VT	N	Prep	D/Art	N
NP:GramSubj	Aux			V:Head	NP::DObj		Det	

MV:PresPass

GerPh

NP:Obj/Prep

PrepPh:Adv-reason

NP:Obj/Prep

PrepPh:Adv-place

VP:Pred

Note: In this sentence and others like it, the superscripted **sub** means subordinator; it indicates here that **-ing** is a subordinator.

But	he	considered	himself	a	singer	and	dancer.
Conj	PersPr	Vc	ReflPr	I/Art	N	Conj	N
	NP:Subj	MV:Past	NP:DObj	Det			NP

NP

NP:ObjComp

VP:Pred

6.
America	cannot	postpone	confronting	environmental	problems.
PropN	M/Neg	VT	VT	Adj	N
NP:Subj	Aux	V:Head	V:Head		

MV:PresCond

NP:DObj

GerPh

NP:DObj

VP:Pred

11. The　　Nicaraguan　refugee　went　to　Los Angeles　to　join　her　sister.
　　　D/Art　　Adj　　　　　N　　　VI　　Prep　PropN　　　Subord　VT　PossPr　N
　　　Det　———NP———　　　MV:Past　　　　NP:Obj/Prep　　　　　V:Head　Det　——NP:DObj——
　　　　———NP:Subj———　　　　　　　　—PrepPh:Adv-place—　　　　　　　————InfPh————
　　　　　　　　　　　　　　　　　　　　　　　　　　　　　　　　—————InfPh:Adv-reason—————
　　　　　　　　　　　　　　　　　　　　　　　　　　　　———Subord———

13. It　　doesn't　take　long　for　Crystal Gayle's　audience　to　understand　that　she　is　Loretta Lynn's　sister.
　　　Expl　Aux/Neg　VI　　Adv　Prep　GenN　　　　　　N　　　　Subord　VT　　　　Subord　PersPr　BE　GenN　　　　N
　　　GrSubj　——MV:Pres——　　　　　———NP:Subj———　　　　　V:Head　　　　　　NP:Subj　MV:Pres　————NP:PredN————
　　————VP:Pred————
　　　　　　　　　　　　　　　　　　　　　　　　　　　　　　　　　　　　————NCl————
　　　　　　　　　　　　　　　　　　　　　　　　　　　　　　　　　———NCl———
　　　　　　　　　　　　　　　　　　　　　　　　　　　　　　　　———NP:DObj———
　　　　　　　　　　　　　　　　　　　　　　　　　　　　　————VP:PartPred————
　　　　　　　　　　　　　　　　　　　　————InfPh————
　　　　　　　　　　　　　—————InfPh—————
　　　　　　　　　———NP:LogSubj———
　　　　　————VPPred————

Note: **Take** and **long** are difficult to define. I've defined **take** as intransitive followed by the adverb **long**. But **long** might be an adjective, making **take** a linking verb, like **become**. The infinitve phrase functions as a complement to **long** (an adv or adj) as well as a logical subject.

17. The　　Israeli　press　chided　the　Syrians　for　what　they　called　. . .　unfriendly　activity.
　　　D/Art　Adj　　N　　VT　　　D/Art　PropN　Prep　Subord　PersPr　Vc　　NP:DObj　Adj　　　　N
　　　Det　——NP——　MV:Past　Det　——NP:DObj——　　　　　NP:Subj　MV:Past　　　　　　　　———NP:ObjComp———
　　　　——NP:Subj——　　　　　　　　　　　　　　　　　　　　　————VP:Pred————
　　　　　　　　　　　　　　　　　　　　　　　　　　———NCl———
　　　　　　　　　　　　　　　　　　　　————NP:Obj/Prep————
　　　　　　　　　　　　　——————PrepPh:Adv-reason——————
　　　　　———————————VP:Pred———————————

23. Calling   a   Texan   a   liar   will   usually   provoke   a   fight.
    Vc   I/Art   N   I/Art   N   M   Adv-frequ   VT   I/Art   N
    V:Head   Det   Det   Aux   Det
          —NP:DObj—   —NP:ObjComp—   —MV:PresCond—   —NP:DObj—
          ——GerPh——
          ——NP:Subj——   ————VP:Pred————

Note: Like **often** in sentence 22, **usually** is attached to the main verb but is not strictly a component of it. You might pattern it with **provoke** as an MV, then include that MV within another MV composed of **will usually provoke**. I've chosen not to, for the sake of simplicity.

25. Father Chabot   wonders   whether   the   city   cares about   kids.
    PropN   VT   Subord   D/Art   N   VT   N
    NP:Subj   MV:Pres   Det   —MV:Pres—   NP:DObj
                                           —NP:Subj—   ——VP:Pred——
                                                              ——NCl——
                                                              ——NP:DObj——
                                  ——————VP:Pred——————

32. It   is   Russian   policy   to   control   oil   production   around   the Black Sea.
    Expl   BE   Adj   N   Subord   VT   N:Adj   N   Prep   PropN
    NP:GramSubj MV:Pres —NP:PredN—   V:Head   ——NP:DObj——   NP:Obj/prep
                                                                                      ——PrepPh:Adv-place——
                                                     ——————InfPh——————
                                            ——————InfPh——————
                                            ——————NP:LogSubj——————
                         ——————————————VP:Pred——————————————

44. Jane Bryant Quinn   makes   money   make   sense.
PropN   Vc   N   VT   N
NP:Subj   MV:Pres NP:DObj V:Head NP:DObj
                                           ——InfPh——
                                           ——NP:ObjComp——
                         ————————VP:Pred————————

47. It   is   clear   that   the South   has   become   a   Republican dominion.
     Expl   BE   Adj   Subord   PropN   HAVE   VL   I/Art   Adj   N
     NP:GramSubj MV:Pres AdjPh:PredAdj   NP:Subj   —MV:PresPerf—   Det   —NP—
                                                                                     ——NP:PredN——
                                                                             ————————VP:Pred————————
                                                                        ——————————NCl——————————
                                                              ————————————NCl————————————
                                                              ——————————NP:LogSubj——————————
                 ————————————————————VP:Pred————————————————————

Note: **That the South has become a Republican dominion** is a complement to the adjective **clear** as well as the logical subject.

Chapter 9. Adding Modifiers to Sentences

1. The   courthouse design …   earned   praise   from   architects   maligned   by   local   residents.
   D/Art   N:Adj   N   VT   N   Prep   N   PastPart   Prep   Adj   N
   Det   ——NP——   MV:Past NP:DObj NP:Obj/Prep   VT   —NP:Obj/Prep—
   ——NP:Subj——   PrepPh:Adv-source   —PrepPh:Adv-agency—
                                                                                                          ——PastPartPh——
                      |———————————MClause———————————| |—————————NonrestrictiveMod—————————|

5. The *J.B. Ford* ... steams no more the freighter I worked on as a teenager.

    - MClause — NonrestrictiveMod
    - The (D/Art, Det) — *J.B. Ford* (PropN, NP:Subj) — steams (VI, MV:Pres) — no more (Adv-frequency, VP:Pred) — the (D/Art, Det) — freighter (N, NP:Head) — I (PersPr, NP:Subj) — worked on (VT, MV:Past) — as (Prep) — a (I/Art, Det) — teenager (N)
    - NP:Obj/Prep — PrepPh:Adv-time — VP:Pred — RelCl:Adj — NP

13. The Range Rover sat near the salt lick, lights off and engine silent, concealing three hunters and their equipment.

    - MClause — NonrestrictiveMod
    - The Range Rover (PropN, NP:Subj) — sat (VI, MV:past) — near (Prep) — the (D/Art) — salt lick (N:Adj N, Det—NP) — lights (N, NP:Subj) — off (Adv-condition, PartPred) — and (Conj) — engine (N, NP:Subj) — silent (Adj, PartPred) — concealing (VT, PresPart) — three (CardN) — hunters (N) — and (Conj) — their (PossPr, Det) — equipment (N)
    - NP:Obj/Prep — PrepPh:Adv-place — VP:Pred — NomAbs — NomAbs — NomAbs — NP — NP:DObj — PresPartPh — NP

20. Since eating well is highly esteemed in New Orleans, restaurant lore is a colorful dimension of social chatter.

    - Since (Subord) — eating (VI, Ger) — well (Adv-manner) — is (BE, Adv-manner) — esteemed (VT, MV:PresPass) — in (Prep) — New Orleans (PropN) — restaurant (N:Adj) — lore (N, NP:Subj) — is (BE, I/Art, MV:Pres) — a (Art) — colorful (Adj) — dimension (N) — of (Prep) — social (Adj) — chatter (N)
    - Ger — GerPh — NP:Subj — VP:Pred — AdvCl — AdvCl:Adv-reason — PrepPh:Adv-place — NP:Obj/Prep — NP:Subj — NP:Obj/Prep — PrepPh:Gen — NP — NP:PredN — VP:Pred

MClause

NonrestrictiveMod

23. | To | defend | the | government | of | South Vietnam, | American | forces | tore | the | country | apart. |
Subord	VT	D/Art	N	Prep	PropN	Adj	N	VT	D/Art	N	Part
		Det			—NP:Obj/Prep—	—NP:Subj—		MV:Past	Det		
					—PrepPh:Gen—				—NP:DObj—		
				—————NP—————				—VP:Pred—		
			—————NP:DObj—————							
		—————————InfPh—————————							
	—————————InfPh:Adv-reason—————————							

Note: **Tore apart** is a two-word verb; the particle **apart** has been disjoined, moved around the direct object NP.

MClause

NonrestrictiveMod

26. | Keeshawna's | birthday | cake | was | like | those | baked | by | my | southern | grandmother— | moist, | rich, | and | sticky. |
GenN	N:Adj	N	BE	Prep	Pron	VT	Prep	PossPr	Adj	N	Adj	Adj	Conj	Adj
			MV:		NP:	Past		Det		N	AdjPh	AdjPh		AdjPh
			Past		Head	Part				—NP—				
—————NP—————						—————PrepPh:Obj/Prep—————				—————AdjPh—————			
—————NP:Subj—————						—————PrepPh:Adv-agency—————							
						—————PastPartPh:Adj—————							
						—————NP:Obj/Prep—————							
					—————PrepPh:Adv-comparison—————							
				—————VP:Pred—————								

Note: The prep phrase **like . . . grandmother** could also be called a predicate adverb.

MClause

```
                                              Seymour    waited    patiently    for    the     next    plane.
                                              PropN      VI        Adv-manner   Prep   D/Art   OrdN    N
                                              NP:Subj    MV:Past                       Det ——— NP
                                                                                       —— NP:Obj/Prep ——
                                                                                       — PrepPh:Adv-intention —
                                                                                    —————— VP:Pred ——————
```

```
37. Although   he        was       anxious          to        see    his     family,
    Subord     PersPr    BE        Adj              Subord     VT     PersPr  N
               NP:Subj   MV:Past   AdjPh:PredAdj                      Det
                                                                      —— NP:DObj ——
                                                                      ——— InfPh ———
                                            —— InfPh:Comp ——
                                          ————— VP:Pred —————
                                        ——————— AdvCl ———————
                            ————— AdvCl:Adv-contrary condition —————
```

Note: The infinitive phrase **to see his family** functions as a complement to the adjective **anxious**. The adjective-infinitive phrase relationship could have been parsed differently. **Anxious to** might be an adjective with a particle, like **afraid of** or **liable to**. That is, there are a number of adjectives in the language that form constituents with particles and that are followed by NP or infinitive complements. Since I didn't introduce the adjective-plus-particle construction in the text, I haven't parsed the construction in this way.

MClause   NonrestrictiveMod

```
40. Cincinnati   public   radio's   series   of     African   American   concerts   was   called        "Karamu,"      the     Swahili   word   for    celebration.
    N:Adj        N:Adj    GenN      N        Prep   Adj       N          N          BE    Vc            PropN          D/Art   Adj       N      Prep   N
    —— NP ——                        Adj                       —— NP:Obj/Prep ——           MV:PastPass    NP:ObjComp     Det ——— NP
    ——— GenNP ———                            —— PrepPh:Gen ——                                                                 —— NP:Head ——       — NP:Obj/Prep —
                                             ——— NP ———                                                                                           —— PrepPh:Adj ——
    ————————— NP:GramSubj —————————                                                       ———————— VP:Pred ————————                         ————————— NP —————————
```

47.

NonrestrictiveMod (over: the Pilgrims)
MClause
NonrestrictiveMod (over: a new promised land)

To	the	Pilgrims,	the	American	continent	was	sacred	soil,	a	new	promised	land.
Prep	D/Art	PropN	D/Art	Adj	N	BE	Adj	N	D/Art	Adj	Adj	N
	Det		Det			MV:Past			Det			
	—NP:Obj/Prep—		—NP:Subj—				—NP:PredN—		—NP—			
PrepPh.:Adv-perception						—VP:Pred—			—NP—			

49.

MClause
NonrestrictiveMod
NonrestrictiveMod

Mickey Mantle	ran	the	bases	like	a	charging	bull,	his	head	down,	his	legs	pumping	furiously.
PropN	VT	D/Art	N	Prep	I/Art	Adj	N	PossPr	N	Adv-place	PossPr	N	PresPart	Adv-manner
NP:Subj	MV:Past	Det			Det			—NP:Subj—		VP:PartPred	—NP:Subj—		VI	
		—NP:DObj—			—NP:Obj/Prep—				—NomAbs—				—VP:PartPred—	
					—PrepPh.:Adv-manner—							—NomAbs—		
		—VP:Pred—												

Index

Absolute phrase, 223–27
  introductory "with," 227
Adjective
  clause. *See* Relative clause, restrictive
  differentiating from determiner, 71
  differentiating from past participle, 110
  differentiating from present participle, 60
  following BE or linking verb. *See* Predicate adjective
  made into adverb, 37
  as object complement, 12, 13
  phrase. *See* Phrase, restrictive
  single word in noun phrase, 165–67
Adverb, 35–38
  of agency, 106
  of attendant circumstance, 219, 226
  clause, 227–37
  explained, 35–38
  following intransitive verb, 6
  of place, unlike adverb of reception, 10–11
  single word in noun phrase, 165–67
Adverbial infinitive, 200
Ambiguity, 173–74
Appositive. *See also,* Modifiers, nonrestrictive
  adjective phrase, 222–23
  noun phrase, 219–22
Article
  definite, 72
  indefinite, 72
Aspect, 55–59. *See also* Auxiliary
  perfective, 55–57
  progressive, 58–59
  putting together with tense and modality, 60–62
Attribute, 24, 30–31
Auxiliary, 48
  BE, 58, 91, 97, 101, 106, 111
  conditional mood, 51–55
  have, 55,58
  to identify subject, 25–26
  modal, 51–53
  not, 91
  perfective aspect, 55–57
  progressive aspect, 58–59
  tense, 48–51
  Semi-modal, 52

Base form of verb. *See* Infinitive
BE
  in auxiliary, 58, 91, 97, 101, 106, 111

deleting from clause, 156, 159, 218, 226
forms of, 13
in negative sentence, 91
in passive, 101
in question, 97, 101
in there-sentence, 112
Brackets, labeled, 32
By prepositional phrase, 106, 108, 161
  deleting, 108, 161

Christensen, Francis, 243, 251
Clause
  adjective. *See* Clause, restrictive
  adverb, 227–31
    words that can introduce, 229–31
  dependent, 130–49, 182–94, 214–17, 227–31
  independent, 131, 135, 136, 147, 148
  matrix. *See* Matrix
  nonrestrictive, 214–17
  noun, 182–94
  relative, 130–49, 214–17
  restrictive, 130–49
  subordinate. *See* Clause, dependent
Closed classes, 71
Combining clauses. *See* Embedding
Commas, 122–23, 228, 256–57
Complement
  to an adjective, 186–87
  to a noun phrase, 186
  object, 12–13
  subject, 14. *See also* Predicate adjective; Predicate noun
Compounding, 117–20
Compounds, punctuating, 120–23
Conjoining, 117–20
Conjunction
  coordinate, 120
  correlative, 120
  subordinate. 183–85, 189, 193. *See also* Subordinator
Conjunctive adverbs, 123–24
Constituency, 23, 31, 162, 164–65, 167, 186. *See also* Constituent
Constituent, 23, 27–30, 196
  disjunctive, 98, 101
  within embedded phrases, 164–65
  and parsing, 167–70
  in passive, 108–109
  problems identifying, 173–74
Copula. See BE
Content words, 71

288